• Studies i utics 15 •

Readi o John

Cover. *St. John on the Island of Patmos,* from a 19th-century, illuminated-Bible woodcut by H. M. Snyder.

"I, John, your brother who shares with you in Jesus the persecution and the kingdom and the patient endurance, was on the island called Patmos because of the word of God and the testimony of Jesus. I was in the Spirit on the Lord's day, and I heard behind me a loud voice like a trumpet saying, 'Write in a book what you see and send it to the seven churches, to Ephesus, to Smyrna, to Pergamum, to Thyatira, to Sardis, to Philadelphia, and to Laodicea.' " (Revelation 1:9-11 NRSV)

• Studies in American Biblical Hermeneutics 15 •

1. *Reimagining America. A Theological Critique of the American Mythos and Biblical Hermeneutics*
   by Charles Mabee
2. *Norman Perrin's Interpretation of the New Testament. From "Exegetical Method" to "Hermeneutical Process"*
   by Calvin R. Mercer
3. *The Community of Interpreters. On the Hermeneutics of Nature and the Bible in the American Philosophical Tradition*
   by Robert S. Corrington
4. *The Poetics of Revelation. Recognition and the Narrative Tradition*
   by Diana Culbertson
5. *Faith and the Play of the Imagination. On the Role of Imagination in Religion*
   by David J. Bryant
6. *The Second Naiveté. Barth, Ricoeur, and the New Yale Theology*
   by Mark I. Wallace
7. *Reading Sacred Texts through American Eyes. Biblical Interpretation as Cultural Critique*
   by Charles Mabee
8. *Hermeneutics as Theological Prolegomena. A Canonical Approach*
   by Charles J. Scalise
9. *A Common Sense Theology. The Bible, Faith, and American Society*
   by Mark Ellingsen
10. *The Politics of Biblical Theology. A Postmodern Reading*
    by David Penchansky
11. *Making Sense of New Testament Theology. "Modern" Problems and Prospects*
    by A. K. M. Adam
12. *Theology as Cultural Critique. The Achievement of Julian Hartt*
    by Jonathan R. Wilson
13. *Beyond the Impasse. The Promise of a Process Hermeneutic*
    by Ronald L. Farmer
14. *The Interior Sense of Scripture. The Sacred Hermeneutics of John W. Nevin*
    by William DiPuccio
15. *Elusive Apocalypse. Reading Authority in the Revelation to John*
    by Greg Carey

• Studies in American Biblical Hermeneutics 15 •

Elusive Apocalypse

Reading Authority in the Revelation to John

by
Greg Carey

MERCER UNIVERSITY PRESS
1979 • 1999
TWENTY YEARS OF PUBLISHING EXCELLENCE

ISBN 0-86554-632-0 MUP/P186

Elusive Apocalypse.
Reading Authority in the Revelation to John

Mercer University Press, Macon, Georgia 31210-3960 USA

Printed in the United States of America

The paper used in this publication meets
the minimum requirements of American National Standard
for Information Sciences—Permanence of Paper
for Printed Library Materials, ANSI Z39.48-1984.

Library of Congress Cataloging-in-Publication Data

Carey, Greg, 1965–
Elusive apocalypse : reading authority
in the Revelation to John / by Greg Carey.
xiv+209pp. 6x9" (15x23cm.) —
(Studies in American biblical hermeneutics ; 15)
Includes bibliographical references and index.
ISBN 0-86554-632-0 (pbk. : alk. paper).
1. Bible. N.T. Revelation—Criticism, Narrative.
2. Bible. N.T. Revelation—Evidences, authority, etc.
I. Title. II. Series.
BS2825.2.C34 1999
228'.07—dc21 99-28149

CIP

Contents

Editor's Preface

Unlike Greg Carey, my appreciation of the Book of Revelation was an acquired taste, rather than one which came naturally. I remember well a conversation with a "former Christian" (his words) who had been driven out of the faith by what he considered irresponsible, if not irrational expressions of apocalypticism. If this be Christianity, said he, then I will have no part of it. For many of us, the Apocalypse of John was the "Haight Ashbury" district of the New Testament, while we yearned for more concrete ethical, moral injunctions that would not make Christians appear to be a kind of "Judaism light." As such, it was more a book to be ignored than to be studied. Of course, all of us know what the biblical literalists continue to do with the book. Our question was, and perhaps is, how can this strange book attain a degree of authority in our Christian lives in spite of its checkered exegetical history?

Several things changed my mind—things that Greg Carey took seriously long before me. The first of these is the well-known fact that the Book of Revelation has played an inordinate role of importance in the American cultural context. The imaginative construct of the New World beckoned forth the New World of biblical imagination. It is well known that these two "realms" have always been intimate bedfellows. Tina Pippan reminded me several years ago that the Book of Revelation is almost always the first book of the Bible suppressed by oppressive governments. A strange phenomenon for a literary perspective that on first brush seems to take flight from reality, rather than engage it heroically, no matter the cost. Perhaps there is something more to the commonality of the machinations of American liberty and the free, fresh air of the Apocalypse than immediately meets the eye.

But, devotee of American readings of the Bible that I am, I was still not convinced that somehow, someone was not pulling the wool over my eyes. I remained dogged in my determined call to my students for the "Deuteronomization" of the faith, thereby avoiding the flights of Christian fancy that avoid the marrow of the realities of human experience.

Then, something unexpected happened. While teaching a survey course on the New Testament (my field of training is Old Testament), I came to a remarkable conclusion. In order to make the Book of Revelation the most important book in the New Testament, yea even the Bible as a whole, only one simple interpretative act need be done. And that act is: reverse the order of the books! If you do that, of course, the Bible begins with the Book of Revelation. I knew that, but I only discovered the importance of it while teaching the Bible "backwards" with my class one semester. This procedure is not absolutely unlike the historical-critical scholar who "unpeels" the onion by ripping ever smaller pieces of a pericope out of its native context.

Why would you want to read the New Testament backward, you may ask? Perhaps now is the time I have to make a public confession. Because my academic field is Old Testament, I allow myself a kind of freedom of interpretation of the New Testament that my colleagues with advanced degrees would probably scoff at (they have not had the chance as yet to do so because this is the first time I have ever revealed outside the classroom my little methodology). You know the expression "all roads lead to Rome." Well that expression came as the summation of my unlicensed foray into New Testament studies. Reversing the order of New Testament books is really only a trick to help us better understand that Rome is the culmination of the movement of the New Testament. I have actually grown quite fond of reading the Bible backwards. But the truth of the matter is, whether the Book of Revelation is either the first, or the last, book of the Bible really does not make much of a difference. The whole point comes down to this fact: for Christians, Rome would be the new Jerusalem. It would be the center of the faith, and the Book of Revelation would lay out an imaginative perspective of what (with God's help) that would someday look like. The book now for me became an incredible affirmation of faith—Christians having the audacity to claim that someday that pagan Rome would be greater than Jerusalem! If God could pull off such a feat in Rome, I thought, there was hope for Philadelphia, Washington, D.C., and Detroit (I won't even mention mention New York and L.A.)! Of course, when I came also to understand more generally that the Apocalypse is the only book in the Bible to really address "systems" in any meaningful way, it only augmented my growing admiration and appreciation for the book.

Greg Carey has made the Book of Revelation even more accessible to me. In this wonderfully written contribution to the study of the Apocalypse, he attempts to deconstruct the various exegetical camps that have contended for the "correct" interpretation of this final addition to the New Testament by centering the discussion in rhetorical authority. I will let him make his own argument for this in the pages that follow.

Suffice it to say that as I write this, we are less than a year away from the new millennium. Perhaps when this book finally reaches your hands, we will know whether or not life still goes on in the face of the Y2K bug. (My hunch is that it probably will.) We are only now beginning to see a spate of publications supercharged with the apocalyptic fever that accompanies the approach of year 2000. In light of all that is beginning to go on, it is vital for all of us involved in Christian thought to put responsible reading material in our hands that deals with this business of the millennium. I am as sure that this book conforms to this requirement as I am that the world will muddle on somehow past the 1,000-year turning of the clock. I wish you good reading, and have a nice third millennium.

Ecumenical Theological Seminary, Detroit *Charles Mabee*
3 January 1999

Acknowledgments

This is my first book, a unique occasion in any scholar's life. As I look back over the entire project, I feel like one of those Academy Award winners who can't keep to the time limit. Without the contributions of many friends, teachers, and family members—many of whom belong in more than one category—I cannot imagine how this project would have turned out as it has. In all things I thank God, in whose grace I have been blessed with the relationships and experiences that have made this book possible.

The book began as a 1996 dissertation in Vanderbilt University's Graduate Department of Religion. My graduate advisor, Professor Fernando F. Segovia, encouraged me to develop an independent voice in the dissertation; his continuing friendship, advice, and professional support are precious to me. My gratitude also extends to Professors Daniel Patte, Amy-Jill Levine, and William Franke, who have fostered my growth as a scholar and contributed to this present effort through their constructive suggestions and responses to my questions. I admire my friend Tina Pippin of Agnes Scott College for modeling engaged reading that is also self-critical.

Wonderful colleagues at both Rhodes College and Winthrop University have also shaped my development and contributed to this work. Rhodes' Department of Religious Studies includes several of my own former teachers—Richard Batey, Michael McLain, and Steven L. McKenzie—as well as delightful colleagues like Ellen Armour, Gail Corrington Streete, Joseph A. Favazza, Stephen R. Haynes, John Kaltner, Darren J. M. Middleton (now at Texas Christian University), and Carey Ellen Walsh. Our conversations about teaching and studying religion continue in a variety of contexts. Truly great teachers like Michael McLain, Milton P. Brown (now retired), and Valarie Ziegler (now at DePauw University)—how do I call them by their first names?—drew me into religious studies in the first place. Daily I look to their examples as I reflect upon my own formation as a teacher and scholar. My Winthrop colleagues Houston Craighead and Bill Daniel, outstanding teachers and philosophers both, have created a stimulating and supportive environment in which I could complete this work. I would also like to thank our departmental administrative assistants, LaShawn Sanders and Althea Hayden, who have painstakingly reviewed various stages of this manuscript.

Charles Mabee, the editor of Mercer's Studies in American Biblical Hermeneutics series, received my proposal with enthusiasm, advocated for it effectively, and has contributed invaluable insights. In particular, he has encouraged me to follow through with my instincts when I have been cautious. Edmon L. Rowell, Jr., senior editor at Mercer University Press, has plowed through the manuscript with scrupulous detail. I appreciate his patience and care.

Most of all, I am singularly grateful for my wife, Laura Briscoe Carey, whose grace and steadfast support have sustained me throughout this effort. Laura captivates my admiration. From graduate school through the birth of two daughters and two teaching positions, she has truly invested as much in this book as I have. Her personal wisdom and authentic ministry have inspired me to do work that is relevant, and I can only hope to have lived up to that challenge. To my occasional frenzies, Laura has responded with tenderness, good humor, and a sense of play that bring balance and joy. Since I began writing we have celebrated the birth of two daughters, Erin and Emily, who also are a continual source of joy to us both. Through Laura, Erin, and Emily I experience the touch of God. I am honored to dedicate this project to Laura, whose love so richly blesses my life.

Finally, I would like to express my love and appreciation to my Mom, Barbara Akin Pace, and my Dad, George Walter Carey, Jr., along with their spouses, Dewey Pace and Diane Carey. My mother is a courageous and virtuous woman who taught me the value of faithfulness and who first showed me the joy of teaching. A single parent from my sixth year through high school, Mom went to hundreds of athletic events, concerts, school functions, and the like, sacrificing her own interests so that I could have every opportunity. My father has always encouraged me to listen to my own spirit and find my own path, even when the results were baffling. My parents' very different contributions came together when I was interviewing for an academic scholarship at Rhodes College (then Southwestern at Memphis). Asked why I had only attained a "B" average in high school, I replied without hesitation, "My parents said I had other things to do." I could tell you how the scholarship worked out some other time, but I am sincerely grateful for their advice.

Greg Carey

Abbreviations

ACNT	Augsburg Commentary on the New Testament
Ad Her.	Pseudo-Cicero, *Rhetorica ad Herennium*
ANRW	*Aufstieg und Niedergang der römischen Welt*
Ant.	Josephus, *Antiquities of the Jews*
BDF	Blass, Debrunner, and Funk, *A Greek Grammar of the NT*
BETL	Bibliotheca ephemeridum theologicarum lovaniensium
BSac	*Bibliotheca Sacra*
CNT	Commentaire du Nouveau Testament
CRINT	Compendia rerum iudaicarum ad novum testamentum
De Or.	Cicero, *De Oratore*
De Part. Or.	Cicero, *De Partitione Oratoria*
De Praescr.	Tertullian, *De Praescriptione Haereticorum*
De Vir. Ill.	Jerome, *De Viris Illustribus*
Ep. Arist.	*Epistle of Aristeas*
GNS	Good News Studies
Haer.	Irenaeus, *Adversus omnes Haereses*
HDR	Harvard Dissertations in Religion
H.E.	Eusebius, *Ecclesiastical History*
Hellholm	*Apocalypticism in the Mediterranean World and the Near East*
HTR	*Harvard Theological Review*
ICC	International Critical Commentary
IDB	*Interpreter's Dictionary of the Bible*
Inst. Or.	Quintilian, *Institutio Oratoria*
JBL	*Journal of Biblical Literature*
JSNTSup	*Journal for the Study of the New Testament* Supplement Series
J.W.	Josephus, *Jewish War*
LCL	Loeb Classical Library
Magn.	Ignatius, *Magnesians*
NASB	New American Standard Bible
NCB	New Century Bible
Neot.	*Neotestamentica*
NJB	New Jerusalem Bible
NTS	*New Testament Studies*

OTP	Charlesworth, editor, *Old Testament Pseudepigrapha*
Phil.	Polycarp, *Philippians*
Phld.	Ignatius, *Philadelphians*
PMLA	Publications of the Modern Language Association
Poet.	Aristotle, *Poetics*
NRSV	New Revised Standard Version
RB	*Revue biblique*
Refutat.	Hippolytus, *Refutation of All Heresies*
Rhet.	Aristotle, *Rhetoric*
SBLSP	*Society of Biblical Literature Seminar Papers*
Strom.	Clement of Alexandria, *Stromateis*
Style	Pseudo-Demetrius, *On Style*
Sublime	Longinus, *On the Sublime*
TCGNT	Metzger, *A Textual Commentary on the Greek New Testament*
UBS	United Bible Societies
USQR	*Union Seminary Quarterly Review*
WBC	Word Biblical Commentary

Chapter 1
Authority of and in the Apocalypse

Authority defines and motivates the Book of Revelation. On at least three primary levels, struggles over authority define the possibilities for reading it. (1) Motivated by a fundamental struggle to legitimate resistance against the imperial conditions of Roman Asia Minor in the late first century CE, Revelation articulates an alternative locus of authority in its vision of the risen Christ. (2) Revelation's critical and popular readers contend for the authorization (academic or spiritual?) to interpret it. (3) And popular readers offer opposed understandings for how to appropriate Revelation, which imply conflicting understandings of authority. For Revelation and its readers, authority is a rhetorical problem, involving religious and political dimensions.

First, the book of Revelation is an example of resistance literature. Written in part to encourage Christians to withstand the demands of life within the Roman Empire, Revelation constructs an alternative locus of authority. Because it embodies the risen Christ's revelation for believers, Revelation transfers authority from the Empire and other likely sources to its own narrating voice, the prophet John. It is John's vision, not Rome or the emperor, that commands absolute obedience.

Second, Revelation may be unique among early Christian literature for the interest its scholarly and popular readers have in one another. Struggles between scholarly and popular readers, particularly those conservative millenarians who listen to television preachers such as Hal Lindsey and Jack van Impe, often involve appeals to authority. A frequent topos among Revelation's critical commentaries is the concern that readers must be led away from the dangers represented in popular millenarian interpretations. Surely, they argue, one would listen to a qualified scholar's exegesis above the extremist readings that whiz through our airwaves and fill the shelves of "Christian bookstores." Likewise, popular prophecy students discriminate between the "true" Bible scholars who see in Revelation a program for the world's imminent end and those "liberal" or "unbelieving" academics who deny that Revelation predicts our immediate future.

Third, Christian readers who seek to appropriate the Apocalypse for contemporary spirituality and practice often disagree about its significance.[1] In my opinion the most obvious point of contention is authority: While some Christians use Revelation to articulate an egalitarian vision for the dismantling of those structures that oppress and dominate people, others find in it authorization for imposing (usually ultraconservative) values upon their own and other societies. According to one reading, Revelation criticizes all claims to supremacy; according to the other, it provides a standard by which claims to authority may be measured. I would also note that most—though not all—scholarly readings are sympathetic toward liberationist interpretations and antagonistic toward millenarian ones. At the same time, one is more likely to find references to critical scholarship in the pages of *Sojourners,* a liberationist magazine, than in *Moody Monthly,* which advocates a more millenarian stance.

What interests me about all these conflicts is that they are conducted through rhetoric. We see them in texts. Implicit in these struggles are various modes of authority—religious, political, and rhetorical—that defy simplistic distinctions.

---

[1]Because of the religious publishing industry, this conflict is especially evident in North America, and I know more about it here than elsewhere. But it also travels worldwide, particularly in struggles over what constitutes liberation in Latin America and South Africa. For a provocative analysis of why some poor Brazilian Christians read the Bible according to a liberation paradigm, while others find hope for heavenly rewards, see Paulo Fernando Carneiro de Andrade, "Reading the Bible in the Ecclesial Base Communities of Latin America: The Meaning of Social Context," in *Reading from This Place,* vol. 2, *Social Location and Biblical Interpretation in Global Perspective,* ed. Fernando F. Segovia and Mary Ann Tolbert (Minneapolis: Fortress, 1995) 237-49, esp. 245-49.

> Rhetoric—the manipulation of the dualisms and dislocations of language—is a weapon of power in the constitution and control of communities, and never more radically so than when communities claim to embody and represent the highest good.[2]

Even for John, Revelation's narrator, the authority to dominate populations along with their commercial and military systems involves both religious and rhetorical dimensions. The Beast and the Whore of Babylon, the Lamb's grotesque opponents, hold power over the marketplace and authority over life and death. They dominate in part through a blasphemous discourse at the intersection of rhetoric, religion, and politics (Rev 13, 17-18). John's reply constructs an alternative authority in the person of Christ, who is both Lamb and Ruler-of-All (παντοκράτωρ).[3] But for John's program to be successful, he must win over his audience by constructing his own rhetorical authority, his ethos (ἦθος).[4]

In response to these three areas of contention, I would offer three theses that motivate this study.

1. We need a thorough rhetorical study of how Revelation constructs authority. John's ethos defines Revelation's rhetorical authority and determines its religious and political strategies. In addition, those who read Revelation, scholarly and popular readers alike, often mimic Revelation's authority rhetoric.

2. Though both scholars and popular prophecy students rigidly define themselves over against one another, it is time to deconstruct those oppositions. Scholarly no less than popular readings depend upon certain interests and reading strategies. It may be that while many scholars downplay their personal interest in

---

[2]David Jasper, *Rhetoric, Power and Community: An Exercise in Reserve* (Louisville: Westminster/John Knox, 1993) 18.

[3]Rev 1:8. Revelation does not distinguish clearly between God, who is παντοκράτωρ and ἄλφα and ὦ in 1:8, and Christ, who names himself ἄλφα and ὦ in 22:13.

[4]Stephen D. O'Leary argues that authority is, along with evil and time, one of the three basic topoi of apocalyptic discourse in *Arguing the Apocalypse: A Theory of Millennial Rhetoric* (New York: Oxford, 1994). While I would suggest that O'Leary's scheme fails to consider the wide variety of apocalyptic rhetorics and their various functions, I agree that the intensity of apocalyptic claims requires that those who make them pay extremely close attention to ethos.

Revelation, certain millenarian preunderstandings enable popular readers to respond to aspects of Revelation's rhetoric that scholars frequently avoid.

3. John's construction of authority may explain certain conflicts among popular readings of Revelation. In particular, "liberationist" interpretations emphasize the Apocalypse's challenge to imperialism and domination, while the "prophecy students" (or "millenarians") apply Revelation to their detailed scenarios concerning the imminent final events. While the focus of this study is exegetical, I will argue that particular tensions within John's rhetoric lead to some of the differences in these religious and social programs. Because Revelation resists the domination represented by Rome and its allies, it lends itself to an egalitarian response. Yet Revelation also establishes an equally absolute locus of authority: a God whose designs are available only through John's representational voice. This dimension of Revelation energizes the claims to final and unique truth that we find among many millenarian readers.

After a methodological discussion concerning "John," these three theses will provide a framework for this introductory chapter, as they motivate the project as a whole. Before I discuss these issues in more detail, I would like to say a word about my own investment in Revelation and its authority problem.

This project is driven by the conviction that our best research usually involves those things we care most passionately about. Biblical scholars typically discount personal experience and seek to distance themselves from popular reading communities;[5] thus, it may seem odd that I care deeply about the book of Revelation and about why particular communities of its interpreters read it in such starkly conflicting ways. But I have wandered through this territory myself. As a high school student and member of a Baptist church in North Alabama, I was a "prophecy student." I bought books by Hal Lindsey and other millenarian authors, consulted my

---

[5]Important challenges to this traditional model include Jeffrey L. Staley, *Reading with a Passion: Rhetoric, Autobiography, and the American West in the Gospel of John* (New York: Continuum, 1995); Janice Capel Anderson and Jeffrey L. Staley, "Taking It Personally: Autobiographical Biblical Criticism," *Semeia* 72 (1995); and Gerald West and Musa W. Dube, eds., " 'Reading with' African Overtures," *Semeia* 73 (1996).

Scofield Study Bible, and paid special attention to sermons and lessons on "the last days."

During college I began to sense an alienation from these interests, an alienation that was probably more cultural than theological or spiritual. A millenarian worldview did not fit well among my teachers and friends who pursued success and "respectable" knowledge, and I simply became less interested in "Bible prophecy." I did become a religious studies major and later a seminary student, however, and I was exposed to other modes of eschatological thought, particularly through liberation theologies and proponents of radical discipleship like Daniel Berrigan. I perceived these liberationist readings as being faithful to the biblical texts, in addition to being spiritually satisfying and socially progressive.

When I entered graduate study in New Testament at Vanderbilt University, I wanted to articulate a critical liberationist reading of Revelation. Readings like those of Elisabeth Schüssler Fiorenza and Allen Boesak encouraged me. But a couple of factors would not allow me to follow through. My encounter with people whose experiences of Revelation had not been so positive led me to a further investigation of the text itself. Within the same week I heard Tina Pippin discuss the misogyny she encountered in the Apocalypse, and Fernando Segovia called my attention to the destructive uses Revelation has served in colonial missionary contexts. When I read it more closely, I found that Revelation can be disturbingly congenial to such dangerous applications.

These experiences have led me to a dimension of Revelation that I believe to be fundamentally important for understanding the conflicts among various reading strategies and for grappling with opposing scholarly interpretations as well: Authority, rhetorically constructed for political and religious ends, presents a fundamental problem for interpreters of Revelation.

The result of this study is my own reading of Revelation. I seek to demonstrate its persuasiveness by arguing that (a) it is a plausible reconstruction of how Revelation might have sounded to John's intended audience and (b) it provides insight into certain conflicts among contemporary scholarly and popular interpretations.

"John" in Theory

I am interested in John, Revelation's ever-present narrating voice, as a means of exploring how the Apocalypse constructs authority. In particular, I want to consider the means by which John constructs his ethos, his authority or credibility as a person to whom his audience should listen. John introduces himself as the recipient and mediator of an extraordinary revelation, an apocalypse (1:1) or a prophecy (1:3). Switching generic indicators, he directly addresses his story as a letter to seven churches in Asia Minor (1:4). Before narrating the vision itself, he identifies himself as brother to his audience and as one who shares in their distress, dominion and endurance, probably as one who suffers persecution (1:9). Throughout the vision John is a constant presence: forty-seven times he stresses having seen ("I saw," εἶδον), twenty-seven times having heard ("I heard," ἤκουσα), the things he describes. And at the end of the narrative, after he emphasizes that it is he who heard and saw the things he relates (22:8), he closes the book with a benediction (22:20-21).

Some readers will notice that I tend to personify John by attributing certain thoughts, intentions, attitudes, and skills to him. Those readers may object that "John" exists only as my own construction, that he is not "real" as a textual property or as a historical figure behind the Apocalypse. They may also protest that my arguments about "John" are circular in the extreme: first I construct him, and then I construct a (hopefully) critical discourse about him.

To offer such objections would be correct, but I doubt it would say much that is particularly interesting or helpful about the Apocalypse. All interpretive discourse is equally constructed, and therefore must be circular to a large degree. The properties that we may ascribe to Revelation are no more or less than those properties that we identify and share with other readers, or those we can persuade other readers to agree upon. Surely the construct that I call John lacks ontological status as a property of the text we call Revelation. However, the textual "properties" certain groups of readers can agree upon often contribute to important cultural legacies.

At the same time, popular and scholarly readers contribute to John's "reality" by appealing to his character and by appropriating his ethos. In other words, his narratorial voice energizes the ways people use the Apocalypse. If John is trustworthy, so is his message. If he is privileged with special knowledge, then his readers should heed him. If he has his audience's best interests in mind, the potentially objectionable aspects of his vision become more palatable. For these reasons, "John" is an appropriate point of entry for any discussion of how religious and rhetorical authority function in Revelation. He provides the energy that is set loose by scholarly and popular readers alike.

In taking John's ethos seriously I am following the lead of literary and cultural critics who share an interest in the rhetorical dimensions of texts. Among these are Kenneth Burke, Wayne C. Booth, Susan Snaider Lanser, and Mikhail Bakhtin, each of whom provides theoretical resources for this project. Even more direct in treating narrative rhetoric as a social and political act are post-colonial and resistance critics, several of whom—including Chinua Achebe, Edward Said, David Spurr, and Richard Terdiman—also contribute to this study. In the next chapter I will sketch the ways in which I draw upon these diverse thinkers in constructing my reading strategy. For now the important thing is to acknowledge John's critical influence on all readers of Revelation. Though the John we encounter in the Apocalypse is several steps removed from the actual person of its author, he nevertheless functions as a powerful rhetorical device.

Rhetorical criticism of the New Testament generally emphasizes textual features above the readers who activate them.[6] Critics of Revelation are no exception. But it is real readers, like myself and Revelation's popular readers, who construct its meaning-potential, and popular readings of Revelation may be just as enlightening as scholarly ones. My position is that real readers produce meaning by identifying and constructing textual properties, properties that become identifiable and debatable.[7] The upshot is a reading

---

[6]The Bible and Culture Collective, *The Postmodern Bible* (New Haven: Yale University, 1995) 164.

[7]In opposition to the Bible and Culture Collective's assessment of reader-

strategy that overturns the hierarchy of critical readers over lay readers by assuming that popular readings may inform critical exegesis. My treatment of John and his intended audience is, then, a construct of my own critical reading and may legitimately (though carefully) be influenced by contemporary North American popular readings.

Thesis One: Authority and Resistance

> The Apocalypse of John is a literary replication of the original and unique revelatory experience of John the Seer which, when performed in a public, probably even a cultic setting, communicates the author's paraenetic message with divine authority.[8]

Critics have reached a fairly strong consensus regarding John's broad historical context and that of his intended audience. They agree that Revelation, addressed to churches in imperial Asia Minor, reflects a colonial situation. It sharply criticizes the Roman Empire and its emperor for oppressing people in general and Christians in particular.[9] Scholars also acknowledge that Revelation offers an oppositional point of view toward the broader society, a dualistic perspective that is common in early Jewish and Christian revelatory literature. They further claim that references to the "synagogue of Satan" in Rev 2:9 and 3:9 most likely indicate a conflict between some Jewish and Christian communities. Finally, they agree that John is concerned with internal as well as external opponents. Especially in the letters to the churches (Rev 2–3) John attacks particular Christian prophets whose teaching he opposes.

---

response criticisms, which collapses the (I think, helpful) distinction between text and reader (*Postmodern Bible,* 51), I maintain that meaning is a negotiation between reader and text. At the same time, I would not go so far in the direction of textual control as does Wolfgang Iser, according to whom the text defines its ideal reader and manipulates or entangles him or her (*The Act of Reading: A Theory of Aesthetic Response* [Baltimore: Johns Hopkins University Press, 1978] 34, 125-34).

[8]David E. Aune, "The Apocalypse of John and the Problem of Genre," *Semeia* 36 (1986): 91.

[9]Scholars do not agree as to whether Revelation reflects a genuine "crisis" situation or simply a "perceived crisis." I will address this question in more detail below.

While I affirm the scholarly consensus about Revelation's likely context, I would like to emphasize its colonial dimension. By colonialism I mean the domination of one culture by another, whether through military, political, ideological, or economic resources.[10] For those who lived under Roman rule, colonialism meant living within what social historian Michael Mann calls the first great territorial empire, possibly the most successful empire in world history at retaining its conquests. Because of the ways Rome managed to absorb conquered elites into the Roman ruling class, the Empire could enjoy ideological hegemony even in its conquered territories.[11] For example, its subjects were generally more impressed by hellenistic culture than resistant to it.[12] Mann describes this dynamic as "authoritative power," the conscious or organized acknowledgement of imperial claims.[13]

There is no "common" colonialism, but particular instances of and responses to colonialism often share common characteristics. Edward Said expresses how colonialism looks to the colonized:

> [T]o be one of the colonized is potentially to be a great many different, but inferior, things in many different places, at many different times.[14]

Revelation reflects tensions similar to those we find in more recent colonial and neocolonial contexts. For one thing, colonialisms create struggles over culture and representation. More contemporary expressions of resistance to colonialism evidence a stronger insider/outsider dynamic than did the more fluid cultures of hellenistic Asia Minor, most of which did not feature a strong

---

[10]See Michael Mann, *The Sources of Social Power*, vol. 1, *A History of Power from the Beginning to A.D. 1760* (New York: Cambridge University Press, 1986). While Mann does not offer a definition of colonialism, he consistently employs the same four factors—military, politics, ideology, and economics—to analyze the development and deployment of international power.

[11]Ibid., 250.

[12]Samuel K. Eddy, *The King Is Dead: Studies in Near Eastern Resistance to Hellenism 334–331 B.C.* (Lincoln: University of Nebraska Press, 1961) 334.

[13]Mann, *Sources of Social Power*, 8-9, 250; cf. Eddy, *The King Is Dead*, 39.

[14]"Representing the Colonized: Anthropology's Interlocutors," *Critical Inquiry* 15 (1989): 207.

sense of national or ethnic identity;[15] however, they share with Revelation a sense that representation involves power.[16] While Roman ideology sought to permeate the worlds of its subjects, cultural resistance did pop up from time to time, notably in Jewish and Christian revelatory literature. Some *Sibylline Oracles*, particularly *Sib. Or.* 3,[17] 5, 8:1-216, and 12,[18] and certain texts from Qumran, notably the *War Scroll*, apply criticisms against Rome that resemble those which Daniel directs toward the Seleucids. Rome is both powerful and arrogant, prosperous and corrupt. For example, *Sib. Or.* 3:175-90 uses Daniel's framework of the successive world kingdoms to combine Rome's power and wealth with its oppression and decadence. Thus, some Jewish subjects contested the Empire's representation of itself. They substituted alternative characterizations of the "real" Rome and envisioned its destruction.

Second, colonialisms often pit their subjects against one another. By offering only one legitimate source for economic resources and commercial validation, colonizers force their subjects to compete for legitimation.[19] And by displacing traditional loci of meaning and authority, colonizers institutionalize cultural confusion. In *Things Fall Apart* the Nigerian author Chinua Achebe portrays this process through Obierika's famous speech:

> But [the white man] says that our customs are bad; and our own brothers who have taken up his religion also say that our customs are bad. How do you think we can fight when our own brothers have turned against us? The white man is very clever. He came quietly and peaceably with his new religion. We were amused at his foolishness and allowed him to stay. Now he has

---

[15]Eddy, *The King Is Dead*, 163-71.

[16]A discussion of representation in postcolonial and resistance theories appears in chap. 2.

[17]According to John J. Collins, *Sib. Or.* 3 includes some oracles from the Roman period (*The Apocalyptic Imagination: An Introduction to the Jewish Matrix of Christianity* [New York: Crossroad, 1984] 101).

[18]Collins maintains that *Sibylline* resistance likely derives from Egyptian models such as the *Demotic Chronicle* and the *Potter's Oracle* (*Apocalyptic Imagination*, 94).

[19]Barbara Harlow, *Resistance Literature* (New York: Methuen, 1987) 5-7, 29; James C. Scott, "Revolution in the Revolution: Peasants and Commissars," *Theory and Society* 7 (1979): 97-134.

> won our brothers, and our clan can no longer act like one. He has put a knife on the things that held us together and we have fallen apart.[20]

Because Revelation is in part a response to imperial realities, it features both these problems. On the one hand, Rome is the enemy, characterized as a Beast and associated with a Whore, both of whom make blasphemous claims, oppress human beings, and persecute Christians. On the other hand, John attacks other colonial subjects—Jews, other Christians, people in general—for their complicity with the Empire. Both dimensions of the colonial condition appear in Revelation: It contests imperial representations even as it promotes division among imperial subjects.

John's most forceful criticisms of Rome occur in chapters 13 and 17-18. Chapter 13 introduces the Beast, whose appearance is foreshadowed in 11:7. The Beast has seven heads and ten horns. Upon each head is a blasphemous name; each horn has a crown. One of the heads has what looks like a mortal wound, a wound that has been healed. Inspired by the Dragon, Satan (12:9), the Beast accepts worship from "the whole world" and persecutes the saints. Then John sees an Other Beast, whose primary role is to promote worship of the first Beast. This Other Beast exercises government authority, excluding from the marketplace anyone who does not have the first Beast's name or number marked on their right hand or forehead (13:17). John then pronounces a riddle—"This calls for wisdom"—the Beast's number is that of a human being. It is six hundred sixty-six (13:18).[21]

One can imagine that scholars and popular readers alike have expended tremendous energy over this riddle, particularly its numerological details. The aim is to identify the Beast by decoding its seven heads, ten horns, and mysterious number, a pursuit that goes at least as far back as Irenaeus,[22] and one that is notoriously

---

[20]*Things Fall Apart*, African Writers Series 1 (repr.: Portsmouth NH: Heinemann, 1962; [1]1958) 124-25.

[21]The overwhelming majority of textual evidence favors the reading ἑξακόσιοι (or ἑξακόσιαι) ἑξήκοντα ἕξ (notably, p[47] C A) over ἑξακόσιοι δέκα ἕξ (for which C is the strongest witness).

[22]Arthur W. Wainwright, *Mysterious Apocalypse: Interpreting the Book of Revelation* (Nashville: Abingdon, 1993) 25; R. H. Charles, *A Critical and Exegetical*

problematic.[23] R. H. Charles's classic exegesis is especially helpful. Charles argues that the seven heads are the sum of the heads on the four beasts in Dan 7:2-7, the ten horns are taken from the fourth beast, and its resemblances to a leopard, a bear, and a lion derive from the first three beasts. Like Daniel's four beasts, the Beast of Revelation rises from the sea. Charles concludes that the Beast is the Roman Empire, read as an even more terrible version of Daniel's fourth beast.[24] Like Daniel's fourth beast, this Beast represents the sum of imperial power, set against the people of God. That the Beast is identified with a single human being in 13:18 (likely Nero) simply indicates a particular instance of its imperious vitality, for John an eschatological configuration of domination and blasphemy.[25]

Nevertheless, the problem of dating the Apocalypse is related to the concern about identifying the Number of the Beast (13:18) and the enumeration of the emperors reflected in 17:9-11.[26] While I join the majority of scholars who maintain that Revelation was written late in the reign of Domitian (i.e. 95-96 CE), a growing number offer strong arguments for an earlier date, probably about 68 CE.[27] Arguments for a Domitianic date usually emphasize the

---

Commentary on the Revelation of St. John, 2 vols., ICC (Edinburgh: T.&T. Clark; New York: Charles Scribner's, 1920) 1:365-67.

[23]Sophie Laws offers a solution to the Beast's number even as she laughs at the difficulties involved (*In the Light of the Lamb: Imagery, Parody, and Theology in the Apocalypse of John*, GNS 31 (Wilmington DE: Michael Glazier, 1988] 47-51). See the helpful discussion in Leonard L. Thompson, *The Book of Revelation: Apocalypse and Empire* (New York: Oxford University Press, 1990) 13-17.

[24]*Revelation*, 1:345.

[25]Ibid., 1:365-67. Thompson argues that Revelation tends to blur the boundaries among the various evil forces it describes (*Book of Revelation*, 79-80), an insight that complements Charles's suggestions and resonates with many of my arguments in chaps. 4 and 5.

[26]The heads "are also seven kings, the five who have fallen, the one who is, the other who has not yet come, and when he comes he will remain only a little while. Now, the Beast which was and is not, it is an eighth and is one of the seven, and it goes to destruction."

[27]The most influential and complete arguments among recent scholars for the later date may be found in Adela Yarbro Collins, *Crisis and Catharsis: The Power of the Apocalypse* (Philadelphia: Westminster, 1984) 54-83; and Thompson, *Revelation*, 13-17. David Aune is notable for his source theory that traces an earlier stage to the 50s and 60s and a final compilation (perhaps by the same author in the 90s

testimony of Irenaeus (*Haer.* 5.30.3) that Revelation was written "toward the end of the reign of Domitian" with external evidence that describes Domitian as a megalomaniac and persecutor of Christians. Arguments that Domitian's claims to divinity were more strident than those of his predecessors or that he fostered systematic persecution of Christians simply do not withstand scrutiny, however.[28] In my opinion, two telling details shift the balance of probability toward Irenaeus's date. First, the use of the codename "Babylon" for Rome reflects a Jewish tradition that presupposes the destruction of Jerusalem in 70 CE and occurs only after that date.[29] And second, Polycarp's letter to the Philippians (11:3) suggests that the church in Smyrna, one of Revelation's seven churches, did not even exist while Paul was writing, presumably before 64 CE.[30] Certainty regarding Revelation's date remains elusive, and I have chosen not to base my interpretation on this issue.

From a literary-rhetorical perspective, however, the date of Revelation and the identities of various Roman emperors—about whose relationship with early Christianity we know almost nothing—are not as important as the Beast's function in John's program. Locating a one-to-one historical correspondence for the Beast

---

(*Revelation 1–5*, WBC 52A [Dallas: Word Books, 1997] lvi-lxx, cv-cxxxiv). Advocates of the earlier date include J. Christian Wilson ("The Problem of the Domitianic Date of Revelation," *NTS* 39 [1993]: 587-605), Christopher Rowland (*The Open Heaven: A Study of Apocalyptic in Judaism and Early Christianity* [New York: Crossroad, 1982] 17), and John W. Marshall ("Parables of the War: Reading the Apocalypse within Judaism and during the Judean War" [Ph.D. diss., Princeton University, 1997]). Advocates of an early date note that: (1) Rev 11:1-2 implies a date before 70 CE, as it may assume the existence of the Jerusalem temple; (2) Rev 13:18, which assigns the number 666 to the Beast, is almost certainly a reference to Nero, whose reign ended in 68 CE; and (3) if the series of emperors enumerated in Rev 17:9-11 begins with Julius or Augustus and continues through every emperor, it must conclude with Galba or Otho, i.e., in 68 or 69 CE.

[28]Thompson, *Book of Revelation*, 95-115.

[29]In 4 *Ezra* 3:1-2, 28-31; 2 *Baruch* 10:1-3; 11:1; 67:7; and *Sib. Or.* 5:143, 159 (cited in Aune, *Revelation 1–5*, lxi).

[30]Though Colin J. Hemer argues that Polycarp may imply only that the Philippian church was older than the Smyrnean (*The Letters to the Seven Churches in Asia Minor in Their Local Setting*, JSNTSup 11 [Sheffield UK: JSOT, 1986] 66), I have followed a more literal reading (cf. Charles, *Revelation*, 1:xciv; Aune, *Revelation 1–5*, lviii).

may be more than we can accomplish anyway.[31] Instead, we may emphasize *why* John is interested in the Beast, which has something to do with worship and blasphemy. The Beast is important not simply as a threatening political figure, but also for its demand of worship.[32] Politically astute, John refuses to discriminate between worship of the emperor and worship of the Empire. As John points out, the Beast has the number of a human being (13:18).

In the cities of late first-century Asia Minor, the cult of the emperor was a prominent feature of civic life. While we lack concrete evidence that John's audience experienced persecution for their refusal to participate in the cult, Pliny's famous correspondence with Trajan reflects how things had developed by 112 CE, within a generation or two of John's audience and just north of their cities.[33] Pliny apparently assumes that the simple identification of a person as "Christian" is cause for severe punishment, and that Trajan is aware of the problem. Pliny allows accused Christians to demonstrate their innocence by cursing Christ and praying to the Roman gods, including the emperor's image. Surprisingly for this early date, Pliny seems to blame the Christians for a decline in traditional piety: temples had been deserted, observance of the sacred festivals had been spotty, and the market for sacrificial meat had fallen sharply.[34]

Pliny's assessment of the Christians may reflect a general opinion that had developed over decades. For most of John's neighbors, the festivals would not have signified mere flattery toward Rome; instead, they were more like a North American city's hosting the Olympic Games, implying civic pride and popular involvement. Cities competed for the privilege of hosting shrines and festivals for the emperor, and the institution eventually became the most

---

[31]If we count its heads as emperors, as the text invites us to do (Rev 17:9), with which emperor should we begin counting, and which ones should we leave out (cf. Thompson, *Book of Revelation*, 14)?

[32]As Charles notes, the Beast's miraculous head is identified with the entire Beast in 13:12, 14 (*Revelation*, 1:349).

[33]Pliny the Younger, *Letters* 10.97.

[34]Pliny's letter may be read as evidence for dating Revelation to the 90s. Pliny indicates that some accused Christians had renounced Christianity "as long as twenty-five years ago," a possible but dubious reference to a Domitianic persecution (Gerhard A. Krodel, *Revelation*, ACNT [Minneapolis: Augsburg, 1989] 40).

important cult in Asia Minor.[35] Persons who refused to participate could be regarded as obstinate, or even subversive. Even if official persecution of Christians did not exist in John's day, conspicuous refusal to participate in the cult[36] would surely bring popular disapproval, perhaps with social and economic consequences or worse. Revelation 13 reflects just such a context: John accuses the Beast of blasphemy, noting that refusal to worship it might imply the risk of death (13:7) and loss of access to essential commercial goods (13:17).

Here the distinction between the Beast and the Other Beast is significant. The first Beast rises from the sea, indicating an international power. But the Other Beast rises out of the land (13:11), likely indicating its indigenous origin. When we recall the popularity of the imperial cult in Asia Minor, John's distinction makes sense. Rome as an oppressive and blasphemous international power is the ultimate Beast; the complicity of John's neighbors is beastly in a derivative sense.

Adela Yarbro Collins and Leonard L. Thompson have advanced the thesis that Revelation reflects not so much an actual historical crisis as a perceived crisis.[37] This argument has dominated

---

[35]S. R. F. Price, *Rituals and Power: The Roman Imperial Cult in Asia Minor* (Cambridge: Cambridge University Press, 1984) 101-32. For the entanglement of the imperial cult with commerce and social life, see J. Nelson Kraybill, *Imperial Cult and Commerce in John's Apocalypse*, JSNTSup 132 (Sheffield UK: Sheffield Academic Press, 1986) 24-101, 121-35. The argument of Donald L. Jones that Domitian's reign (81–96 CE) did in fact bring persecution to those Christians in Asia Minor who refused to participate in the cult now seems dated ("Christianity and the Roman Imperial Cult," *ANRW* 2.23.2, 1032-35).

[36]We do not know how some Christians might have avoided participation, whether openly or by stealth.

[37]Collins, *Crisis and Catharsis*; Thompson, *Book of Revelation*. Drawing from contemporary sociological research, Stephen L. Cook has recently demonstrated that some Hebrew Bible and early Jewish apocalyptic literature did not arise from contexts of absolute deprivation, as most biblical scholars have assumed (*Prophecy and Apocalypticism: The Postexilic Social Setting* [Minneapolis: Fortress, 1995]). Instead, relative deprivation, which occurs when persons or groups perceive their situations as being inconsistent with their expectations or hopes, is often the social context for apocalyptic or millenarian movements. However, the explanatory power of relative deprivation theory is limited, as almost anyone can *feel* deprived or dissatisfied. Among the important studies from sociology and social psychology are Yonina Talmon, "Pursuit of the Millennium: The Relation between

recent discussions of the Apocalypse, as scholars take sides for or against a real crisis. Noting the lack of evidence that Christians (or Jews for that matter) in late first century CE Asia Minor suffered systematic persecution, and the problems of trusting the Roman and Christian historians who blame Domitian for every evil of the period, Collins and Thompson argue that John's program involves a kind of social radicalism. John, they say, is not describing an ongoing official persecution of Christians, but is predicting what he believes is the inevitable conflict between John's churches and the rest of society. Indeed, John promotes such a conflict by calling Christians to withdraw from all entanglements with the Empire.

Systematic persecution or no, John and his audience had reason to be anxious. John certainly knew of some Christian martyrs; Antipas (Rev 2:13) is only one recent example. And it is likely that John himself was a political exile (1:9).[38] But for John the critical source of crisis involves more than instances of martyrdom; it is his perception of an imperial world that is entirely corrupt. Whether or not his criticism is accurate,[39] it certainly would create a crisis for John and those whom he could persuade.[40]

Religious and Social Change," *Archives Européennes de Sociologie* 3 (1962): 125-48; Sylvia L. Thrupp, "Millennial Dreams in Action: A Report on the Conference Discussion," in *Millennial Dreams in Action: Studies in Revolutionary Religious Movements*, ed. Sylvia L. Thrupp (New York: Shocken, 1970) 11-27; David F. Aberle, "A Note on Relative Deprivation Theory as Applied to Millenarian and Other Cult Movements," in *Millennial Dreams in Action: Studies in Revolutionary Religious Movements*, ed. Sylvia L. Thrupp (New York: Shocken, 1970) 209-14; Bryan R. Wilson, *Magic and the Millennium: A Sociological Study of Religious Movements of Protest Among Tribal and Third-World Peoples* (New York: Harper & Row, 1973); and Charles B. Strozier, *Apocalypse: On the Psychology of Fundamentalism in America* (Boston: Beacon, 1994).

[38]Again, this is a disputed point, which I will discuss in chap. 4.

[39]According to Ernest P. Janzen, "The numismatic data . . . strongly suggest that many of the claims made about [Domitian's] megalomania are solidly grounded" ("The Jesus of the Apocalypse Wears the Emperor's Clothes," *SBLSP* 33 [1994]: 643).

[40]I am not convinced by Philip F. Esler's suggestion that Rome is not among John's pressing concerns ("Sorcery Accusations and the Apocalypse," in *The First Christians in Their Social Worlds: Social-Scientific Approaches to New Testament Interpretation* [New York: Routledge, 1994] 131-46). Drawing upon contemporary cases in which individuals or groups accuse individual outsiders of sorcery in order to deal with internal threats to the group or community, Esler argues that Rome serves as a scapegoat in Revelation. John's accusations against Rome are "in

In addition to characterizing Rome as the Beast, John uses another image: the Whore. How do these grotesque representations relate to one another? For one thing, boundaries among the representations of John's enemies are often blurred.[41] John tells us that the Whore is seated on the Beast (17:3), implying intimacy but not identity. According to Richard Bauckham the Whore represents Roman civilization in general: "Roman civilization, as a corrupting influence, rides on the back of Roman military power."[42] But perhaps the Whore embodies something more specific than Roman civilization: She is a city; the Beast is an institution. Though drunk with the blood of Jesus' witnesses (17:6), her primary associations are political and economic.[43] But in another sense, the Whore is greater than the Beast. While the Beast represents only one person, city, or institution, the Whore connotes an entire imperial political and economic network, one that results in immense wealth for some and death for others.

So John's problem with Rome is political, economic, and religious. The Empire uses its power to dominate people; it demands not just submission but worship. For John the Empire is so evil as to be beyond redemption, so powerful that Christians must reckon with it. The Empire and John's churches are, or, from John's perspective, ought to be on a collision course. Revelation is resistance literature.

One effect of John's response to Rome is his assessment of humanity in general, the "inhabitants of the earth" whose names

---

response to internal tendencies toward disintegration and ennui" (146), and they remind the churches of their fragility as communities. In my opinion, Esler's parallels are inappropriate: Rome is not an individual, and John has no cultural resources by means of which his accusations against Rome may be resolved. Revelation's attack against Rome does indeed promote heightened community solidarity, but only insofar as it represents the Empire as a genuine threat.

[41]Thompson, *Book of Revelation*, 79-80.

[42]"The Economic Critique of Rome in Revelation 18 [with note on Sibylline Oracles]," in *Images of Empire*, ed. Loveday Alexander, JSOTSup 122 (Sheffield UK: Sheffield Academic Press, 1991) 52.

[43]Rev 17:2, 18; 18:3, 9-19. Cf. Néstor Míguez, "Apocalyptic and the Economy: A Reading of Revelation 18 from the Experience of Economic Exclusion," in *Reading from This Place*, vol. 2, *Social Location and Biblical Interpretation in Global Perspective*, ed. Fernando F. Segovia and Mary Ann Tolbert (Minneapolis: Fortress, 1995) 250-62.

are not included in the Book of Life. John does not discriminate among them. They have collaborated with the Beast, making them deserving of punishment. Not only do they worship the Beast (13:12-14; 17:8) and become intimate with the Whore (17:2), they themselves are guilty of the saints' blood (6:10). So depraved are they that even when confronted by Revelation's cosmic plagues, they do not repent (9:20-21) and curse God for their pain (16:9). Commentator Wilfrid J. Harrington follows John's assessment of the "inhabitants of the earth": "throughout the book these are the enemies of God, the oppressors of God's people."[44] For these people John imagines destruction: "Woe, woe, woe to the earth's inhabitants" (8:13). So John predicts their final judgment: "If anyone was not found to be written in the Book of Life, that one was thrown into the lake of fire" (20:15).

In effect, John has not merely chosen to resist the Empire's political and economic systems, he also advocates a revolutionist stance toward society in general.[45] The only evidence that could mitigate the severity of John's view is the assertion that people are deceived by the Other Beast's miraculous signs (13:14). To the extent that John perceives the Empire to be absolutely evil, and to the extent that most people in Asia Minor were favorable toward Rome, so John justifies dreams of destruction for the world's population.

In addition to Rome and humanity in general, John specifically alludes to conflict with what appear to be Jewish communities in Smyrna and Philadelphia, calling them "the synagogue of Satan" and "those who say themselves to be Jews and are not" (τῶν λεγόντων Ἰουδαίους εἶναι ἑαυτοὺς, καὶ οὐκ εἰσίν, 2:9; 3:9). What could be the problem here? In both contexts the apparent references to Jews are followed immediately by allusions

---

[44]*Revelation*, Sacra Pagina 16 (Collegeville MN: Michael Glazier, 1993) 93.

[45]David A. deSilva speculates that one source of pressure for John and his audience would have been the expectation that they participate in trade guilds and their ritual meals ("The Revelation to John: A Case Study in Apocalyptic Propaganda and the Maintenance of Sectarian Identity," *Sociological Analysis* 53 [1992]: 381-82). His suggestion largely depends upon the assumption that the situation reflected in 1 Cor 8 and 10 involves these issues and is analogous to that in Rev 2-3.

to particular trials. In the letter to Smyrna John accuses the Jews of slander, then exhorts his audience not to fear their impending suffering, which will include imprisonment, perhaps even death, for some (2:9-10). John promises that the Jews will prostrate themselves before the feet of his Philadelphian audience, then notes that the Philadelphians have kept the word of endurance, a word John associates with trial and danger (ὑπομονή, 3:9-10).

Could it be that some Jews are instigating problems for the Christians in these cities? In the light of comments like those of G. B. Caird and Colin J. Hemer, one should hesitate before blaming Jews for John's problem. While Caird would be describing John's perspective, he twice says that by rejecting their Messiah Jews had lost the right to that name.[46] Perhaps more chilling is his comment that, "There is no indication that the Jews at Philadelphia were any better than Jews in other parts of Asia. . . ."[47] Hemer, who may be correct in supposing that Jewish "rejection of the Christians placed the latter outside the protection and toleration which the Jews themselves enjoyed,"[48] also accounts Jewish influence in Philadelphia to the fact that it was "an economically weak city" and to Jewish pursuit of "opportunities for exploitation by the less scrupulous by the sale of necessities at extortionate prices."[49]

Caird and Hemer's comments may seem mild when compared to those of popular readers like Grant R. Jeffrey, but the similarity is instructive. Jeffrey asserts not only that some Jews were persecuting the Christians in Smyrna (Rev 2:9), but also that their actions were a blasphemy against God. Moreover, he somehow knows that in Smyrna "many Jews listened to the message of the gospel and accepted Christ as their Messiah." As for the others,

---

[46]*The Revelation of Saint John*, Black's New Testament Commentary (Peabody MA: Hendrickson, 1966) 35, 52.

[47]Ibid., 52.

[48]*Letters*, 68.

[49]Ibid., 160. I had not noticed this quote in Hemer until I read Jack T. Sanders, who calls attention to Hemer's prejudice, as well as to similar statements from other scholars (*Schismatics, Sectarians, Dissidents, Deviants: The First One Hundred Years of Jewish-Christian Relations* [Valley Forge PA: Trinity Press International, 1993] 176-78, 318-22).

they were tools of Satan: "Although Satan used human instruments to oppress the Church, their real enemy was the Devil."[50]

Some have suggested that the problems in Smyrna and Philadelphia were internal to the churches. Due to their status as an ancient and respectable people, Jews enjoyed certain privileges within the Empire, notably an exemption from the emperor cult. Perhaps John condemns those Christians who were claiming identity as Jews in order to benefit from this exemption.[51] Such behavior *could* draw John's criticism that these persons claimed to be Jews when in fact they were not.[52] I find this conclusion unlikely. The contexts of Rev 2:9 and 3:9 tell against this suggestion. In each case John associates these "so-called Jews" with dangers faced by his audiences. It is unlikely that some Christians, persons who were identifying themselves as Jews in order to protect *themselves*, would provoke hostility to other Christians who did not follow the same strategy.

So we are left with the likelihood that some Jews were causing problems for members of John's audience. But why? And how? Even if Christians were not identifying themselves as Jews, and some may have been, their presence would have been confusing to many Gentiles.[53] For one thing, while Jews represented a sizable

---

[50]Jeffrey, *Apocalypse: The Coming Judgment of the Nations* (New York: Bantam, 1992) 76.

[51]Such claims could be based upon conviction, given Christianity's relationship with Judaism. Or they may simply have been expedient. For a strong argument for the possibility that John is accusing Gentile Christians who have also identified themselves as Jews, see Stephen G. Wilson, *Related Strangers: Jews and Christians, 60–170 C.E.* (Minneapolis: Fortress, 1995) 162-63. But one should also note that Domitian at least was opposed to Gentiles "who drifted into Jewish ways," as testified by the fates of Flavius Clemens, whom Domitian executed, and his wife Flavia Domitilla, who was exiled, for adopting Jewish practice (Dio Cassius, *Epitome* 67.14.1-3). Of course, the execution of a member of the Roman elite does not necessarily indicate any level of systematic persecution.

[52]Ignatius makes a similar complaint concerning the same region around 110 CE (*Phld.* 6:1; *Magn.* 8:1; cf. Wilson, *Related Strangers*, 163-65). For a discussion of Ignatius's response to Christians who adopted distinctive Jewish practices, see Adela Yarbro Collins, "Vilification and Self-Definition in the Book of Revelation," *HTR* 79 (1986): 311; and Peder Borgen, "Polemic in the Book of Revelation," in *Anti-Semitism and Early Christianity*, ed. Craig A. Evans and Donald A. Hagner (Minneapolis: Fortress, 1993) 210.

[53]Gentiles in Asia Minor may have found it difficult to distinguish some Chris-

section of the population in any major city in Asia Minor and likely saw themselves as the civic equals of their Greek neighbors, Christians did not.[54] Christians, particularly when they claimed to be the true heirs to the Jewish heritage, and especially if they sought Jewish legal privileges, probably represented a threat to Jewish security.[55] With Christians reaching for the limited security available to Jews, it would be perfectly understandable for Jews to identify them as being outsiders to their communities.[56] From a Jewish point of view, such a decision would have seemed a reasonable act of self-preservation. For Christians, it would have implied exposure to public scrutiny.[57] And for John, it was an act of slander, or blasphemy.

A final category of John's opponents includes other Christians. We find them among the letters to the churches in chapters 2 and 3. John's most obvious concerns are with those he names Nicolaitans (2:6, 15) and the prophets Balaam (2:14) and Jezebel (2:20-24). In addition, John mentions the presence of false apostles (2:2). Against the Nicolaitans John says nothing direct, though it is possible he associates them with Balaam in 2:14-15. But the individual prophets he names Balaam and Jezebel are identified with identical offenses: teaching people to eat food that has been sacrificed to idols and to commit sexual immorality. Jezebel's

---

tians from Jews (Adela Yarbro Collins, "Insiders and Outsiders in the Book of Revelation and Its Social Context, in *"To See Ourselves as Others See Us": Christians, Jews, "Others" in Late Antiquity*, ed. Jacob Neusner and Ernest S. Frerichs, Scholars Press Studies in the Humanities [Chico CA: Scholars Press, 1985] 196-97).

[54]S. Appelbaum, "The Legal Status of the Jewish Communities in the Diaspora," in *The Jewish People in the First Century: Historical Geography, Political History, Social, Cultural, and Religious Life and Institutions*, ed. S. Safrai and M. Stern, CRINT (Assen: Van Gorcum & Comp. B.V., 1974) 1:451; Wilson, *Related Strangers*, 25.

[55]While they enjoyed some privileges within the Empire, Jews were also subject to suspicion and violence. What John G. Gager says of Rome may generally apply to the Empire as a whole: "Roman public opinion was deeply divided on the matter of Judaism" ("Judaism as Seen by Outsiders," in *Early Judaism and Its Modern Interpreters*, ed. Robert A. Kraft and George W. E. Nickelsburg (Atlanta: Scholars Press, 1986) 111. Not only during the Jewish War, but throughout the first century, Jewish communities in some parts of the Diaspora were subject to urban violence (Philo, *In Flaccum* and *Ad Gaium*; Josephus, *Ant.* 18.8.1; *J.W.* 2.18).

[56]Collins, "Vilification and Self-Definition," 313; Borgen, "Polemic," 211.

[57]Borgen, "Polemic," 211.

teaching also appears to involve knowledge of "the deep things of Satan" (2:24).

What can we make of these various attacks? M. Eugene Boring argues that, "Since these [figures] are described in identical terms, they are probably all designations of the same group or movement."[58] While most commentators would agree with Boring that these opponents share a common teaching, caution is in order. For one thing, Revelation does not describe John's opponents in identical terms. We know nothing about the Nicolaitans, except through their likely association with Balaam (2:15). And while Balaam and Jezebel are both associated with idolatry and *porneia*, the link with esoteric knowledge applies to Jezebel alone. Finally, there is no firm evidence that these figures have anything to do with the false prophets of 2:2.

For our purposes, which do not include an exhaustive study of John's historical context, we may limit ourselves to John's clearest assertions. John says that some of his opponents advocate eating food sacrificed to idols, sexual immorality, and esoteric knowledge. Here we find help from two sources: the Hebrew Bible and an analogy with 1 Corinthians. In the Hebrew Bible, both Balaam and Jezebel are outsiders to Israel who promote assimilation with other peoples and worship of gods other than YHWH.[59] The Hebrew Bible often characterizes idolatrous practices as adultery, making it extremely likely that John's pairing of eating food sacrificed to idols with sexual misconduct is actually a case of emphasis by repetition. For John they are one and the same: to eat food that had been sacrificed to idols is to show complicity with the idolatrous practices that define the Empire and the larger society.

A look at one of Paul's problems in 1 Corinthians fills in the picture. Some of the Corinthians, with whom Paul agrees, defend the eating of food sacrificed to idols by appealing to knowledge (1 Cor 8:1-7). And yet some of them apparently were involved in

---

[58]*Revelation*, Interpretation (Louisville: John Knox, 1989) 92.

[59]Balaam's account is included in Num 22-24 and 31:8; Num 31:16 blames Balaam for the people's worship of Baal at Peor (25:1-9). Jezebel becomes most famous as the enemy of the prophet Elijah. She is introduced through her marriage to Ahab king of Israel, which leads immediately to his worship of Baal and an Asherah (1 Kgs 16:31-33).

pagan worship, a practice Paul condemned (10:14). When we note that John links Jezebel's teaching with esoteric knowledge (Rev 2:24), a possible connection presents itself. Perhaps some members of John's audience defended their diets by appealing to special knowledge, though most likely in a different form than that we find in 1 Corinthians.[60]

So far as we can tell, John's complaint is that some Christian leaders are advocating an accommodation to popular practice, in particular the eating of food that had been offered to idols. Indeed, such food was common in Asia Minor, often served in cultic contexts as well as in private banquets and parties.[61] To abstain from such food implied removing oneself from one's larger network of friends and allies; it could mean giving up one's social and material security. As we have seen, Pliny's letter to Trajan indicates that by around 112 CE some Christians in Asia Minor had indeed refused to eat such meat. In opposing those who advocate accommodation, John calls for a hazardous deviance.

John's complaints against humanity in general and against Jews and other Christians in particular are marked by his colonial context. Perhaps his stance against popular practices such as eating food from cultic settings would imply an opposition to everyone, regardless of the imperial presence. But it is the Empire that requires its citizens to worship Caesar, and it is the Empire that defines Jews as a special people by exempting them from such responsibilities. Without the Empire, tensions between some Jews and Christians would amount to no more than infighting between a venerable tradition and one of its sects, altogether lacking the dangers a Christian might face through being exposed by Jews. Apart from the Empire and its determination to stamp out deviance and disloyalty, John's antipathy toward society would not have had life and death connotations.

Scholarly as well as popular readings have drawn upon John's struggle for authority. We are hardly surprised when popular

---

[60]It is a long but conceivable journey from knowledge that "an idol is nothing in the world" (1 Cor 8:4) to familiarity with "the deep things of Satan" (Rev 2:24).

[61]Thompson, *Book of Revelation*, 122-23; cf. Gerd Theissen, *The Social Setting of Pauline Christianity* (Philadelphia: Fortress, 1982) 127-32.

readers describe John as God's faithful prophet. And we expect that conservative scholars may appeal to John's authority through characterizations of his identity. For example, G. B. Caird insists that it is "unjust" to link John with the Jewish apocalypticists (except for the author of Daniel, which "is the product of an original mind"). The Jewish apocalypticists were "for the most part imitative and pedestrian," and their works lack literary quality and religious worth. In contrast, "John, though he adopts the apocalyptic form, claims over and over again to be a prophet."[62] Caird's assertions may be extreme, but Robert W. Wall's more measured assessment conveys the same sense that John speaks out of a genuinely prophetic authority.

> There is a sense in which Revelation represents the best illustration in the NT of a book whose authority derives from its revelatory content rather than from its author's status. . . . The authority of Revelation does not derive from an apostle who writes his visions down; rather, it derives from their source, God, and from the one who commissions their writing, the risen Christ.[63]

Conservative critics are not the only ones who buy into John's authority rhetoric. Appeals to John's character and authority are common even among Revelation's most rhetorically sensitive readers. Gerhard A. Krodel, who highlights the rhetorical dimensions of John's self-characterization, also maintains that John's authority comes from below (through his shared experiences and privileges with his audience) and from above (through his visionary experiences).[64] And David E. Aune, whom I quoted at the beginning of this section, knows that John works to "legitimate his prophetic role" by appealing to shared values and experiences with his audience.[65] At the same time, however, Revelation is empowered by an "egalitarian notion" that all Christians share the same status and obligations.[66]

---

[62]*Revelation*, 10.

[63]*Revelation*, New International Biblical Commentary (Peabody MA: Hendrickson, 1991) 9.

[64]*Revelation*, 54.

[65]"The Social Matrix of the Apocalypse of John," *Biblical Research* 26 (1981): 22.

[66]Ibid., 24.

These critical readings convey the sense that we might "know" John's values and intentions. While Krodel defends John against accusations that he was "possessed by a 'perfervid and psychotic imagination,' " Harrington suggests that John, "profoundly concerned that the communities [he addresses] be united in face of the all-out persecution he felt sure was at hand," had "no time for internal conflict."[67]

These examples demonstrate the importance of John's authority for Revelation's critical readers. In an indirect way, they also testify to authority as a critical dimension of the Apocalypse itself. To counter perceived threats from the Empire, the larger society, Jews, and other Christians, John presents an authoritative discourse of his own. John's characterization of himself becomes fundamental to his resistance.

Thesis Two: Scholars and Millenarian Readers

What is it about Revelation that prompts its scholarly readers to be so interested in what its popular readers are doing? A thoroughly rhetorical criticism of Revelation demands that we treat critical interpretations as rhetorical acts in themselves. They possess

> historical sets of topics, arguments, tropes, ideologies, and so forth which determine how texts are established as meaningful through rhetorical exchanges.[68]

A quick survey of the commentaries reveals that Revelation's critical readers are looking over their shoulders. There are certain topoi one expects of commentaries, like discussions of author, date, place, situation, and genre, to which Revelation's critics have added a new topos: misguided popular readings, especially those of dispensational premillennialists.

Dispensational premillennialists believe that the Bible accurately predicts this aeon's final events. By combining a wide range of

---

[67]Krodel, *Revelation*, 63; Harrington, *Revelation*, 66.

[68]Steven Mailloux, *Rhetorical Power* (Ithaca NY: Cornell University Press, 1989) 15.

biblical texts—especially readings from Daniel, Ezekiel, the Synoptics, 1 Thessalonians, and of course Revelation—they work out a coherent scheme for the world's end. In addition, dispensational premillennialists stress that human history has been divided into seven dispensations, that in each dispensation God relates to people differently, and that the present age is the penultimate dispensation. They further believe that the parousia will precede Christ's millennial reign. While millenarian readings of Revelation are nothing new, dispensational premillennialism is a more recent development, with origins in late nineteenth century Britain and North America.

The scholars' complaint appears to have two dimensions. First, many popular readings represent poor exegesis. They neglect the Apocalypse's larger historical and social context and fail to treat the entire Apocalypse with integrity, instead finding key passages to cut and paste into a millenarian framework. Second, millenarian readings are perceived to offer poor practical theology, encouraging all sorts of social and religious dysfunctions: (a) a pessimism about prospects for social change that leads to inactivity or worse; (b) a fascination with the obscure that distracts people from life's more important dimensions; and (c) a dualism that depersonalizes nonbelievers by constructing them as objects of missionary activity, as passive participants in the inevitable cosmic catastrophe, or even as enemies of God and God's people.

Some scholars appear to have more at stake than others. Gerhard A. Krodel devotes nineteen pages to the "Sorry Story of Misinterpretation" that runs from Victorinus of Pettau (d. 303 CE), Revelation's first commentator, to our own era's Hal Lindsey.[69] Perhaps accurately, Krodel characterizes premillennialist use of the Bible "as God's gigantic jigsaw puzzle" to help us "figure out" the final events.[70] But other than being poor exegesis, what is wrong with premillennialist readings?

> The notion of divine rapture from the inevitable holocaust buttresses self-righteous, narcissistic smugness; the rejection of

---

[69]*Revelation*, 14-32.

[70]Ibid., 28. The mixed metaphor is Krodel's.

> negotiations and compromise with our international opponents divides nations among lines of absolute good and absolute evil. The premillennialist ideologies concerning the State of Israel have made its devotees deaf to the cries of Palestinians and to the need of a shared humanity.[71]

And Wilfrid J. Harrington assigns the "premillennial dispensationalist" label to "the teaching of the major contemporary television evangelists," without discriminating among their various systems. Then he calls this teaching a "gross misinterpretation" that is "unsavory and even dangerous."[72] Likewise, Elisabeth Schüssler Fiorenza associates these readings, which she characterizes as "often very farfetched," with "imperialist politics."[73] David L. Barr presses even harder, intimating "a history of deception" in America, with people like Hal Lindsey who "have become wealthy [by] selling false scenarios" to a desperate public.[74] In each case the issue is that poor exegesis results in poor theology, or worse.

Disdain for the prophecy teachers has trickled down to the level of New Testament introductory texts. Some ignore millenarian interpretations altogether, choosing instead to begin by locating the Apocalypse within the imaginations and historical and literary contexts of early Christians.[75] When these texts refer to popular impressions of Revelation at all, they do so by noting how it baffles modern readers. Others, who cannot resist the temptation to take the prophecy teachers head-on, find a variety of ways in which to deal with them. (One textbook even devotes a full-page

---

[71]Ibid.

[72]*Revelation*, 15-16.

[73]*Revelation: Vision of a Just World*, Proclamation Commentaries (Minneapolis: Fortress, 1991) 8.

[74]*Tales of the End: A Narrative Commentary on the Book of Revelation*, Storytellers Bible 1 (Sonoma CA: Polebridge, 1998) 152-54.

[75]E.g., Stephen L. Harris, *The New Testament: A Student's Introduction* (Mountain View CA: Mayfield Pub. Co., 1988); Howard Clark Kee, *Understanding the New Testament*, 4th ed. (Englewood Cliffs NJ: Prentice-Hall, 1983); Robert A. Spivey and D. Moody Smith, *Anatomy of the New Testament: A Guide to Its Structure and Meaning*, 2nd ed. (New York: Macmillan, 1974). Cf. Susan R. Garrett, "Revelation," in *The Women's Bible Commentary*, ed. Carol A. Newsom and Sharon H. Ringe (Louisville: Westminster/John Knox; London: SPCK, 1992) 377-82.

box to its discussion of futuristic interpretations.)[76] Here one might (a) argue that futuristic readings of Revelation are actually misreadings,[77] (b) point to the religious and political dangers of these readings,[78] (c) provide absurd examples from popular interpretations,[79] (d) mock the people who hold to them,[80] or (e) simply allude to them in passing.[81]

In addition to the New Testament introductions, a recent wave of popular commentaries on the Apocalypse also engages the prophecy teachers. Each of these works attacks millenarian readings precisely on the issue of *ethos*. Bruce M. Metzger worries that millenarian readings often stunt the spirituality of their adherents, who concentrate "all their reading of Scripture on this one book alone."[82] Perhaps more seriously, while C. Freeman Sleeper admits that Revelation has often been used to authorize violence, he blames those who have taken the Apocalypse "as a literal blueprint for revolution or a religious reform."[83] Charles H. Talbert is even more explicit:

> My aim is twofold: to offer aid to those who are scarred by harmful readings of Revelation and to encourage mainstream Christians to deal with the Apocalypse in ways other than ignoring it.[84]

---

[76]Bart D. Ehrman, *The New Testament: A Historical Introduction to the Early Christian Writings* (New York: Oxford University, 1997) 407.

[77]E.g., Ehrman, *The New Testament*, 407; Pheme Perkins, *Reading the New Testament*, rev. ed. (New York: Paulist, 1988) 312.

[78]E.g., Luke Timothy Johnson, *The Writings of the New Testament: An Interpretation* (Philadelphia: Fortress, 1986) 512.

[79]E.g., Ehrman, 407; Norman Perrin and Dennis C. Duling, *The New Testament: An Introduction*, 2nd ed. (San Diego: Harcourt Brace Jovanovich, 1982) 123.

[80]E.g., Perkins, *Reading*, 327.

[81]Russell Pregeant, *Engaging the New Testament: An Interdisciplinary Introduction* (Minneapolis: Fortress, 1995) 507.

[82]*Breaking the Code: Understanding the Book of Revelation* (Nashville: Abingdon, 1993) 9.

[83]*The Victorious Christ: A Study of the Book of Revelation* (Louisville: Westminster/John Knox, 1996) 125.

[84]*The Apocalypse: A Reading of the Revelation of John* (Louisville: Westminster/John Knox, 1994) ix.

Perhaps millenarian readings are so dangerous that their proponents must be working from false motives. In reply, James M. Efird cautions, "One must have some integrity and honesty with regard to dealing with the biblical texts."[85]

Not surprisingly, popular millenarian writers are highly concerned with "unbelieving" or "liberal" scholars, distinguishing them from "real students of Bible prophecy." To acknowledge that most scholars reject their teachings would diminish their own credibility, so prophecy students rarely confront biblical criticism head-on. Instead, they discuss the inevitable apostasy of the last days, which is already becoming visible, especially in the rejection of millenarian doctrine. In his "Prophetic Checklist for the Church," John F. Walwoord cites liberalism, the ecumenical movement, and "open denial of biblical truth" as tragic signs of the end times.[86] And Charles C. Ryrie identifies a liberalism that "has long denied the deity of Christ and the return of Christ" as contributing to the general apostasy that will appear in the last days.[87]

Perhaps Hal Lindsey, the most famous of the popular prophecy teachers, best exemplifies what they have to say about their critical counterparts. Writing in 1970, Lindsey notes the apostasy spreading through churches in the United States, particularly through false eschatologies.[88] Moreover, adherence to a futuristic understanding of prophecy marks the line between the true biblical scholars and their apostate counterparts.

> For many years prior to 1948 some Christian scholars denied the possibility of accepting the prophecies concerning the restoration of Israel as a nation in Palestine. As a matter of fact, many Bible teachers taught that all prophecy relating to Israel's future was fulfilled in Israel's past. Others taught that the promises made to Israel must be applied to the church (since Israel rejected her Messiah). Some theologians of the liberal school still insist that

---

[85]*Revelation for Today* (Nashville: Abingdon, 1989) 37.

[86]*Armageddon, Oil, and the Middle East Crisis* (Grand Rapids MI: Zondervan, 1990) 219-21.

[87]*The Final Countdown* (Wheaton IL: Victor, 1982) 69-73.

[88]*The Late Great Planet Earth*, with C. C. Carlson (Grand Rapids MI: Zondervan, 1970) 117-19.

> prophecy has no literal meaning for today and that it cannot be taken seriously. It is difficult to understand this view if one carefully weighs the case of Israel's rebirth as a nation.[89]

And,

> Many so-called biblical scholars today try to "late date" such predictions as Isaiah's [concerning Cyrus] to make his prophecies seem to be after the fact. To do this not only violates the consistent witness of the history of those times, but also makes the Jewish people religious charlatans and deceivers.[90]

Lindsey continues by distinguishing between those "liberal professors" who date Daniel to about 165 BCE from the real scholars who have maintained Daniel's traditional sixth century date.[91] Critical interpreters will be surprised, then, when Lindsey cites Wilhelm Gesenius as a "great Hebrew scholar of the early nineteenth century" and W. F. Albright as an "eminent archaeologist."[92] Of course, Lindsey is using Gesenius to support his identification of Gog and Magog (of Ezek 38–39) to refer to the Soviet Union and Albright to document that foretelling was a dimension of Hebrew Bible prophecy.

So a struggle for authority defines the conflict between Revelation's scholarly and popular interpreters. While scholars appeal to their knowledge of ancient apocalyptic conventions and historical contexts, prophecy students appeal to their "literal" strategy of biblical interpretation.[93] But the struggle may not be as simple as it seems. Scholarly readers like Krodel, Harrington, and Schüssler Fiorenza appeal to theological and political as well as technical considerations, and we have seen that Lindsey documents scholarly sources whenever they suit his purposes. Scholars may rely upon an opposition between their "critical" pursuits and

---

[89]Ibid., 38.

[90]Ibid., 15.

[91]Ibid., 80.

[92]Ibid., 53, 34.

[93]As attested in: Lindsey, *Late Great Planet Earth*, 38-40; Walwoord, *Armageddon*, 23; Ryrie, *Final Countdown*, 16-19; cf. Jeffrey, *Apocalypse*, 6-7, 19-22; Tim LaHaye, *No Fear of the Storm: Why Christians Will Escape All the Tribulation* (Sisters OR: Multnomah, 1992) 240-42.

more popular reading strategies, but in practice the wall between "critical" and popular readings reveals signs of erosion.

Daniel Patte and Brian K. Blount offer justifications—though from different theoretical backgrounds—for bringing popular and scholarly interpretations into critical conversation.[94] Patte argues that all critical interpretations are the bringing to critical understanding of interested interpretations. The biblical text offers several dimensions of meaning potential. What scholars do is to apply particular reading strategies—which already embody particular interests and assumptions—to elucidate some of the texts' meaning potential.[95] The important difference between a critical reading and a popular one (what Patte calls "ordinary readings") is that the critical reading claims to demonstrate its own interpretive legitimacy through the disciplined application of critical methods.[96] What separates critical from popular readings is not a lack of bias or interest, but simply the rigorous application of method.

Blount's sociolinguistic model for what he calls cultural interpretation also assumes a multivalent text. According to Blount, the text includes textual and ideational dimensions. While the textual dimension includes diction and syntax, the ideational involves the conceptual implications behind those terms and phrases. "In both textual and ideational categories, meaning is understood to reside within the boundaries of a particular text's language."[97] But meaning also involves an interpersonal dimension. Just as the interaction between an original author and his or her audience (macrointerpersonal dimension) defined a range of meanings in that context, so contemporary readers bring their own life situations and preunderstandings (microinterpersonal dimension) to

---

[94]Patte, *Ethics of Biblical Interpretation: A Reevaluation* (Louisville: Westminster/John Knox, 1995); idem, "Textual Constraints, Ordinary Readings, and Critical Exegesis: An Androcritical Perspective," *Semeia* 62 (1993): 59-79; Blount, *Cultural Interpretation: Reorienting New Testament Criticism* (Minneapolis: Fortress, 1995). Though their theoretical backgrounds differ—Blount uses sociolinguistics while Patte is grounded in structuralist and semiotic theory—Blount's sociolinguistic framework reflects influence from semiotics.

[95]*Ethics*, 37-71; "Textual Constraints."

[96]*Ethics*, 102; "Textual Constraints," 58.

[97]*Cultural Interpretation*, 8.

bear upon the text.[98] The result is that while the text offers a limited range of possible meanings, contemporary interpretations do in fact draw upon that potential.

Blount's program would have readers attend fully to all three dimensions of a text: textual, ideational, and interpersonal. But scholarly no less than popular readers fail in this attempt. Scholarly readers pay attention to textual and ideational respects, but they often fall short just where popular readers excel—the interpersonal dimensions. The "fullest possible meaning," then, results from careful attention to various readings as they express different aspects of a text's meaning potential.[99]

I am less optimistic than Patte and Blount that one may discriminate among the diverse factors of which a text is composed, and I am especially doubtful of Blount's suggestion that one should strive for a finally "more complete" reading on the basis of other interpretations. But Patte and Blount do provide insight into the conflict between scholarly and millenarian readings of Revelation, especially with respect to the question of authority. I would argue that both groups reflect particular biases and assumptions: Critical readings are by no means neutral or objective, while the prophecy students do in fact draw upon aspects of Revelation's textual and ideational rhetoric for their readings. Critical readers like myself can learn about Revelation from people like Hal Lindsey.

Thesis Three: Liberationist and Millenarian Readers

One key moment in Chinua Achebe's *Things Fall Apart* involves a conflict of interpretations. Through an interpreter a European missionary addresses his audience for the first time. The interpreter speaks the audience's language, Ibo, awkwardly. When he means to say "myself," he says "my buttocks," provoking laughter from the audience. Within the audience are a father and his son. The father is a self-made man who through management skills and strength has made a prominent place for himself. But his son has

---

[98]Ibid., 92-96.
[99]Ibid., 176.

been a mild disappointment, too lazy and not quite masculine enough to please his father. And the son has some nagging questions about his society's values: why would they abandon twins to die, and why would they kill a young man from another village in order to appease a deity?

The father and son hear the sermon differently. The missionary's preaching sounds ridiculous to Okonkwo, the father, as it does to many members of the crowd. How can a god have a son but no wife? Convinced that the missionary has lost his mind, Okonkwo walks away to tap his afternoon palm wine. But to his son Nwoye, the sermon brings hope. It somehow addresses his nagging questions.

> It was not the mad logic of the Trinity that captivated him. He did not understand it. It was the poetry of the new religion, something felt in the marrow. The hymn about brothers who sat in darkness and in fear seemed to answer a vague and persistent question that haunted his young soul—the question of the twins crying in the bush and the question of Ikemefuna who was killed. He felt a relief within as the hymn poured into his parched soul. The words of the hymn were like the drops of frozen rain melting on the dry plate of the panting earth. Nwoye's callow mind was greatly puzzled.[100]

The conflict of interpretations ultimately causes alienation between Okonkwo and Nwoye. Upon hearing that Nwoye has been seen with the Christians, Okonkwo grabs Nwoye and beats him. Nwoye leaves the household, and never returns.[101]

Disputes among interpretations of Revelation can be just as sharp as that between Okonkwo and Nwoye. I would like to focus upon one particular conflict, involving the prophecy students and the liberationists. Both groups claim that their readings of Revelation legitimate their spirituality and practice, yet their interpretations and practice differ dramatically. I am interested in the conflict between these reading strategies because they reflect different

[100]*Things Fall Apart*, 103-104.
[101]Ibid., 107.

responses to Revelation's construction of authority, responses that emphasize conflicting dimensions of the Apocalypse.

As Stephen D. O'Leary has shown, demonstration of authority is a basic problem for millenarian rhetoric, primarily because precise predictions about the end of the world sound dubious in the first place.[102] So prophecy students almost always affirm that the Bible is entirely and literally true, and they also pay special attention to demonstrating the accuracy of their interpretive methods.[103] Perhaps their most common strategy is to appeal to the 100 percent success rate of the biblical prophets, particularly by saying that Jesus fulfilled every prophecy about the messiah. Because many of the Bible's "prophecies" obviously remain unfulfilled, they are assumed to refer to events still in the future.[104] For example, Lindsey acknowledges that there may be more "prophecies" about the Messiah that have yet to be fulfilled. No problem! Since Jesus has fulfilled so many other prophecies, Lindsey argues, we should understand the rest to apply to his second coming.[105]

But the Bible's predictive accuracy is not enough to ground the prophecy students' claims; they must establish that they are interpreting the Bible correctly. Generally, they advance strategies much like the "Rules of Interpretation" used by William Miller over a hundred years ago.[106] They read the Bible literally, bringing diverse passages together when necessary to build a complete picture. Since God is the Bible's ultimate author, whose desire is to communicate with human beings, one may expect the Bible to present a coherent program for the last days. Lindsey cites earlier prophecy students who predicted the founding of a Jewish nation in Palestine: "They prove that these prophetic passages are clear and could be understood if taken literally."[107] By presenting careful

---

[102]*Arguing the Apocalypse*, esp. 51-60.

[103]Cf. LaHaye, *No Fear*, 234-40; Moishe Rosen, *Overture to Armageddon? Beyond the Gulf War*, with Bob Massie (San Bernardino CA: Here's Life, 1991) 62-91; Ryrie, *Final Countdown*, 16; Walwoord, *Armageddon*, 18-22.

[104]I place the term "prophecies" within quotation marks to indicate that I am following the usage of the prophecy teachers, who use the term to refer to predictions of future events.

[105]*Late Great Planet Earth*, 31.

[106]O'Leary, *Arguing the Apocalypse*, 116-20.

[107]*Late Great Planet Earth*, 40.

readings of an enormous range of biblical texts, then connecting those readings with respected sources and current events, prophecy students legitimate their interpretations.

In the end, prophecy students seem almost as confident of their interpretations as they are of the Bible. Such high claims to authority have serious implications. For one thing, they are congenial with imperialistic missions practices. Millenarian or not, Christian missions have often followed the "we know best" approach, thus placing their religious endeavors in an imperialist context.[108] Chinua Achebe characterizes this attitude through a missionary, Mr. Brown, who "saw all things in black and white. And black was evil."[109] From the prophecy students' camp, Grant R. Jeffrey argues that a literal hermeneutic and premillennial doctrine were critical to the missionary movements of the last two centuries.[110] And one of the justifications of inerrancy often presented by fundamentalist scholars is that global missions efforts could not be sustained without it. In making that point, John Floyd, then Professor of Missions at Mid-America Baptist Theological Seminary, clarified the implications of an absolutist approach to the Bible:

> This institution offers a course in World Religions and one in Modern Cults. In the missiological structure of these courses, they are eclectic in nature. They are not taught with a view on gleaning philosophical truths from them [other religions], but with a view of winning them to faith in Christ.[111]

---

[108]Edward Said, *Orientalism* (New York: Random House, 1978) 100. For the complexities faced by missionaries and their audiences alike, see Elizabeth Isichei, *A History of Christianity in Africa* (Grand Rapids MI: Eerdmans, 1995) 233-35; Kwok Pui Lan, "Discovering the Bible in the Nonbiblical World," *Semeia* 47 (1989): 25-42; and Pablo Richard, "The Hermeneutics of Liberation: A Hermeneutics of the Spirit," in *Reading from This Place*, ed. Segovia and Tolbert, 2:263-80.

[109]*Things Fall Apart*, 130.

[110]*Apocalypse*, 19-20.

[111]"The Relevance of Inerrancy for Missions," *Mid-America Theological Journal* 6 (1982): 79; cf. J. I. Packer, "Implications of Biblical Inerrancy for the Christian Mission," in *The Proceedings of the Conference on Biblical Inerrancy, 1987* (Nashville: Broadman, 1987) 245-50.

Second, prophecy students tend to withdraw from efforts toward progress. Their knowledge that the world is headed for imminent catastrophe leads them to be skeptical of efforts toward peace or justice. Charles B. Strozier's psychological study of millenarian fundamentalists reveals a consistent problem among them: a "deadening effect," marked by political quietism and a diminished sense of efficacy.[112] Dave Hunt argues:

> Are we saying that the world's leaders shouldn't even try to achieve global peace? Of course they must try. But those who are not Christians don't realize the futility of their efforts, and are driven by the necessity to use every possible means to establish peace.[113]

Hunt goes on to argue that Christians should also work for peace, but primarily through evangelistic efforts.[114]

Third, the disregard for entire people groups we find among prophecy students is particularly frightening. Throughout the prophecy movement's history, Jews have been assigned a special role in last days. While Jews are viewed as God's chosen people, they will also endure incredible suffering.[115] In the wake of the Soviet Union's disintegration, Islam and Islamic nations have become the key villains in the end-time drama. For example, Walwoord predicts that the nation of Israel will come to possess "all the holdings of present-day Israel, Lebanon and the West Bank of Jordan, plus substantial portions of Syria, Iraq, and Saudi Ara-

---

[112]*Apocalypse: On the Psychology of Fundamentalism in America* (Boston: Beacon, 1994) 73. The contemporary surge of the religious right is marked by an ambivalence toward progress. Perhaps, the argument goes, an America that turns to God in that last days will be on the winning side in the final conflict (cf. Paul Boyer, *When Time Shall Be No More: Prophecy Belief in Modern American Culture* [Cambridge MA: Harvard University Press, 1992] 298-304; O'Leary, *Arguing the Apocalypse*, 172-93; Lindsey, *Late Great Planet Earth*, 150; idem, *The Final Battle* [Palos Verdes CA: Western Front, 1995] 213-32).

[113]*Global Peace and the Rise of Antichrist* (Eugene OR: Harvest House, 1990) 14.

[114]Ibid.

[115]See Boyer, *When Time Shall Be No More*, 181-224; Grace Halsell, *Prophecy and Politics* (Chicago: Lawrence Hill, 1986); and Stephen R. Haynes, *Reluctant Witnesses: Jews and the Christian Imagination* (Louisville: Westminster/John Knox, 1995) 141-70. Prophecy students often identify Jews with the state of Israel.

bia,"[116] without regard for the population groups that have long inhabited these areas. Hal Lindsey, who in 1970 used the chapter title "Sheik to Sheik" to predict affairs in the Middle East,[117] now predicts a future pan-Islamic attack on Israel as a key to the final events. Calling it "The New Islamic Global Threat" and an "evil empire . . . more than 1,300 years old," Lindsey argues that Islamic fundamentalists, driven by hatred for Jews, will kick start the final chain of events.[118] In the process, Lindsey marks the state of Israel for devastation, and Russia and China for failed invasions.

Fourth, prophecy students share the conviction that they represent the only truly saved community. Strozier's study of millenarian evangelicals repeatedly involves their justification of God's end-time violence, a conviction that creates a certain "dissociated quality" in otherwise peaceful and gentle people.[119] But, as the premillennialists teach and many of Strozier's subjects believe, the true believers will be delivered from the worst aspects of the last days, the Tribulation.[120] So not only do believers escape damnation, they are taken to heaven before the final events even begin. As believers are doubly lucky, unbelievers will suffer an extra share: the Tribulation precedes their judgment.[121] Their certainty about the message of Revelation, with its images of judgment and condemnation, often leads to impassioned evangelistic invitations. "At any moment it may be too late to respond,"[122] but for now Walvoord includes a guide for "How to Be Sure of Our Eternal

---

[116]*Armageddon*, 69. Grace Halsell cites a personal interview with Walwoord, who says of Palestinians, "Frankly, God didn't have them in His master plan. His concern was for the Jews, to whom He had given the Holy Land" (*Prophecy and Politics*, 12). Even with his low regard for Muslims, one wonders whether Walwoord was aware that many Palestinians are Christians?

[117]Lindsey also used "The Yellow Peril" for China (*Late Great Planet Earth*).

[118]*Final Battle*. Lindsey interchanges two pairs of terms: "Jews" with "Israel," and "Islam" with "Islamic fundamentalism."

[119]*Apocalypse*, 70.

[120]See LaHaye, *No Fear*, for a monograph-length argument that Christians will escape Revelation's catastrophes.

[121]Cf. Strozier, *Apocalypse*, 120-22, for diverse ways prophecy students cope with the tensions built into these concepts.

[122]Hunt, *Global Peace*, 290.

Destiny" at the end of his book.[123] And Hal Lindsey ups the stakes for those considering whether to ask God to save them:

> If you pray and ask God to do what I've just explained, then you will not be here for the Final Battle. You will be in heaven with Jesus. We will witness this terrible period of history from the presence of God.[124]

And that sums up the prophecy students' reading of Revelation: either one accepts truth on their terms, or one faces final judgment.

At first glance, liberationist interpretations of Revelation appear to be different. Whether in contexts of struggle such as Apartheid South Africa or Latin America, or even among the prosperous in North America, some readers use Revelation to reject systems of domination and to imagine a peaceful and egalitarian world community. By a hermeneutical leap, they construct Revelation's meaning for today as parallel with that of its original context. However, a profound tension lies beneath the surface of these readings. Though they would promote human liberation, their claims to authority mirror Revelation's absolutist rhetoric and differ little from what we find among the prophecy students.

One of the fascinating things about liberationist interpretations is how they have reversed the usual colonial process.[125] North American interest in Latin American and South African liberation theologies has been reflected in the major religious publishers, introductory texts by North American scholars, and public appearances by liberation theologians at major American institutions. Also interesting has been the delayed resistance to liberation theology among millenarians.[126] In 1990 and 1991 the Dallas Theological Seminary periodical *Bibliotheca Sacra* featured two critiques of liberation theology. While one author criticizes liberationists for their relatively low view of biblical authority and

---

[123]*Armageddon*, 229-34.

[124]*Last Battle*, 286.

[125]Perhaps not entirely, however. Interest in liberation theology may be on the decline in North America.

[126]In 1984 Harvey G. Cox made the connection between Latin American liberation theologies and North American fundamentalisms (*Religion in the Secular City: Towards a Postmodern Theology* [New York: Simon & Schuster, 1984).

their failure to recognize that the meaning of the Bible is fundamentally clear,[127] another arrives more precisely at the point: the liberationists place too much emphasis on social change at the expense of otherworldly salvation.

> By restricting their analyses and cures so stringently to historical time and earthly reality, liberationists have neglected the eternal dimension and divine intervention.[128]

Thus, liberationists and millenarians must struggle for the authority to interpret Revelation. The result is that while liberationists espouse egalitarian values, liberationists must assert their authority over against their opponents. Chilean liberation theologian Pablo Richard is aware of this tension. Richard, who "reject[s] every kind of fundamentalist, dispensationalist, or neoconservative interpretation of Revelation,"[129] finds good news in the Apocalypse: "the resurrection of Christ in the present history of our world." According to Richard's Apocalypse, we live in the "time . . . in which it is possible to build the reign of God in history."[130] It calls us to work toward utopia,[131] while at the same time standing over against the beasts, "symbol of empires,"[132] of John's day and our own.

While Richard also acknowledges that parts of Revelation endorse violence and hatred, he minimizes these factors by suggesting that Revelation's violence results from "the limit situation of extreme oppression," and that it is "more literary than real."[133] His judgment that Revelation reflects the limits of oppression does not match what we can know of Revelation's audience, some of whom John calls "rich" (3:17), and the opposition between the literary and the real is highly problematic. Richard recognizes

---

[127]Larry D. Pettegrew, "Liberation Theology and Hermeneutical Preunderstandings," *BSac* 148 (1991): 284-86.

[128]J. Ronald Blue, "Major Flaws in Liberation Theology," *BSac* 147 (1990): 102.

[129]*Apocalypse: A People's Commentary on the Book of Revelation* (Maryknoll NY: Orbis, 1995) 5.

[130]Ibid., 171.

[131]Ibid., 172.

[132]Ibid., 100.

[133]Ibid., 4; cf. 31-32.

an ambivalence within Revelation, but his acknowledged engagement on behalf of liberation leads him to stifle its more dangerous dimensions.

Néstor Míguez, an Argentine liberationist reader, emphasizes the economic dimension of the Apocalypse. Assuming that biblical apocalyptic embodies the perspective of the poor,[134] Míguez argues that Rev 18 condemns global economic systems that reduce life to commerce at the expense of the poor and discloses another possibility, life with "music, craftsmanship, production, light, and family."[135] Avoiding the violent imagery of Rev 18, Míguez suggests that "the system" devours itself.[136] Míguez's reading legitimizes life outside the global economy, but it offers nothing but doom for those who find themselves contributors to and victims of that system.

Allan A. Boesak's reading of Revelation grew out of his own struggles with apartheid, including tear gas and imprisonment, solitary confinement, and watching far too many deaths and funerals.[137] Boesak advocates a "contemporary-historical" reading that moves between the present and the time when Revelation was written.[138] By correlating these contexts, Boesak arrives at a message: "the Apocalypse speaks not only of the suffering of the faithful. It speaks also of the destruction of evil and the victory of the Lamb."[139] Unlike Richard, Boesak does not withdraw from Revelation's violence: "If [Christ's] cloak is spattered with blood, it is the blood of his enemies, the destroyers of the earth and of his children."[140] Those readers who reject Revelation's violence do not know genuine oppression or suffering.[141] For Boesak, Revelation provides its own locus of authority. Those who hear will work for justice; those who oppose its vision must face ultimate destruction.

---

[134]"Apocalyptic and the Economy," 252-53.

[135]Ibid., 262.

[136]Ibid.

[137]*Comfort and Protest: Reflections on the Apocalypse of John of Patmos* (Philadelphia: Westminster, 1987) 13-14.

[138]Ibid., 28-29.

[139]Ibid., 39.

[140]Ibid., 124.

[141]Ibid., 72.

North American resistance readers have taken a cue from their international counterparts. Daniel Berrigan and Dale Aukerman seek to subvert imperial powers from within. Berrigan's reading of Rev 15:2-4 is overtly political: atomic weapons and the state are one with the Beast.[142] Only the church that says a prophetic no to the United States has the right to sing the Lamb's song.[143] Though written fifteen years later, Aukerman's interpretation strongly resembles Berrigan's. Revelation embodies "God's continuing word to his people and to the nations . . . throughout history."[144] While the United States and other imperial powers practice "terminal politics" that can lead to one version of apocalypse,[145] Aukerman confesses that the world is ultimately subject to God.[146] While Aukerman rejects human attempts at revenge or violence, he affirms "God's recompense."[147]

Berrigan and Aukerman both resist imperialism and other violent systems. Revelation provides ultimate legitimation for their practice as it presents the final critique of global evil. While both discard violence as a means of making things right, neither takes Revelation's violence seriously. Berrigan simply avoids the question, while Aukerman removes destruction from human hands and entrusts it to God. Unfortunately, Aukerman has not solved the problem. His own claim to absolute truth, "God's continuing word . . . to the nations," connotes a coercive force of its own.

Liberationists abhor the prophecy students' systems and their implications. Because the premillennial system requires that the human world decline rapidly during the last days and that an Antichrist will control most of the world, conspiracy theories abound among millenarians. Common arguments are that the European Union or the Roman Catholic Church, or both, will be the seat of Antichrist's rule, that Russia will form an international

---

[142]*Beside the Sea of Glass: The Song of the Lamb* (New York: Seabury, 1978) 96, also cited in Wainwright, *Mysterious Apocalypse*, 184.

[143]*Beside the Sea of Glass*, 64.

[144]*Reckoning with Apocalypse: Terminal Politics and Christian Hope* (New York: Crossroad, 1993) 10.

[145]Ibid., 27.

[146]Ibid., 128-30.

[147]Ibid., 158.

conspiracy against Israel, and that the ecumenical movement will erode true Christianity. Liberationists respond by identifying these suspicions with those of other conspiracy hunters in the political sphere and by complaining that the prophecy students' interpretations foster a dangerous dualism. "There's a disturbing similarity between the apocalyptic conspiratorial worldviews of some on the extreme Political Right with some on the Religious Right," suggests Tom Sine in a 1995 issue of *Sojourners*.[148] Sine continues, "By viewing foes as the adherents of absolute evil, apocalypticism provides a rationale for 'total opposition and dire vengeance on the wicked.' "[149]

Liberationist readings are marked by a passion for justice, particularly through resistance against oppression. They call for an egalitarian practice, utopian in the case of Richard. This vision is consistent with Revelation. But these readings follow the Apocalypse in another sense as well: they make extremely high claims to authority. Their analyses of Revelation's social program may be more sophisticated than those of the prophecy students, but they are just as exclusionary.

In the final analysis, one must accept their version of a just society in order to avoid becoming an opponent of God. While liberationists and prophecy students have radically different programs, with different implications for authority and legitimation, their own discourses participate in Revelation's rhetoric of ultimate authority.

Critical scholarship is by no means neutral in this struggle. Critics uniformly reject millenarian interpretations, and many of their readings sound much like those of the liberationists. Notable among these is Elisabeth Schüssler Fiorenza, who acknowledges that Revelation can be dangerous, yet chooses to read it for liberation.

> Such a liberationist reading of Revelation's rhetoric subordinates the book's depiction of cosmic destruction and holy war to its desire for justice, which is repeated throughout the book. It puts

---

[148]"Suspicions of Conspiracy: How a Spirit of Fear Can Distort Scripture and History," *Sojourners* 24 (July–August 1995): 26-30.

[149]Ibid., 29, quoting Bernard McGinn.

> in the foreground those rhetorical features of the text that aim at moving the audience to practical engagement in this struggle for God's qualitatively new world of salvation.[150]

Schüssler Fiorenza's reading has a long heritage, one we can trace at least as far back as R. H. Charles, who also found continuing significance in Revelation's critique of Rome.

> There is to be no legislation, no government, no statecraft which is not finally to be brought into subjection to the will of Christ. J^ap is thus the Divine Statute Book of International Law, as well as a manual for the guidance of the individual Christian.[151]

While Charles sounds much more triumphalist than Schüssler Fiorenza, their point is essentially the same. Revelation judges all oppressive dominions as subject to its vision of Christ. The tension between the liberating and the coercive is obvious. Could it be that we critical readers have something to learn from the prophecy students?

Conclusion

Intentionally or otherwise, Revelation's readers mirror John's rhetoric of authority. As John struggles to legitimate his message over against competing voices from the Empire, the larger culture, Jewish communities, and other Christian prophets, so do critical scholars, prophecy teachers, and liberationists use the Apocalypse to construct their own privileged perspectives. While popular readers use Revelation for different purposes, they draw upon particular facets of John's authority rhetoric in actualizing their own readings. Just as the Apocalypse blurs the lines that would divide religious and political from rhetorical authority, the same slippage occurs among those who use Revelation to authorize their own programs.

This study is concerned primarily with John's ethos, not those of his readers. The following chapters will present a critical assessment of how John builds his authority. At the same time, I

---

[150]*Revelation*, 122.
[151]*Revelation*, 1:ciii.

am convinced that conflicts among Revelation's scholarly and popular readers embody tensions within John's own rhetoric. John resists Rome's coercive power. He describes himself as a brother and fellow servant, no greater than other priestly members of God's dominion (1:6; 5:10), and he imagines an eschaton in which those who endure the present will inherit God's blessings (22:7). But John's ethos has another side. John curses anyone who veers from his program in the slightest way.

We begin by trying to understand rhetorical authority through various perspectives. Chapter 2 builds a model of *narrative ethos* as a means of investigating how ancient authors may have woven authority into narrative form. The model reflects how Greek and Roman rhetorical practices constructed ethos and employs insights on narrative authority from contemporary literary criticism and resistance or postcolonial theories. In chapter 3, applying the model of narrative ethos to early Jewish apocalyptic discourse reveals some of the ethical conventions available to John as an apocalyptic narrator. A thorough exegetical examination of John's ethos follows in chapters 4 and 5. Chapter 4 is concerned with John's positive ethos, how he represents himself as brother to his audience and the sole mediator of divine truth, and chapter 5 is directed toward John's negative task, his attack on competing loci of authority. Chapter 6, the conclusion, integrates the results of this study. It considers how several critics have sought to mitigate perceived ethical problems in Revelation and offers John's ethos as a key to understanding these dilemmas. Drawing upon Jürgen Habermas's discourse ethics, I pose ethos as a problem that permeates Revelation, requiring continuing negotiation among its contemporary readers.

Chapter 2
Narrative Ethos: Reading Authority

I have argued that authority is a basic problem for readers of Revelation. If I am right, the means by which John constructs his own authoritative voice merit our special attention. The ancient rhetoricians had a special term for how speakers characterized themselves in the attempt to earn an audience's trust and goodwill—*ethos* (ἦθος).[1] Ethos, then, is an attempt to grasp power, the authority to represent oneself and the world in a given rhetorical situation. In seeking a rhetorical understanding of authority as it works in Revelation and in contemporary readings, ethos is the place to start.

Fortunately, ethos has been a recurring theme in rhetorical and literary criticism from the Greek rhetoricians to the present. Nevertheless, Revelation presents several challenges to the interpreter. For one thing, the Apocalypse emerges from the ancient Mediterranean world. Its conventions of character, authority, and persuasion differ vastly from those of contemporary North American readers. Since John and his audience would have had some familiarity with the devices of *classical ethos,* the ancient Greek and Latin rhetorical handbooks will provide important insights into the ethical conventions of the era. Cicero's political speeches offer a more specific picture, as they represent how one famous speaker constructed ethos, often in the midst of intense conflict. But Revelation is not

---

[1]The term ἦθος applies of course to character in general, in the sense of a person's nature, qualities, or disposition, but in rhetorical theory its special significance relates to the persuasive capacity of a speaker's character.

simply an example of Greek rhetoric; it is largely narrative as well.[2] While the classical rhetorical handbooks did not address narrative authority systematically, twentieth-century *literary criticism* has developed models for how authority is constructed through narrative. More specifically, contemporary ideological criticisms theorize narrative voice as an act of power: contributions from *postcolonial and resistance theorists* are particularly helpful in this regard.

From these three resources—classical ethos, literary criticism, and postcolonial and resistance theory—I have constructed an interpretive framework that (a) respects Revelation as literature from an altogether distant time and place and (b) takes seriously its character as narrative. I call this model *narrative ethos*. In chapter 3, I draw upon a fourth resource, the conventions of Jewish *apocalyptic* literature. These conventions provide much of the literary and imaginative fuel that energizes Revelation. In particular, I will investigate how ancient Jewish apocalypses built ethos and how apocalyptic experiences provided a crucial ground for authority in early Christianity as a background against which to read John's ethos.

Classical Ethos

Greek and Latin rhetorical theorists recognized that ethos was an essential element of persuasive speech. While ethos may have meant different things in different contexts, no ancient theorist denied how important it is for a speaker to hold an audience's attention, trust, and in some cases sympathy.

The goal of this section is to identify how persons living in the Roman Empire of the late first century, the time when Revelation was probably written, may have understood the importance of a speaker's character in making an argument. This investigation draws upon two resources. The Greek and Latin rhetorical hand-

---

[2]For this reason the groundbreaking work of Bruce J. Malina and Jerome H. Neyrey (*Portraits of Paul: An Archaeology of Ancient Personality* [Louisville: Westminster/John Knox, 1996]) has not been particularly helpful to this study. Apocalyptic discourse is rarely as direct about ethos as are the *encomia* and public defense speeches.

books offer systematic ethical theories, while Cicero's speeches exemplify actual practice. Admittedly, neither John nor many persons in his audience would likely have read Aristotle's *Rhetoric* (edited about 341 BCE), Cicero's *De Oratore* (54 BCE), the *Rhetorica ad Herennium* (around 84 BCE), or Quintilian's *Institutio Oratoria* (around 94 CE).[3] But these texts reveal more than abstract theory produced by Greek and Roman elites; they claim to represent what was commonly practiced in the public courts and assemblies of the day. As Cicero pointed out,

> to my thinking the virtue in all the rules is, not that orators by following them have won a reputation for eloquence, but that certain persons have noted and collected the doings of men who were naturally eloquent. (*De Or.* 1.146)[4]

Admittedly, most persons in the ancient Mediterranean world did not have formal education, much less training in rhetoric, which represented the secondary stage of hellenistic education. However, rhetoric was a part of daily life for the average citizen. Wandering philosophers and teachers were common, as were public declamations and performances.

To complement the handbooks, I have chosen one example of ethos in action—Cicero's political speeches—in which these techniques are clearly at work.[5] Cicero so well represents Latin oratory that Quintilian cited his name "not as the name of a man, but as the name of eloquence itself" (*Inst. Or.* 12.1.112).[6] Though many of Cicero's techniques would offend modern rhetorical tastes, these speeches provide an especially helpful witness to the interaction between ethos and polemic contexts in classical rhetoric. Most

---

[3]Dates taken from George A. Kennedy, *Classical Rhetoric and Its Christian and Secular Tradition from Ancient to Modern Times* (Chapel Hill: University of North Carolina Press, 1980).

[4]Cited in Brian Vickers, *In Defence of Rhetoric* (Oxford: Clarendon, 1988) 1. Cf. *Rhet.* 1.1.1; *Inst. Or.* 1.10; *Ad Her.* 1.1–2.2.

[5]From Cicero's huge body of work (twenty-eight volumes in the LCL) I have chosen to examine *Selected Political Speeches of Cicero*, rev. ed., ed. and trans. Michael Grant (New York: Penguin, 1973). Citations include page numbers in Grant's edition.

[6]Cited in Kennedy, *Classical Rhetoric*, 102; cf. Vickers, *In Defence of Rhetoric*, 76-77.

striking is the contrast between contemporary standards of restraint and the intensity characteristic of ancient polemics. Though Luke T. Johnson generalizes that, "Abuse tends to gain in volume when it is powerless,"[7] Cicero could be extremely vicious in states of relative power as well as weakness. Extreme polemic was common in the ancient Mediterranean, particularly among philosophers and religionists.[8]

If these sources provide a background for understanding ethos in the ancient Mediterranean, how are we to go about using them? I have chosen a synchronic approach. While it would be possible to trace the development of ethos through antiquity, what is needed here is a field of rhetorical conventions and expectations that John and his intended audience might well have shared. As we shall see, theoretical expositions of ethos did not all agree, and the concept appears to have changed over time, but we are concerned more with the general terrain of classical ethos than with features of its particular maps. I am not claiming that John adopted some monolithic ethos theory, only that he and his audience likely shared certain sensibilities about how speakers and authors might represent themselves in various contexts.

1. The handbooks indicate that *ethos was a priority for every ancient speaker*, performing an essential function in any speech act. Aristotle laid the groundwork for this view by naming ethos along with logos, an argument's rational force, and pathos, its emotional effect upon the audience, as his three categories of argumentative proof (πίστεις, *Rhet.* 1.2.3).[9] He even goes so far as to call ethos

---

[7]"The New Testament's Anti-Jewish Slander and the Conventions of Ancient Polemic," *JBL* 108 (1989): 424.

[8]Ibid., 430-41; George A. Kennedy, *Comparative Rhetoric: A Historical and Cross-Cultural Introduction* (New York: Oxford University Press, 1998) 221. Cf. Borgen, "Polemic"; and Sean Freyne, "Vilifying the Other and Defining the Self: Matthew's and John's Anti-Jewish Polemic in Focus," in *"To See Ourselves as Others See Us": Christians, Jews, "Others" in Late Antiquity*, ed. Jacob Neusner and Ernest S. Frerichs, Scholars Press Studies in the Humanities (Chico CA: Scholars Press, 1985) 117-43. It is evident from Cicero's speeches that at least in the Rome of the late Republic extremely serious charges were a common means of rhetorical and legal attack.

[9]Aristotle distinguishes between inartificial proofs, which are readily available to the speaker (contracts, testimony, etc.), and artificial proofs, which the speaker must develop (*Rhet.* 1.2.2).

"the most effective means of proof" (1.2.4). This scheme is consistent with Aristotle's analysis of the rhetorical situation, which involves speaker, audience, and argument.[10] Each category of proof relates to one of the essential aspects of the rhetorical situation; theoretically, the three proofs are equally important. Quintilian went even farther, subordinating logical proof as less effective than ethos and pathos as a means of convincing an audience.[11]

The Latin tradition lacks any cognate word for ἦθος.[12] But, heavily influenced by Aristotle, it agrees on ethos's critical role in persuasion. Cicero, for example, maintained not only that winning over the audience was one of the three sources of persuasion (*De Or.* 2.114-15) but also that it could be more compelling, "when agreeably and feelingly handled . . . , than the merits of the case" (2.184).

> Now nothing in oratory . . . is more important than to win for the orator the favor of his hearer, and to have the latter so affected as to be swayed by something resembling a mental impulse or emotion, rather than by judgement or deliberation. (*De Or.* 2.178)

Here we see how Ciceronian ethos is associated with pathos through its appeal to an audience's emotions. The goal is to attain the audience's goodwill (*benevolentia*) through careful portrayal of character:

> A potent factor in success, then, is for the characters, principles, conduct and course of life, both of those who are to plead cases and of their clients, to be approved, and conversely those of their opponents condemned; and for the feelings of the tribunal to be won over, as far as possible, to goodwill towards the advocate and the advocate's client as well. (2.182)

---

[10]τοῦ λέγοντος καὶ περὶ οὗ λέγει καὶ πρὸς ὅν, καὶ τὸ τέλος πρὸς τοῦτόν ἔστι, λέγω δὲ τὸν ἀκροατήν; 1.3.1.

[11]Cited (but with an incorrect reference to *Inst. Or.* 5.19.29-31) in Vickers, *Defence of Rhetoric*, 77. The correct reference is 5.14.29-31.

[12]Quintilian admits as much, saying that while *adfectus* is a fine and appropriate rendering of πάθος, it is better to give the sense of ἦθος than to translate it into Latin (*Inst. Or.* 6.2.8-9).

The extended discussion of character sketches in the *Rhetorica ad Herennium* indicates the importance of ethos for that system (3:4-15; 4.63-66). Character delineation (*notatio*) involves a description of the properties distinctive to an individual (4.63-66). Such descriptions are both charming and effective, highlighting a person's ruling passion. Quintilian maintains that ethos (and here he uses the word) is most effective in "making it seem that all that we say derives directly from the nature of the facts and persons concerned and in the revelation of the character[13] of the orator in such a way that all may recognize it" (6.2.13). In Quintilian's system, an appeal to ethos is absolutely necessary when moral character[14] is at issue (6.2.17).

Among Cicero's virtues are his vigilance and willingness to risk his own welfare. Against Catalina's revolt he risks his own life, but danger only steels his determination:

> In this war, Romans, it is I who offer myself as your commander. The hostility of these criminals I take upon myself. What can be healed I will somehow contrive to heal, and what must be cut away I shall not allow to spread and involve our country in mortal peril. (99; cf. 87, 136-37, 139, 144)

This is the sort of rhetoric Cicero uses repeatedly, and, though it may seem exaggerated, Cicero did eventually suffer exile and execution for his political activity. Still, one has the sense that Cicero intends his courage to serve as an ethical resource. He admits a desire to be famous, but, "This is a passion which may seem exaggerated; but I am sure it is not dishonorable" (162).

2. One might build ethos through the *speaker's formal self-characterization* or through *appeals to the audience's emotions*. These options reflect a conceptual shift that occurred between Greek and Latin understandings of ethos.[15] Tracing this shift might enable us to

---

[13]*Mores*, the word which, according to Quintilian, usually translates ἦθος (6.2.8-9).

[14]*Mores* again.

[15]The distinction between Greek and Latin approaches to ethos is by no means neat or absolute. Latin rhetoric was heavily influenced by Aristotle, Isocrates, and other Greek figures, and the Greek tradition was by no means univocal. Still, the

locate classical approaches to the problem in a broad perspective.[16] First, the very definition of ethos moved from Aristotle's focus on the content of the speech itself to a Latin sense that ethos primarily involved an effect on an audience. We might describe this trend as movement from a logos-oriented ethos to one that is more pathos-oriented. A second modification was the Latin inclusion of factors external to the speech itself, such as the speaker's reputation. Third, Aristotle's ambition that a speaker should *seem* to be a good person eventually becomes Quintilian's doctrine of "a good man, skilled in speaking" (*Inst. Or.* 12.1.1), the orator who actually *is* good.

First, ethos moved from a message orientation toward an audience orientation, from association with logos toward an emphasis on pathos. For Aristotle, ethos consisted of the means by which speakers could characterize themselves as persons of good sense, virtue, and goodwill (φρόνησις καὶ ἀρετὴ καὶ εὔνοια; *Rhet.* 2.1.5). This characterization amounted to what we might call an argument; only through the speech itself may orators construct their characters (1.2.4). Convinced that solid arguments have tremendous power on their own, Aristotle excludes external factors from his ethical theory. We may therefore characterize Aristotle's approach as logos-oriented, that is, associated primarily with the content of the speech itself.[17]

But by Cicero's time, ethos theory had moved away from logos toward pathos, a speech's emotional effect upon an audience. Ethos was a matter of winning an audience's feelings—its goodwill—with respect to a speaker or client (*De Or.* 2.115). While Aristotelian ethos sought to establish conviction regarding the speaker's character, Ciceronian ethos developed into "something resem-

---

distinction does provide heuristic value for understanding how ethical theory developed over time.

[16]Again, we are not choosing from among classical options, but marking a field of ancient cultural convention.

[17]Aristotle's systematic discussion of ethos is brief, perhaps due to an assumption that ethos is a simple matter and the association of a speaker's ethos with the problem of character in general. At any rate, Aristotle refers the reader to his discussion of the virtues (found in *Rhet.* 1.9), and argues that the means of one's own characterization are no different than for the depiction of others (2.1.7).

bling a mental impulse or emotion, rather than . . . judgement or deliberation" (*De Or.* 2.178). By the time we reach Quintilian, ethos could even be secured by praise of the audience (*Inst. Or.* 4.1.16). This had become possible because Quintilian aligns ethos so strongly with pathos that they differ more in degree than in kind, with ethos designating the calm and gentle emotions (6.2.9-12).[18]

Second, external items such as a speaker's reputation became more important in Latin rhetoric than they had been in the Greek tradition. Aristotle intentionally excluded external factors such as a speaker's reputation or the difficulties of the case from his exposition of ethos (*Rhet.* 1.2.4);[19] the Latin tradition did not.[20] While the *Rhetorica ad Herennium* argues that references to the speaker's person should be pertinent to the case at hand (1.8), it also recognizes that orators must adapt to their circumstances. Sometimes a speaker starts off at a disadvantage; how one addresses ethos depends upon the broader context (1.6-11). External factors had become so important that for Cicero ethos could become a career project: once one has built one's own ethos, the effect continues through time and in future contexts.[21] Once one has developed one's reputation, or *dignitas,* one may properly play the part of an orator: "when advising on affairs of supreme importance, to unfold his opinion as a man having authority" (*dignitas, De Or.* 2.35).

There is a third and related facet to ethos's development: a transition from *seeming* good to *being* good.[22] Cicero's argument—that orators could establish a career reputation that would lend credibility to all their speeches—constitutes the background for

---

[18]Cf. Vickers, *Defence of Rhetoric,* 74.

[19]Oddly enough, Isocrates did include a speaker's cultivated character as an essential component of ethos, even arguing that speakers needed to *be* good in order to *seem* good (James S. Baumlin, "Introduction: Positioning *Ethos* in Historical and Contemporary Theory," in *Ethos: New Essays in Critical and Rhetorical Theory,* ed. James S. Baumlin and Tita French Baumlin, SMU Studies in Composition and Rhetoric [Dallas: Southern Methodist University Press, 1994] xiv-xv).

[20]Jakob Wisse, *Ethos and Pathos from Aristotle to Cicero* (Amsterdam: Adolf M. Hakkert, 1989) 245-46.

[21]Richard Leo Enos and Karen Rossi Schnakenberg, "Cicero Latinizes Hellenic *Ethos,*" in *Ethos: New Essays in Critical and Rhetorical Theory,* ed. Baumlin and Baumlin, 203.

[22]I have borrowed this terminology from James S. Baumlin ("Introduction," xv), who actually applies this distinction to Aristotelian versus Isocratean ethos.

Quintilian's famous slogan: "a good man, skilled in speaking" (*Inst. Or.* 12.1.1). (Indeed, Cicero taught that only persons of good character should receive oratorical training [*De Or.* 2.85]). Quintilian agreed with Aristotle that ethos could be represented in speech, but only as a display of the speaker's actual character (6.2.13): "ethos in all its forms requires the speaker to be a man of good character and courtesy" (6.2.18).[23] Here Quintilian is far removed from Aristotle, who emphasized the mere appearance of good sense, virtue, and goodwill:

> These qualities are all that are necessary, so that the speaker who appears (δοκοῦντα) to possess all three will necessarily convince his hearers. (*Rhet.* 2.1.6)[24]

Aristotle's speaker, who was "a signifier standing *inside* an expanded text,"[25] has become a signified—Quintilian's "man of good character and courtesy."

These three developments are related. Aristotle's emphasis upon the speech act itself creates a sort of fictional world within the speech, much like the world of Aristotle's own system. In this world speakers become whoever they represent themselves to be, relatively unconstrained by external factors. The Latin tradition is more attuned to the larger rhetorical situation; speakers' already established reputations limit their self-representations for good or ill. The traditional scholarly line has been that Aristotelian theory was transformed into Latin (or Ciceronian) practice.[26]

This theoretical distinction also has implications for how we read apocalyptic ethos. Aristotle's more intratextual approach will be appropriate for most of the apocalypses, which are pseudonymous, while Paul's apocalyptic ethos is more clearly linked to an

---

[23]Quintilian's position may not be as unqualified as is commonly supposed. In the same passage (6.2.18) he leaves room for those who "possess *or be thought to possess* those virtues" which they would attribute to their clients.

[24]In this passage (2.1.4-7) Aristotle uses three verbs to demonstrate ethos's intratextuality: φαίνομαι, δοκέω, and κατασκευάζω.

[25]Baumlin, "Introduction," xvi; Baumlin's emphasis.

[26]Enos and Schnakenberg, "Cicero Latinizes Hellenic *Ethos*," 191. For a monograph that argues precisely this point, see Wisse, *Ethos and Pathos from Aristotle to Cicero*.

elusive world of extratextual relationships. On the other hand, the distinction between Greek and Latin ethical theory is not absolute. Several common motifs run throughout the rhetorical handbooks, and these themes provide the background against which to assess hellenistic texts such as Revelation.

3. Speakers sought to identify themselves as persons of *virtue, knowledge, and pure motives*. These values, modified from Aristotle's trilogy of good sense, virtue, and goodwill (*Rhet.* 2.1.5), may be variously expressed but are common among all the handbooks. Virtue and pure motives are most prominent in the tradition, as Aristotle argued that the moral purpose of a speech should be clear in order to establish the speaker's character (*Rhet.* 2.21.16; 3.16.8). The Latin handbooks share a concern that speakers ought to remind audiences of their meritorious service in the past (*Ad Her.* 1.8; 3.6.10-12; *De Or.* 2.182; *Inst. Or.* 4.1.7; 6.2.13). At the same time, they argue that speakers do well who demonstrate that they are speaking not out of greed or hope of glory but due to duty, friendship, patriotism, or some other altruistic motivation. It is even desirable that speakers should express their own reluctance to take the floor in the first place (*Ad Her.* 3.6.10-12; *De Or.* 2.182; *Inst. Or.* 4.1.7-10). Virtue and proper motives come together when one speaks from a sense of moral obligation:

> For as everything treated by the orator may be regarded from the ethical standpoint, we may apply the word *ethos* whenever he speaks of what is honorable and expedient or of what ought or ought not to be done. (*Inst. Or.* 6.2.11)

The religious dimension of Cicero's ethos provides a prime example of virtue and pure motives. Not only does Cicero frequently praise the gods, he often identifies himself with their favor and authority. The gods direct Cicero (108; 119); he appeals to them frequently (69; 93; 109; 126); his efforts cooperate with their love for Rome (110; 120-21); and his opponents are their enemies (121-22).

Such a pious man must surely be working from pure motivations. Indeed, Cicero thinks of Rome before he thinks of himself (142). He represents peace rather than war (108), seeking reconciliation for his enemies (102). He holds pity for his enemies rather than hate (84), and though he is fearful he remains faithful to his duty (85; 135; 217; 318). He turns down opportunities for glory and power in order to serve Rome (69); all he asks is that the people keep his memory (144).

Crisis rhetoric also confirms Cicero's pure motives. Like the apocalyptic visionaries, Cicero could envision grand destruction and wrap it in the rhetoric of ultimacy.

> And yet I also have a vision of this city, the light of the world and the stronghold of every nation, suddenly plunged into all-engulfing flames. I see, in my mind's eye, our country reduced to a graveyard. I see the corpses of unburied citizens lying in miserable heaps. . . . I shudder at the wails of mothers, the panic flight of girls and boys, the rape of Vestal Virgins. (137)

When Cicero defends Titus Annius Milo, he pictures a Rome in which all citizens consider Milo's fate their own and the fate of their country and see the murder of which he is accused as Rome's salvation (218-19). As Ch. Perelman and L. Olbrechts-Tyteca point out, the urgent—the unique, the precarious, and the irremediable—is a rhetorical commonplace (topos) sure to get attention.[27] While the primary effects of crisis rhetoric relate to pathos, there is also an ethical dimension: The speaker is represented as someone who is speaking from pure motives, someone who must be heard because she or he is addressing important issues.

Cicero repeatedly emphasizes his own virtue, especially his vigilance and willingness to risk his own welfare. Against Catalina's revolt he risks his own life, but danger only steels his determination:

> In this war, Romans, it is I who offer myself as your commander. The hostility of these criminals I take upon myself. What can be healed I will somehow contrive to heal, and what must be cut away I shall not allow to spread and involve our country in mortal peril. (99; cf. 87, 136-37, 139, 144)

---

[27]*The New Rhetoric: A Treatise on Argumentation* (Notre Dame IN: University of Notre Dame Press, 1969) 91-92. Aristotle would call this the topos of magnitude (*Rhet.* 2.19.26-27).

Though he may seem brash, Cicero did eventually suffer exile and execution for his political activity. Still, one has the sense that Cicero intends his courage to serve as an ethical resource. He admits a desire to be famous, but, "This is a passion which may seem exaggerated; but I am sure it is not dishonorable" (162).

Of virtue, knowledge, and pure motives, the least discussed is knowledge, though the Latin handbooks agree that speakers ought to be broadly educated (cf. *Ad Her.* 1.2; *Inst. Or.* 12.2.1-10). The need for knowledge among orators may be the primary concern in Cicero's *De Oratore*:

> No man can be an orator complete in all points of merit, who has not obtained a knowledge of all important subjects and arts. For it is from knowledge that oratory must derive its beauty and fullness, and unless there is such knowledge, well grasped and comprehended by the speaker, there must be something empty and almost childish in the utterance. (*De Or.* 1.20)

Speakers in the hellenistic world sought to present themselves as persons who could be trusted because of their exemplary character, command over the subject matter, and blameless motivation.

4. Ancient rhetorical theorists approached ethos *cautiously*. Aristotle hints that building ethos is actually a sly operation:

> And you should at once introduce yourself and your adversary as being of a certain character, that the hearers may regard you or him as such; *but do not let it be seen* (λανθάνων δὲ ποίει). *Rhet.* 3.16.10, emphasis mine)

The theorists advised speakers to construct ethos with great care; after all, boasting would be a sign of *hybris* (ὕβρις), one of the most despised personality traits in the hellenistic world. This caution is related to the issue of proper motivation as well, since judicial and deliberative speeches were not primarily meant to glorify the speaker. As the *Rhetorica ad Herennium* demands self-praise without arrogance (1.8) and Quintilian forgoes pride and elevated rhetoric (*Inst. Or.* 6.2.19), we see the dilemma the ancient speaker faced: How does one praise oneself without sounding too proud? So Cicero advocates a gentle style (*De Or.* 2.129), tempered with a modest approach (2.182), as an indication of goodwill.[28] And in *De Partitione Oratoria* he suggests that both praise and blame are achieved through narrative rather than propositional argument, thus "gently influencing the emotions" (71).

As an indirect means of building ethos, Aristotle suggests mentioning witnesses. If by speaking too well of oneself the speaker may incite envy—or even outright contradiction!—perhaps "we must make another speak in our place" (*Rhet.* 3.17.16). Ever the wise strategist, Cicero takes Aristotle's advice. Appealing to witnesses as a means of praising himself indirectly, he reminds the city that it had held a special day to honor his supression of Catalina's rebellion. Such praise he did not confer upon himself; instead, it was granted by the very audience he is addressing. Significant for our purposes is that, while Cicero's interpretation of the events emphasizes his own virtue and importance in the strongest terms, it relies upon the testimony of his audience.

> In the first place, you expressed gratitude to myself in superlative terms, and declared that it was my courage and energy which enabled the machinations of these traitors to be revealed. . . . And above all you decreed a thanksgiving in my name, an honor which no man acting in a civil capacity had ever been awarded before.[29] (132)

We should not overemphasize Cicero's caution. The same Cicero who advocated a mild tone in establishing ethos (*De Or.* 2.129; but 2.200) could be astonishingly bold in praising his own importance, even resorting to obvious hyperbole. After his suppression of Catalina's rebellion, he describes himself as a person of superhuman vigilance and skill, admonishing Catalina that "No single thing you do, nothing you attempt or even contemplate, escapes my notice" (79). Nevertheless, in both practice and theory, Cicero also testifies to the caution that often distinguished ancient ethos.

---

[28]As we shall see below, in practice Cicero's "modesty" is often what we might call audacity.

[29]In an earlier speech Cicero reminds the audience of what the thanksgiving said: "because I had saved the city from the flames, the citizens from massacre and Italy from war" (118).

5. The handbooks all agree: ethos applies to speakers as well as their *opponents* (*Rhet.* 3.19.1; 3.17.16; *Ad Her.* 1.8; *De Or.* 2.182).[30] Speakers are to discuss their opponents' past conduct, habits, character traits, and motivations, simply using the same techniques they would employ in praising themselves (*Inst. Or.* 4.1.14-15). As we shall see, the caution appropriate to one's own self-characterization became less important when assailing someone else.

6. *Vivid characterization* was a prominent feature of ancient stylistics. Though this characteristic stands in some tension with the tentative nature of ancient ethical theory, ancient speakers and writers desired ἐναργείας, the vivid sort of description which places things "before the eyes." A characteristic of ancient literary theory in general (*Style* 208-22; *Poet.* 17.1; *Sublime* 15.1), it was effectively appropriated by the rhetorical tradition (*Rhet.* 1.9-10; 3.16.10; *Inst. Or.* 4.1.15).[31] Cicero advised speakers to "paint their characters in words" (*De Or.* 2.184; cf. 3.202), and even Quintilian approved of exaggeration in characterization (*Inst. Or.* 4.1.15).

In the *Rhetorica ad Herennium* we find lengthy discussions of Portrayal, representing a person's bodily form, Character Delineation,[32] the depiction of someone's distinctive traits, Dialogue, imitation of a person's speech, and Personification,[33] which among other things is "representing an absent person as present" (4.63-66). Ancient characterization tended to identify a subject with a single

---

[30]According to *Ad Her.* (1.8) and Quintilian (*Inst. Or.* 4.1.16), goodwill may also be obtained through discussing one's audience (1.8).

[31]Beth Innocenti ("Towards a Theory of Vivid Description as Practiced in Cicero's *Verrine* Orations," *Rhetorica* 12 [1994]: 355-81) argues that vivid description does not receive full theoretical treatment in the Latin handbooks, then goes on to fill in the gaps by connecting the references from the handbooks themselves. In my opinion, the treatment in *Ad Her.* is indeed systematic. At any rate, vividness was a feature of both theory and practice in ancient literature.

[32]ἠθοποιία in the Greek tradition according to Harry Caplan, the translator of the LCL edition of *Ad Her.* Cf. *De Or.* 3.204.

[33]According to Caplan, προσωποιία in the Greek tradition.

attribute,[34] making Character Delineation especially valuable as a means of exposing a person's ruling passion in the public light:

> Character Delineations of this kind which describe the qualities proper to each man's nature carry very great charm, for they set before our eyes a person's whole character . . . in short, by such delineation any one's ruling passion can be brought into the open. (*Ad Her.* 4.65)

Simplicity combined with vividness is the mark of ancient characterization, a feature we should expect to find applied to speakers as well as to their opponents.

Vivid characterization was especially effective in attacking one's opponents. Cicero could adapt a mild tone when speaking of himself and even his opponents (302), but his moderation does not always carry the day, especially in relation to his adversaries. Cicero's vivid characterization often takes the form of demonization and debasement.[35] He freely sketches his opponents' motives, often associating them with debauchery. His characterization of Catalina provides one example:

> For imagine every type of criminality and wickedness that you can think of; he is behind them all. In the whole of Italy there is not one single poisoner, gladiator, robber, assassin, parricide, will-forger, cheat, glutton, wastrel, adulterer, prostitute, corrupter of youth, or youth who has been corrupted, indeed any nasty individual of any kind whatever, who would not be obliged to admit he has been Catalina's intimate. (*Political Speeches*, 97)

Cicero goes on, elaborating on Catalina's sexual offenses:

---

[34]The most famous examples might be Theophrastus's *Character Sketches* and Homer's Achilles (cf. Robert Scholes and Robert Kellogg, *The Nature of Narrative* [Oxford: Oxford University Press, 1966] 88, 161-65). Aristotle argues for the persuasive power of drawing upon "what is specially characteristic of yourself or of the adversary" (*Rhet.* 3.16.10).

[35]I have adapted debasement as a rhetorical category from David Spurr, *The Rhetoric of Empire: Colonial Discourse in Journalism, Travel Writing, and Imperial Administration*, Post-Contemporary Interventions (Durham NC: Duke University Press, 1993).

> Not one single act of filthy lechery has been committed without him being its guiding spirit. For no one has had such a talent for seducing young men. He himself became the lover of a number of them, in the most repulsive fashion; and he disgustingly allowed others to make love to himself. (97)[36]

The ultimate result of such characterization is a kind of dualism: Cicero represents the side of good against absolute evil (e.g., 234).

7. Though Cicero argued that ethos should be constructed throughout the speech (*De Or.* 2.184), most theorists especially identified ethos with the *beginning and end* of speeches.[37] Quintilian exemplifies this tension between ethos as it works throughout an address and ethos concentrated in beginnings and endings. Though he locates ethos in his discourse on the exordium (*Inst. Or.* 4.1.7-29), he acknowledges that ethos is continuous, relevant whenever one speaks of what is right or expedient (6.2.10-11). According to the *Rhetorica ad Herennium*, the introduction (exordium) and conclusion of the speech bear the primary task of making the audience become attentive, receptive, and well disposed (*benivolos*).[38] One builds goodwill (*benivolentia*)[39] primarily by directly discussing one's own person, the characters of one's adversaries, the persons who compose the audience, and the facts themselves (1.5.8).

Sometimes ethos is covered in discussions of arrangement, as is the case for Aristotle (*Rhet.* 3.14.7; 3.19.1) and the *Rhetorica ad Herennium* (1.8; 2.50). Quintilian also discusses *benivolentia* in the context of the exordium, arguing that the exordium should work

---

[36]Most offensive among these charges may have been the accusation that Catalina had allowed himself to be sexually penetrated by social inferiors such as young men. This would have been a serious charge in ancient Greece (John J. Winkler, *The Constraints of Desire: The Anthropology of Sex and Gender in Ancient Greece*, New Ancient World Series [New York: Routledge, 1990] 46-54), and probably was in Rome as well (Dale B. Martin, "Heterosexism and the Interpretation of Romans 1:18-32," *Biblical Interpretation* 3 [1995]: 344-46).

[37]Edward P. J. Corbett maintains that though ethos must be sustained throughout a speech, the introduction and conclusion are especially important (*Classical Rhetoric for the Modern Student*, 2nd ed. [New York: Oxford University Press, 1971] 95).

[38]For the importance of the introduction, see 1.4.6; for the conclusion, see 2.50.

[39]The word is spelled *benevolentia* in Cicero, *De Or.* and *benivolentia* in *Ad Her.* and Quintilian, *Inst. Or.*

to establish an attentive, receptive, and well-disposed audience (*Inst. Or.* 4.1.5). While ethos is embedded in the entire text, we should be particularly alert to beginnings and endings.

Though Cicero the theorist noted that ethos belongs to the entire speech, Cicero the orator concentrates his ethical appeal at the beginnings and endings of his speeches. Even his argument that Rome should send Pompey against Mithridates VI concludes not with a summary of Pompey's qualifications but with Cicero's single-minded devotion to Rome (*Political Speeches*, 70). Ethical appeal, present throughout his speeches, is most explicit in making the audience well disposed (beginnings) and in leaving them with positive feelings (endings).

Summary

This survey of classical ethos has sought to sketch the broad field of conventions and expectations shared by ancient speakers and audiences. Perhaps the most important issue is the universal recognition that the speaker's relationship to the audience is extremely important. While conceptions of ethos varied and developed, we observe several other motifs: concern with the speaker's character (virtue, knowledge, and pure motives); cautious approaches to the issue; attacks upon opponents; vivid characterization; and an emphasis on the speech's beginning and end.

Narrators in Literary Theory

The book of Revelation is probably not literature in the sense of a work produced for a general or literary audience. And it certainly does not resemble the prose novels of the past three centuries. Instead, Revelation addresses a particular audience, the churches of Asia Minor in the first century CE, and calls upon that audience to respond to its message in particular ways. So, while it may be fairly obvious why the categories of ancient apocalyptic discourse and rhetorical theory would be relevant for our investigation, why introduce contemporary literary theory?

The body of Revelation is a narrative. It is told by a narrator, John, who is also its implied author. John's point of view dominates the text. Though John promises to tell everything he sees right from the beginning (1:2), his audience in fact only learns what John chooses to or is allowed to tell them. And what John does tell is still mediated through John's own visual and evaluative point of view. John's ethos, then, is a narrative construct if it is anything at all. In the language of ancient ethos: How does John manipulate narrative to represent himself as a person of virtue, knowledge, and pure motives?

These questions have often been assigned to the literary-critical category of point of view. But they need not be restricted to the formalist context with which they are often associated, a setting in which texts are detached from their historical contexts and audiences.[40] Instead, point of view may serve as a rhetorical category, a means of analyzing a narrative's ethos through the voices that present it.[41] While we do not have direct access to Revelation's author, we may assess how that author constructs ethos through the narrator, John. And we may treat this device as a rhetorical act with genuine social and ideological implications.[42]

---

[40]The Bible and Culture Collective (*The Postmodern Bible* [New Haven CT: Yale University Press, 1995] 84-85) associates point of view and critics such as Wayne C. Booth with formalism, neglecting Booth's own self-identification with ethical (in the sense of values and morals) and rhetorical criticism. They do not mention the use of point of view as a category for feminist and ideological criticisms, as in the case of Susan Snaider Lanser, whose works do not appear in their impressive bibliography. Booth and Lanser are critical figures for my own approach to ethos through narrative criticism. It is ironic that the Collective neglects this category's potential for postmodern and liberating practice, since Michel Foucault's work on the power of looking and writing is a prominent feature of much postmodern criticism (cf. Edward W. Said, *Orientalism* [New York: Random House, 1978]; Spurr, *Rhetoric of Empire,* 11).

[41]Frederic Jameson argues that point of view as practiced in formalist criticism is an ideological act in its own right: an attempt to reconstitute the subject through textuality when the bourgeois individualist subject is disintegrating (*The Political Unconscious: Narrative as a Socially Symbolic Act* [Ithaca NY: Cornell University Press, 1981] 220-21).

[42]Wayne C. Booth, *The Company We Keep: An Ethics of Fiction* (Berkeley: University of California, 1988) 80-122; and "Are Narrative Choices Subject to Ethical Criticism?" in *Reading Narrative: Form, Ethics, Ideology,* ed. James Phelan (Columbus OH: Ohio State University Press, 1989) 57-78; Susan Snaider Lanser, *The Narrative Act: Point of View in Prose Fiction* (Princeton NJ: Princeton University Press, 1981) 8, 48-49, 57-60. To continue the conversation with *The Postmodern Bible,* this is how its authors would see rhetorical criticism developing (161, 166).

With the movement of literary criticism toward more rhetorical ways of understanding meaning over the past three decades[43] has come a renewed interest in the narrating voice. Who tells a story? How does this narrator establish relationships to the story being told and to its characters, as well as to the audience? Contemporary literary critics have offered several important insights for addressing such questions.

1. *A narrator's activity is subject to analysis* along multiple axes. Wayne C. Booth and Susan Snaider Lanser have both developed proposals for evaluating narrative activity, not only in terms of literary-rhetorical devices, but also as ethical and ideological acts.[44] While their proposals differ in terms of theoretical background,[45] scale, and vocabulary, Booth and Lanser share the conviction that stories and how they are narrated can have important consequences for their audiences.

Booth began with the insight that novels are produced for certain rhetorical ends, and that whatever narratorial devices best serve those ends are appropriate. The narrator is the agent employed by the implied author (direct access to the real author being impossible) to carry out the novel's tasks.[46] The reader, then, depends upon the narrator for his or her experience of the story.

---

[43]Wayne C. Booth's *The Rhetoric of Fiction*, 2nd ed. (Chicago: Univ. of Chicago Press, 1983; [1]1961) may have been the catalyst for the revival of rhetorical modes of literary criticism. For general announcements and retrospectives on this trend, see Susan R. Suleiman, "Introduction: Varieties of Audience-Oriented Criticism," in *The Reader in the Text: Essays on Audience and Interpretation*, ed. Susan R. Suleiman and Inge Crosman (Princeton NJ: Princeton Univ. Press, 1980) 7-11; Jane P. Tompkins, "The Reader in History: The Changing Shape of Literary Response," in *Reader-Response Criticism: From Formalism to Post-Structuralism*, ed. Jane P. Tompkins (Baltimore: Johns Hopkins Univ. Press, 1980) 201-26; Terry Eagleton, *Literary Theory: An Introduction* (Minneapolis: Univ. of Minnesota, 1983) 203-12; and Bryan C. Short, "Literary *Ethos*: Dispersion, Resistance, Mystification," in *Ethos: New Essays in Rhetorical and Literary Theory*, ed. Baumlin and Baumlin, 367.

[44]I will refer to the following texts: Booth, *Rhetoric of Fiction*; *Company We Keep*; "Narrative Choices"; and "Distance and Point of View: An Essay in Classification," *Essays in Criticism* 11 (1961): 60-79; Lanser, *Narrative Act*; and *Fictions of Authority: Women Writers and Narrative Voice* (Ithaca NY: Cornell Univ. Press, 1992).

[45]Booth adapts essentially formalist and audience-oriented categories; Lanser is influenced by structuralist narratology.

[46]The distinction between implied author and narrator is not entirely appropriate to Revelation, since the two figures amount to almost the same character.

In general, he or she learns only what the narrator reveals and perceives characters and events as mediated by the narrator's point of view. Booth is not so naive as to overlook the possibility of and need for resisting readers; nevertheless, even those readers begin with their experience of the text as narrated.[47]

Booth's project implies a thorough study of the various modes of narration. The categories he provides include: (a) person; (b) dramatized or undramatized narration; (c) narrators as observers or as agents; (d) scene or summary narration; (e) commentary; (f) self-consciousness in narrating or the lack thereof; (g) distance (intellectual, moral, spatial, or temporal) between the narrator and the author, reader, or the characters, a category which encompasses reliability and unreliability; (h) isolation (being unsupported or uncorrected by other narrators) or its opposite; (i) privilege or limitation in knowledge; and (j) depth and axis of inside views of characters.[48]

For example, we may say that John is a first-person, dramatized narrator-agent who: uses scene more than summary; is frequently self-conscious; maintains various degrees of moral and intellectual distance from his audience and characters; is sometimes corrected and frequently supported by other voices; is extremely privileged; and almost never provides deep views of his characters.[49] We may say all these things, but it is also necessary to employ them in a way that provides insight into John's attempt to win his audience's trust. For our purposes, the critical thing is not so much where John might fit into each these fields, but how these categories might enlighten our reconstruction of John's character.

Though the ethics of narration has been important to Booth's project from the beginning,[50] some of his more recent work has

---

[47]Booth calls this process surrendering to the text (*Company We Keep*, 32), a task which must be performed even in the act of resisting it (257). For example, according to Jonathan Culler: "The practitioner of deconstruction works within the terms of the system in order to breach it" (*On Deconstruction: Theory and Criticism after Structuralism* [Ithaca NY: Cornell University Press, 1982] 86).

[48]"Distance and Point-of-View." This article is an expanded version of chap. 6 of *Rhetoric of Fiction*.

[49]These observations contribute to the conclusions of the next chapter.

[50]*Rhetoric of Fiction*, 376-98.

foregrounded ethical (by which he means moral) considerations.[51] Booth argues that narrative techniques often have moral implications, and that readers should judge texts in such terms. In *The Company We Keep: An Ethics of Fiction*, Booth characterizes ethical criticism as the attempt to "describe the encounters of a storyteller's ethos with that of the reader or listener."[52] In other words, the implied author (the construct held responsible for the narrative choices sketched above) is treated as a character. And the question becomes: Is this implied author a good friend with whom to spend time?[53] How valuable (or detrimental) are the things this implied author asks me to desire?[54] Such evaluation should be complex,[55] and it ought to be conducted through a negotiation among interested readers.[56] But just as it is inevitable that authors will promote values, so is ethical evaluation implied in the reading act. The goal is to be aware of what one is doing.

Lanser's project is similar to Booth's in that she works to identify how narrative techniques serve rhetorical ends. But her work is more systematic than Booth's in that she develops a more complex multidimensional scheme for assessing the possibilities for narration, a framework couched less in alternative terms (e.g., dramatized versus undramatized narrators) than in positions on relative poles (e.g., degree of privilege). Lanser is also more engaged in a specific mode of ideological analysis: she wants to know how gender interacts with authorial authority.[57]

Before we move into Lanser's framework, we should review some of her key assumptions. First, Lanser employs speech act theory as a means of assessing narration: fictions seek to perform specific actions.[58] This reading strategy tends to close the distance between author and audience, as every aspect of a text is the

---

[51]*Company*; "Narrative Choices."
[52]*Company*, 8.
[53]Ibid., 174-79.
[54]Ibid., 201-206.
[55]Ibid., 336.
[56]Ibid., 70-76.
[57]This interest is the focus of her *Fictions of Authority*.
[58]*Narrative Act*, 67-73.

author's ideological product.[59] Unless a text indicates otherwise, the narrator is directly identified with the implied author.[60] Still, Lanser is aware of the multiple levels of narrative discourse. It is essential to distinguish among author, implied author, narrators, narrating characters, and so forth down the scale of knowledge and responsibility for the work as a whole.[61] The goal is to assess ideology at work in narrative, "the act of using language . . . defined, constrained and conventionalized according to a system of values, norms, and perceptions of the world."[62]

Lanser divides the modalities of narration into three categories: status, contact, and stance. Each of these fields includes many more subgroups. (These are too many to be summarized here, but we will introduce several as they become relevant.) *Status* pertains to the narrator's qualifications: his or her identity, credibility, sincerity, and skill. This category somewhat resembles Aristotelian ethos, and it addresses the narrator's representation as a person who knows what she or he is talking about. The difference is that Lanser is describing fiction rather than prescribing rhetoric: she does not judge more knowledge or skill as necessarily better than less. *Contact* involves the narrator's relationship to an audience, a concern similar to that of the Latin tradition. Is the narrator self-conscious, confident, formal? Does she address the audience directly? Does she show respect for them? *Stance* reflects the narrator's perspective toward the message, including her or his ideological and psychological point of view. Of course, narrators may employ the points at which their stance coincides with the audiences' as a step toward transforming the audiences' view on other matters.[63] On the other hand, narrators who seem particularly concerned with their audiences' response, or who go out of their way to

---

[59]Cf. ibid., 18, 32, 64.

[60]Ibid., 151; *Fictions of Authority*, 16.

[61]*Narrative Act*, 146, 242.

[62]Ibid., 64.

[63]Ibid., 216-17. Cf. Kenneth Burke, *A Rhetoric of Motives* (repr.: Berkeley: University of California Press, 1969; [1]1950) 46; Perelman and Olbrechts-Tyteca, *New Rhetoric*, 320.

defend themselves, may lack confidence that their messages will be well received.[64]

Booth and Lanser enable us to make careful discriminations concerning how John's storytelling serves his own ethos. What does John know and what does he tell? How does he align his perceptions with those of God and his audience? How does John's angle of vision manipulate his audience's perception of himself and his opponents? When we ask questions like these, we are applying Booth and Lanser's insights to an understanding of John's ethos.

2. *Identification* is a universal dimension of rhetoric. Kenneth Burke's analysis of identification in philosophical, economic, and other cultural texts as well as literary works has been described as a precursor to some contemporary cultural criticism.[65] According to Burke, the realm of rhetoric is division among people. When there is division, rhetoric's task is to move people to identify with one or another set of symbols.[66] By identifying themselves with their audiences' prejudices, writers and speakers may enlist them in a "partnership" of interest. Speakers may invite audiences to identify with their goals and values, or they may identify their opponents with symbols which will repulse their audiences. Quoting Augustine's *De Doctrina Christiana*, Booth suggests that a person is persuaded who

> likes what you promise, fears what you say is imminent, hates what you censure, embraces what you commend, regrets whatever you built up as regrettable, rejoices at what you say is cause for rejoicing, sympathizes with those whose wretchedness your words bring before his very eyes, shuns those whom you admonish him to shun . . . and in whatever other ways your high eloquence can affect the minds of your hearers, bringing them not merely to know what should be done, but to do what they know should be done.[67]

---

[64]*Act of Narrative*, 178. Cf. Booth, *Rhetoric of Fiction*, 179.

[65]Vincent B. Leitch, *Cultural Criticism, Literary Theory, Poststructuralism* (New York: Columbia University Press, 1992) 43-44.

[66]Ibid., 25.

[67]Ibid., 50, quoting Augustine, *On Christian Doctrine* 4.12.

For readers of the Apocalypse, Burke's rhetoric is especially helpful when John builds complicated webs of association. John employs identification in positive and negative ways. On the one hand, John employs identification in aligning himself with Jesus, prophets and apostles, and the martyrs. Especially important are the bridges he builds to his audience. On the other hand, John links his opponents to villains from the Hebrew Bible and the contemporary imagination. Exalting himself and debasing his opponents, John uses identification to his advantage.

3. *Multiple voices* inhabit narratives. Mikhail Bakhtin's work, which calls attention to the relationships between the narrating voice and other voices in modern novels, has become extremely influential in postmodern discussions of narrative voice. Only in the last two decades has Bakhtin's work become widely known in North America. It is not so much his theses that the novel is the most advanced and still developing literary genre and that Dostoevsky is the model of polyvocality that make Bakhtin's work significant for this project. Instead, what is important are the questions he raises, questions concerning the relationship of authorial voice to the other voices in a work. Bakhtin describes the dialogic novel, in which an author incorporates many diverse voices in the same text. Vincent B. Leitch correctly characterizes Bakhtin's insight: "the [literary] text is part of the social text, an arena of struggle."[68] As Michael Holquist has put it, for Bakhtin, "Dialogue is real; monologue is not."[69] Bakhtin's ideal novel would give full voice to a variety of competing modes of discourse, making no attempt to force them to serve a dominant authorial point of view. While Bakhtin privileges those novels in which all voices are allowed to express themselves fully, we may adapt his insights as we investigate how John uses levels of discourse to enhance the status of his own voice.[70]

---

[68]*Cultural Criticism*, 56. Leitch goes on to criticize Bakhtin for privileging the novel and opposing monologic and dialogic discourse (56-57).

[69]*Dialogism: Bakhtin and His World*, New Accents (New York: Routledge, 1990) 59.

[70]*The Dialogic Imagination: Four Essays*, Slavic Series 1 (Austin: University of Texas Press, 1981); and *Problems of Dostoevsky's Poetics*, Theory and History of

As we shall see, Bakhtin's proposal raises sharp questions for John's narrative ethos. For in Bakhtin's world, "snuffing out the 'I' of other subjects" is both bad aesthetics and bad politics.[71] Does John use other voices in his Apocalypse? How do they relate to one another, and to his own voice? Revelation is filled with voices human, heavenly, mythological, and divine. It even characterizes the voices of John's opponents. While I do not intend to evaluate John according to Bakhtin's prescient standards, Bakhtin does suggest a helpful strategy for reading Revelation. What does John do with the voices he incorporates? What might John's construction of those voices have meant to his own audience, and what are its implications for contemporary readers?

Summary

Insights from contemporary literary criticism enhance the sophistication of our investigation of John's ethos. While the ancient rhetoricians developed careful ethical models for the speaking situation, their attention to narrative ethos was much less thorough. We may analyze how John constructs his narrative point of view through categories such as privilege, participation, status, contact, and stance. We will also explore the webs of identification—positive and negative—with which John links himself and his opponents. And we may ask about John's relation to other voices in his narrative.

Narrative Authority in Theories of Resistance Literature

The Apocalypse is resistance literature set in a colonial context. In it Rome is characterized as a colonial and commercial power riding on the back of its empire and killing those who refuse to take part. The book calls its audience to withdraw from participation in the colonial culture and envisions the empire's self-destruction. Though we have no evidence that the many ancient writers who opposed the Empire had access to theories of resis-

---

Literature 8 (Minneapolis: University of Minnesota Press, 1984).

[71]Holquist, *Dialogism*, 34.

tance literature, their texts may be illuminated by insights from contemporary resistance literature and criticism.

1. Postcolonial or resistance literature and theory share an assumption with rhetorical theory and the literary theorists we have reviewed above: *Textual strategies reflect and affect social and political conditions and behaviors.* "Worlds exist by means of languages," according to one team of postcolonial critics,[72] and the textual construction of worlds is a site of struggle.[73] This conviction stands in opposition to two common cultural myths: the myth of pure fiction and the myth of the objective reporter. Resistance literatures tend to reject purely aesthetic understandings of literature,[74] arguing that the literary is the political and literary techniques are ideology in action. An emphasis on the connection between a text and its historical world need not erase that text's status as art. Precisely because of its situatedness, the text grows, rather than decreases, in interest and value.[75]

Because he takes literature deadly seriously, a postcolonial author like Chinua Achebe must attack works like *Heart of Darkness*. Achebe judges that Conrad's novel cannot be considered a work of art because it celebrates "the dehumanization of Africa and Africans."[76] Just as important for this project, Achebe struggles with the question of authorial voice and Conrad's fictional first-person narrator, Marlow. Is Conrad responsible for Marlow's story?

> But if Conrad's intention is to draw a *cordon sanitaire* between himself and the moral and psychological malaise of his narrator, his care seems to me totally wasted because he neglects to hint however subtly or tentatively at an alternative frame of reference by which we may judge the actions or opinions of his characters. It would not have been beyond Conrad's power to make that provision if he had found it necessary.[77]

---

[72]Bill Ashcroft, Gareth Griffiths, and Helen Tiffin, *The Empire Writes Back: Theory and Practice in Post-Colonial Literatures*, New Accents (New York: Routledge, 1989) 44.

[73]Barbara Harlow, *Resistance Literature* (New York: Methuen, 1987) 2.

[74]Ibid., 40.

[75]Edward W. Said, *Culture and Imperialism* (New York: Knopf, 1993) 13.

[76]"An Image of Africa," *Massachusetts Review* 18 (1977) 788.

[77]Ibid., 787.

Achebe even goes so far as to notice similarities between Conrad's career and that of his fictional narrator. Achebe's bottom line: Authors are responsible for their representations of the world, even across fictional levels of discourse.

So it comes as no surprise that Achebe's own novels manage to combine fictional characterization with real-world concerns. Achebe, like other postcolonial writers, uses fiction as a means of critique toward relations of domination.[78] His novel *Things Fall Apart*, the first of four novels which represent Nigeria in successive stages of colonialism and independence,[79] presents a complex but coherent portrait of an Ibo culture before contact with European colonizers as well as a representation of the Europeans themselves. He often uses inside views of characters to demonstrate African ambivalence toward Europeans and vice versa. For example, a first encounter with white missionary preaching leads one village leader to conclude that the Europeans are crazy, while his son sits captivated.[80] And many of Achebe's Europeans believe they embody liberal or progressive values even though they actually slander Ibo culture. While one European administrator reflects on his bringing civilization to Africa, he plans a book: *The Pacification of the Primitive Tribes of the Lower Niger*.[81] His plan, literally the projected book's title, provides the novel's last words just as it expresses Achebe's salient conviction: that books function within and contribute to relations of domination and resistance.

Parody and irony often accompany Achebe's representation of the European consciousness. White missionaries wrongly assume that Umuofia, the village at the novel's center, has a king. Apparently, European forms of government are universal.[82] The citizens of Umuofia have tremendous fun with the missionaries' poor command of their language, mocking them and calling them

---

[78]Cf. Harlow, *Resistance Literature*, 36-37; Ashcroft, Griffiths, and Tiffin, *The Empire Writes Back*, 32-33.

[79]*Things Fall Apart*, African Writers Series 1 (repr.: Portsmouth NH: Heinemann, 1962; [1]1958).

[80]Ibid., 101-104.

[81]Ibid., 148.

[82]Ibid., 105.

names such as "Ashy Buttocks."[83] Some mock the European religion as well.[84]

Achebe refuses to settle for simplified oppositions. The Ibo people he represents are not perfect, nor are they entirely unified. Women frequently suffer abuse, and infanticide is common. Still, Achebe also presents an Ibo culture that is both viable and mature. It is keenly democratic and features highly developed oral literature and rhetoric. The culture has dignity. And not all European persons and institutions are evil. One missionary, Mr. Brown, encouraged village leaders to send their children to his school, arguing that unless their children could read and write "strangers would come from other places to rule them."[85] While Mr. Brown (Could the in-between color of his name be symbolic?) certainly contributed to the cultural demise of the village, his policy was "compromise and accommodation"; he wanted as much autonomy for the village as possible. His replacement, however, "saw things as black and white. And black was evil."[86]

2. Achebe's emphasis upon the representing consciousness through inside views and his use of irony and parody contest representation by the colonizers. In response to the myth of the objective reporter, resistance literatures emphasize *the intimate relationship between representation and power*. This is a critical issue for postcolonial and resistance theory, as "Postcolonial criticism bears witness to the unequal and uneven forces of cultural representation involved in the contest for political and social authority within the modern world order."[87]

Representation can become reality; the authority to represent implies power. Perhaps the critic who makes this point most strongly is Edward W. Said. Said argues that texts are acts of power from the beginning, that the relationship between writing

---

[83]Ibid., 102, 123.

[84]Ibid., 103.

[85]Ibid., 128.

[86]Ibid., 130.

[87]Homi K. Bhabha, "Postcolonial Criticism," in *Redrawing the Boundaries: The Transformation of English and American Literary Studies*, ed. Stephen Greenblatt and Giles Gunn (New York: Modern Language Association of America, 1992) 437.

about and being written about is one of domination.[88] In Said's view, the ability to represent requires a *strategic location* with respect to one's object. This location commits the observer to certain perspectives and means of expression.[89] The scary thing is that over time representation becomes "reality."[90] A deeply entrenched discipline such as Orientalism is at the same time its own product and enabling factor, censor and creator. An abstract and arbitrary construct such as the Orient becomes less an object of study than a means by which the West discovers and confirms itself.[91] It also becomes a system of political relationships and effects.

Because resistance theorists take seriously the power of representation, one of their primary enterprises is to point out contradictions in the representing consciousness. As we have observed in Achebe's use of parody, satire, and point of view, this activity destabilizes the apparent monolithic authority of narrators, reporters, and other experts. For example, Gayatri Chakravorty Spivak uses deconstruction to identify "traces" left over in what seem to be self-contained descriptions.[92] While the project is always incomplete—traces always remain—it does allow for persistent critique of what must seem "natural and self-evident" to a dominant group.[93] Spivak's treatment of "womb envy" exemplifies this strategy. Spivak "speculate[s] that the womb has always been defined as a lack *by* man in order to cover up the lack *in* man, the lack, precisely, of a tangible place of production."[94] The idea is that when one group characterizes itself as superior to another, it is often avoiding its own insecurity.

David Spurr's analysis of colonial journalism and travel writing also demonstrates the impulse to destabilize the narrating voice.[95]

---

[88]Cf. *Orientalism*, 32, 308; "The World, the Text, and the Critic," in *Critical Theory Since Plato*, rev. ed., ed. Hazard Adams (Fort Worth TX: Harcourt Brace Jovanovich, 1992) 1218. Both Said and David Spurr (*Rhetoric of Empire*) rely heavily upon Michel Foucault for their perspectives.

[89]*Orientalism*, 20.

[90]Cf. "Orientalism Reconsidered," *Cultural Critique* 1 (1985): 92.

[91]*Orientalism*, 115.

[92]*In Other Worlds: Essays in Cultural Politics* (New York: Routledge, 1988) 46.

[93]Ibid., 119.

[94]Ibid., 45.

[95]*Rhetoric of Empire*.

Spurr identifies twelve tropes according to which colonial subjects were represented.[96] The interesting thing is that these tropes often attempt to cover European insecurity. The debasement of colonized subjects in terms of filth or sex betrays a western longing for a return to a savage state.[97] Idealizing the colonized provides a means of compensation for the damage inflicted upon them.[98] And so forth. As Said indicates, confrontation with the Orient creates an anxiety which must be accounted for, whether by comparing colonized to colonizer[99] or by projecting one's fear and desire onto the colonial subject and landscape.[100] I have noted the same sentiment in the work of Booth and Lanser: When a narrator goes to great lengths to demonstrate control over the subject matter, it likely belies a concern for his or her own authority.[101]

3. Counterdiscourses such as postcolonial and resistance literatures struggle with their *hybrid nature.* They generally find it necessary to appropriate the language and techniques of the center which they oppose.[102] Perhaps even more important for this project are the ways in which counterdiscourses and resistance movements often (always?)[103] duplicate not simply diction and genre but the very oppressive structures they would oppose as well. Well known is the phenomenon of division between elite and populist elements of resistance movements.[104] But there is also a tendency within

---

[96]These are surveillance, appropriation, aestheticization, classification, debasement, negation, affirmation, idealization, insubstantiation, naturalization, eroticization, and, finally, resistance. I have referred to his work on debasement in our study of Cicero above. While space will not allow a review of these tropes, I will refer to several of them later.

[97]Ibid., 79.

[98]Ibid., 132.

[99]*Orientalism*, 152.

[100]Ibid., 167.

[101]Lanser, *Act of Narrative*, 178; Booth, *Rhetoric of Fiction*, 179.

[102]This theme permeates Ashcroft, Griffiths, and Tiffin, *Empire Writes Back*. Cf. Linda Hutcheon, *The Politics of Postmodernism*, New Accents (New York: Routledge, 1989), for the thesis that one is always implicated in the object of criticism, what she calls "complicitous critique."

[103]Richard Terdiman argues that "counterdiscourses are always interlocked with the domination they contest" (*Discourse/Counter-Discourse: The Theory and Practice of Symbolic Resistance in Nineteenth-Century France* [Ithaca NY: Cornell University Press, 1985] 16).

[104]Cf. James C. Scott, "Revolution in the Revolution: Peasants and Commis-

counterdiscourses to reinscribe the oppositions they resist. Though asserting difference from the center may be an effective rhetorical device,[105] difference always defines itself by what it excludes.[106] The danger is what Ashcroft, Griffiths, and Tiffin call "counterdetermination," the symmetry between a resistance discourse and that which it seeks to decenter.[107]

The problem for resistance and postcolonial literatures is how to counter an imperial center without reinscribing an oppressive center of their own. This is precisely what Averil Cameron says happened in early Christian discourse. Christians began by asserting their difference within the Empire, claiming that they were different because they had encountered the truth. But over time, "Christians . . . talked and wrote themselves into a position where they spoke and wrote the rhetoric of empire."[108] Eventually the Christian claim to truth became a totalizing discourse.

Postcolonial and resistance perspectives contribute several important dimensions to our study of narrative authority in Revelation. First, they emphasize that textual strategies are social and political acts. Second, they underscore the power implied by the representing voice and provide tools for its analysis. And finally, they raise a fundamental problem: is it necessary for a counterdiscourse to mirror the oppressive structures it protests? Early Christian rhetoric certainly moved from the margins of the Roman Empire to its center. Is this process already at work in Revelation?

Conclusion

In this chapter I have reviewed three perspectives which I believe will contribute to an analysis of the narrative ethos at work in Revelation. These are: ancient ethical theory, literary criticism on narration, and postcolonial and resistance theories. In the next

---

sars," *Theory and Society* 7 (1979): 97-134; Bhabha, "Postcolonial Criticism," 452-53; Harlow, *Resistance Literature*, 160.

[105]Cf. Harlow, *Resistance Literature*, 29; Neil ten Kortenaar, "Beyond Authenticity and Creolization: Reading Achebe Writing Culture," *PMLA* 110 (1995): 41.

[106]Terdiman, *Discourse/Counter-Discourse*, 278.

[107]*Empire Writes Back*, 170.

[108]*Christianity and the Rhetoric of Empire*, Sather Classical Lectures 55 (Berkeley: University of California Press, 1991) 14.

chapter I will discuss a fourth ingredient—ethos in early Jewish and Christian apocalyptic discourse.

A simple review might be helpful. I am employing these disparate perspectives to address two major problems. First, I want to explore the conventions available to John and his audience as he struggled to identify himself as a person of authority. Early Jewish and Christian apocalyptic literature and ancient rhetorical conventions provide a background against which to read Revelation. I do not wish to argue that I now understand how any actual historical audience might have heard some historical figure named John. Instead, I am using a broad historical context as my own heuristic device: How *might* such a hypothetical audience—one which had experienced apocalyptic literature and public rhetoric—have understood Revelation's narrative voice?

My second concern has been that Revelation is largely a narrative. To my knowledge, ancient Greek and Latin critics did not discuss narrative voice much, and not at all in terms of authority. But contemporary literary critics do, and some of them connect what would seem to be stylistic insights on point of view with acute ethical and ideological analysis. It is even reasonable to construe this aspect of literary criticism as a return to rhetoric, as several critics have already suggested. The intersection between rhetorical and literary criticism is becoming busier as authority and narrative ethos receive more and more attention. This work is pressed even further in postcolonial and resistance discourses. These movements identify narrative voice with power, and they question whether and how representation can be liberative.

This study will employ these perspectives in order to assess John's narrative ethos. I want to learn how Revelation's narrating voice claims its authority to be heard. Addressing a context marked by conflicting claims to power and authority from both within and beyond his audience, John shouts for attention. His cry is an assertion of power, an attempt to reconfigure himself, his audience, and the world. Before we move our attention to John, however, one more context against which to read his ethos still deserves attention: the world of early Jewish and Christian apocalyptic discourse.

Chapter 3
Apocalyptic Ethos

Stephen O'Leary has shown that authority is a fundamental building block of all apocalyptic argumentation. Claims about the end of the world, the nature of heavenly or hellish realms, or the ultimate fate of human beings necessarily rely on revelatory experience or downright speculation. To such claims most hearers respond with skepticism. After all, "We do not readily accept epochal pronouncements from simply anyone who claims to have discovered the cosmic significance of evil or to have calculated the remaining duration of the cosmos."[1] More specifically, authority—imperial, divine, and prophetic—represents a fundamental site of struggle in Revelation and its contemporary appropriations. When John claims to reveal "the things that must happen shortly" (1:1), one can imagine the audience's response: "Who says so?" or "How do you know?"[2] For John, the answer must lie in his character and experience. "I was in the Spirit on the Lord's day" (1:10), he writes, and "I saw, and behold, a door opened in heaven" (4:1).

But John's ethos does not develop out of pure logical necessity, nor in a cultural vacuum. As we have seen, ethos was surely on the mind of every ancient speaker or writer. Moreover, by the time Revelation was composed, apocalyptic literature and motifs were thriving among Christians and Jews. The working canon included apocalyptic and protoapocalyptic passages such as Isaiah 24–27, 56–66, Ezekiel 37–38, Zechariah 9–14, and the book of Daniel. Jewish responses to the fall of Jerusalem included apocalypses such as *2 Baruch*, *3 Baruch*, and *4 Ezra*. That at least some early Chris-

---

[1]*Arguing the Apocalypse: A Theory of Millennial Rhetoric* (New York and Oxford: Oxford University Press, 1994) 51.

[2]Ibid., 203.

tians knew and respected Jewish apocalyptic literature such as *1 Enoch* and the *Assumption of Moses* is evident from the epistle of Jude. Paul, in fact, argued for his own authority on the basis of apocalyptic and visionary experiences (2 Cor 12:1-10; Gal 1:12), and the Synoptics characterize Jesus as one who experienced otherworldly visions (Mark 1:10-13 par.; 9:2-13 par.; Luke 10:17-20).

Given that first century Jews and Christians were familiar with apocalyptic texts and motifs, it is appropriate to locate Revelation within the flow of Jewish apocalyptic literature of the period. Despite the absence of a highly developed ethical theory, Jewish visionaries employed a distinctive cluster of ethos-enhancing techniques.[3] The question here is not one of literary dependence. Instead, it concerns the conventions available to Revelation's implied author and intended audience. Specifically, how do the Jewish apocalypses dated near or before the composition of Revelation address ethos?[4] And how did first century Christians employ apocalyptic to authorize their own messages?

It would seem that familiarity with apocalyptic literature and its modes of authority would distinguish scholarly from popular readers. Commentaries and critical studies are full of allusions to early Jewish and apocalyptic literature; however, popular authors who dare to use extrabiblical sources in explicating Revelation's internal dynamics would open themselves to a variety of charges. Not only would they fail to allow the Bible to "speak for itself," they would yield some of their own authority as well. I suggest that this distinction can be misleading. Many critical readers lack the rhetorical sensitivity to recognize John's use of standard apocalyptic resources—self-characterization, dialogues with heavenly beings, and the like—as literary devices. Instead, many critics speak of these motifs as John's "experiences," and for this reason their characterizations of John differ little from those of their popular counterparts. Eugene Boring claims:

---

[3]George A. Kennedy demonstrates the global contribution of ethical proof, even where rhetorical theories are lacking (*Comparative Rhetoric: A Historical and Cross-Cultural Introduction* [New York: Oxford University Press, 1998] esp. 223).

[4]Prominent among these would be Daniel, *1 Enoch*, *2 Baruch*, *3 Baruch*, and *4 Ezra*, as well as literature from Qumran such as the *War Scroll* (1QM) and the *New Jerusalem* (5Q15).

> John writes with the authority of a prophet, but John's prophetic role does not have for him the dimension of over-againstness, does not separate him from the members of his churches. He writes as a pastor who shares the life of his congregations.[5]

And Robert W. Wall suggests that "John is a pilgrim in a strange world—a world constructed by dramatic visions and impressive sounds." Revelation becomes John's travel report, an innocent collection of John's visionary experiences.[6] Surely a rhetorically sensitive model for understanding John's apocalyptic ethos is in order.

Ethical Topoi in Apocalyptic Discourse

1. The most prominent and universal means of achieving ethos in Jewish apocalyptic literature was *pseudonymity*, "a constant feature of Jewish apocalypses."[7] Jewish apocalypses (those usually defined as members of the genre) claim to report visions of venerable figures of the distant past, especially persons with mystical associations such as Enoch, Moses, Baruch, or Daniel. That "Enoch walked with God—and then he was not, for God took him" (Gen 5:24) was ample cause for mystical and even eschatological speculation. And Moses, besides being an authoritative figure through the Exodus and his reception of the Torah, had his own apocalyptic credentials. Not only had he heard God's voice, he had even seen God (Exod 34:6-9). In addition, God had once ambushed Moses with the intent to kill him (Exod 4:24). As for Baruch, God had promised him safety "wherever you might go" even in the midst of worldwide judgment (Jer 45:5). But the book of Jeremiah does not tell us where Baruch finally settled, thus making him a fitting object of mystical speculation. And Daniel appears to have been a legendary figure associated with wisdom and righteousness, as we may see from Ezek 14:14; 28:3, and the

---

[5]*Revelation*, Interpretation (Louisville: John Knox, 1989) 80-81.

[6]*Revelation*, 13.

[7]John J. Collins, *The Apocalyptic Imagination: An Introduction to the Jewish Matrix of Christianity* (New York: Crossroad, 1984) 211.

Ugaritic tale of Aqhat.[8] Other figures who had mystical associations and became "authors" of apocalyptic literature include Adam, Shem, Abraham, and Elijah.

We can only guess whether the first audiences of *1 Enoch* or Daniel considered the names on their title pages to represent their authentic authorship. We can conclude, however, that pseudonymity played a necessary role in these texts' self-representation. Pseudonymity is so universal among ancient apocalypses as to be listed among their defining characteristics.[9] Yet despite its widespread occurence, little has been done to identify the role of pseudonymity toward the rhetorical effect of ancient apocalypses.[10]

Kenneth Burke's rhetoric of identification may provide a clue as to pseudonymity's contribution to apocalyptic rhetoric. Speakers identify themselves with persons, figures, or concepts to which their audiences are sympathetic. By identifying apocalypses with prominent legendary figures, their authors sought instant identification with specific mystical traditions. In some cases, pseudonymity automatically offers the audience a sense of the author's character. By the time *1 Enoch* had approached its present form, Enoch, never a developed character in the Hebrew Bible, had become a topos of speculation with a tradition: "Enoch pleased the Lord, and was transformed, as an example of repentance to the nations" (Sir 44:16). And, "No one has been created upon the earth the like of Enoch, for he was taken up from the earth" (Sir 49:14).

2. *Legends* concerning an apocalypse's implied author or the origin of its revelation provided a second standard apocalyptic ethical technique. The case of Daniel, whose story fills about half of the book's twelve chapters, is the best-known example, but many other apocalypses narrate how pious persons receive

---

[8]Ibid., 69.

[9]Philipp Vielhauer and Georg Strecker list pseudonymity first among the fixed features of Jewish apocalypses ("Apocalypses and Related Subjects: Introduction," in *New Testament Apocrypha*, vol. 2, *Writings Related to the Apostles; Apocalypses and Related Subjects*, rev. ed., ed. Wilhelm Schneemelcher, trans. R. McL. Wilson [Louisville: Westminster/John Knox, 1994] 545), while Klaus Koch listed it among the six typical features of apocalypses ("What Is Apocalyptic? An Attempt at a Preliminary Definition," in *Visionaries and Their Apocalypses*, Issues in Religion and Theology 2, ed. Paul D. Hanson [Philadelphia: Fortress, 1983] 23).

[10]Koch, "What Is Apocalyptic?" 23.

supernatural revelation. Several apocalypses, including *2 Baruch, 3 Baruch,* and *4 Ezra,* depict how sincerely their protagonists mourn Jerusalem's fate. Fasting and prayer mark their preparation for the mystical experience, as they do for Daniel (6:10-13; 9:3-21) and for Enoch (*1 Enoch* 12-13; 39:9-14; 84).[11]

As a result of their prayer and fasting, visionaries often receive words of divine commendation. After Daniel's prayer of confession, he learns that he is chosen to receive the revelation:

> Daniel, I have now come forth to instruct you in wisdom. At the beginning of your prayer a word came forth, so I came to announce it to you; for you are the chosen person (ἀνὴρ ἐπιθυμιῶν, Dan 9:22-23 LXX).[12]

Daniel's designation as a specially chosen visionary is reemphasized by the repetition of the phrase ἀνὴρ ἐπιθυμιῶν at 10:11 and 10:19.

Particularly flattering to the protagonists is the narration of their intercession on behalf of the people. This device demonstrates not only their piety, but it also reveals their intimacy with God and access to divine knowledge. *Fourth Ezra* is perhaps the finest example of this process, though we may observe similar devices in *1 Enoch,* Daniel, *2 Baruch,* and *3 Baruch.*[13] *Fourth Ezra* is largely structured as a dialogue: Ezra intercedes with God on Israel's behalf.

---

[11]Christopher Rowland argues that apocalyptic visions probably did follow preparation by meditation and fasting (*The Open Heaven: A Study of Apocalyptic in Judaism and Early Christianity* [New York: Crossroad, 1982] 215-31).

[12]Both Theodotian's Greek (ἀνὴρ ἐπιθυμιῶν σὺ εἶ) and the Hebrew (חמודות אתה) are syntactically problematic, as is reflected in the various translations. The NRSV reads, "you are greatly beloved"; the NJV, "You are a man specially chosen"; the NASB, "you are highly esteemeed." For the Hebrew, Joüon-Muraoka locate the phrase as an example of a "plural of abstraction," presumably leading to the translation, "You are an excellent person" (Paul Joüon, *A Grammar of Biblical Hebrew,* Subsidia Biblica 14, 2 vols., trans. and rev. T. Muraoka [Rome: Editrice Pontificio Istituto Biblico, 1991] §136e). For the Greek, the phrase represents a genitive of quality (BDF §165), implying a translation like that rendered here.

[13]Note especially *1 Enoch* 12:1-6; 13:6-7; 84:5-6; Dan 9; *2 Baruch* 6:2; 21:1-26; *3 Baruch* 1.

> I was troubled as I lay on my bed, and my thoughts welled up in my heart, because I saw the desolation of Zion and the wealth of those who lived in Babylon. My spirit was greatly agitated, and I began to speak anxious words to the Most High . . . (3:1–3).[14]

In reply, God sends Uriel as an angelic mediator of the revelation.[15] But Ezra is still dissatisfied: Why are things going so poorly for Israel?

> I beseech you, my lord, why have I been endowed with the power of understanding? For I did not wish to inquire about the ways above, but about those things which we daily experience: why Israel has been given over to the gentiles as a reproach; why the people whom you loved has been given to godless tribes, and the Law of our fathers has been made of no effect and the written covenants no longer exist; and why we pass from the world like locusts, and our life is like a mist, and we are not worthy to obtain mercy. But what will he do for his name, by which we are called? It is about these things that I have asked. (4:22-25)

These dialogues reveal a pious person who is at once humble before the divine but tenacious regarding Israel. Ezra resembles other great characters like Abraham (Gen 18:16-33) and Moses (Exod 33:12-23) who step between God and the people. These characters are specially favored, even chosen, by God and mediate knowledge of God's purposes that would otherwise be inaccessible to their communities. Their compassion moves them to risk their own welfare in an effort to address God.

Occasionally a prophetic call might precede the apocalyptic vision. Such is the case in the *Apocalypse of Abraham* (9:1-10), which

---

[14]Quotations from the Jewish pseudepigrapha follow *OTP*.

[15]One of the curious things about apocalyptic literature is the confusion among levels of discourse. The reader is often unsure whether God is speaking directly or through an intermediary, nor is one sure whether God is being addressed directly. In *4 Ezra*, the word of the Lord comes to Ezra (1:4), Ezra responds by consulting an angel (2:44), Ezra addresses the Most High (3:3), and is answered by the angel Uriel (4:1).

probably postdates Revelation, as well as in *4 Ezra* (1:4-11), which is roughly contemporary. These calls echo canonical models. In the *Apocalypse of Abraham,* Abraham twice hears a voice calling his name. That the allusion is to the call of Samuel is reinforced by Abraham's reply, "Here I am" (9:1; cf. 1 Sam 3). In Ezra's case, the word of the Lord comes commanding him: "Go and declare to my people their evil deeds" (1:4), vaguely echoing Isaiah 58:1.

Prophetic calls and divine commendations are ethical devices. By setting visionaries apart as persons especially meriting divine revelation and by aligning their knowledge and point of view with that of God, these methods certify their character and access to hidden knowledge.

3. *Modes of revelation* through which the visionary gains access to knowledge and the *nature of that knowledge* provide another cluster of ethical devices, especially in the formal apocalypses. The types of knowledge vary, including dreams, dialogues with heavenly figures, tours of heavenly regions, and esoteric knowledge concerning primeval history or the fundamental elements of the universe. What does not vary is that the knowledge is otherwise inaccessible. Christopher Rowland's shorthand definition of apocalyptic as "knowledge of the divine mysteries through revelation"[16] may appear reductionist, but it emphasizes the power of apocalyptic rhetoric to represent itself through the absolute certainty of eyewitness accounts.

Knowledge is crucial to any speaker's credibility. But in apocalyptic literature it often takes complicated forms. In *3 Baruch,* Baruch passes through four heavens and stands at the gate of the fifth, where God dwells. In the first four heavens Baruch sees things that are hidden from other mortals. What he does not understand an angel interprets for him. But there are secrets even Baruch cannot know. When he arrives at the fifth heaven, the gate is closed so that Baruch cannot see what is going on. Baruch's relation to his audience, then, is that of an especially privileged human being. He is willing to tell what he has learned about the most holy of realities, but there are limits to what even he can

---

[16]*Open Heaven,* 9.

know. Those boundaries strengthen Baruch's contact with the audience.

Knowledge rarely comes easily for the visionaries. Quite often they need help in understanding their revelations. Daniel, for example, struggles to understand a vision, so God sends Gabriel (8:16) to explain things. In another case, Daniel hears ambiguous references to the amount of time for the eschtological tribulation. When Daniel asks for specifics, they are not available: "Go, Daniel, for the words are sealed up tight (ἐμπεφραγμένοι καὶ ἐσφραγισμένοι; Theodotian) until the end time" (12:9).

Fourth Ezra may present the most graphic struggle for heavenly insight among the major Jewish apocalypses. God approaches Ezra to condemn Israel for its transgression. Ezra confesses that Israel has indeed been sinful, but he questions why Babylon should prosper while Zion is desolate. Surely Babylon is no less sinful than Jerusalem? But the angel Uriel challenges Ezra.

> Uriel: Your understanding has utterly failed regarding this world, and do you think you can comprehend the way of the Most High?
> Ezra (always humble): Yes, my lord.
> Uriel: I have been sent to show you three problems. If you can solve one of them for me, I also will show you the way you desire to see, and will teach you why the heart is evil. (4:1-4)

Confronted by his inability to pass the tests or to understand the divine ways (4:10-11), Ezra falls on his face and says, "It would be better for us not to be here than to come here and live in ungodliness, and to suffer and not understand why" (4:12). This, then, is the plot of *4 Ezra*: Ezra seeks understanding, and he receives revelations, but the process is a constant negotiation between Ezra and the Most High. Finally, almost as a necessary conclusion, Ezra is given a drink which instills in him (and five accomplices) the wisdom necessary to restore the Bible and to draft seventy books fit only for the wisest of the people.[17]

Sometimes the revelation overcomes the visionary physically.[18]

---

[17]What Bruce M. Metzger calls, "esoteric, apocalyptic books" (*OTP* 1:555n.o).
[18]For a discussion of the similar physical effects of *merkabah* experiences, see

As Ezra awakens after the conclusion of one vision, his "body shuddered violently, and my soul was so troubled that it fainted" (*4 Ezra* 5:14). What happens then is common for those points when a visionary is overwhelmed: the angel holds him, strengthens him, and sets him on his feet (5:15).[19] Daniel is likewise overcome by his visionary experiences. After the vision in ch. 7, his face pales but he discusses the experience with no one (7:28). A similar pattern occurs in 10:7-10, in which Daniel loses his strength and becomes extremely pale before entering a trance. When the angel touches him, all Daniel can do is rise to his hands and knees. And when Daniel hears the heavenly voice addressing Gabriel he is frightened and falls on his face. The angel comforts him, puts him into a deep sleep, and causes him to stand (8:16-18). The effects become even more severe after the vision, when Daniel becomes exhausted and remains ill for several days (8:27).

These physical effects contribute to the authority of the revelation in at least four ways. First, they confirm the authenticity of the revelatory event. It is not only in the mind, but also it has palpable effects. Second, we see that the visionary enjoys divine favor in that the angel usually intervenes so as to preserve him from overwhelming fear or severe physical harm. The visionary physically experiences the touch of the divine, sometimes with words of comfort or commission. Third, these experiences lend verisimiltude to the visionary's character. How else should one respond to a radical encounter with the divine? Again preserved is the delicate balance between extraordinary privilege and human limitation. And fourth, the visionary's response echoes that of biblical characters who have encountered the divine glory, most notably Ezekiel (Ezek 1:28–2:2).[20] The visionary receives an experience of biblical significance and responds like a biblical character.

What are we to make of apocalyptic modes and levels of knowledge in terms of ethos? The visionaries, though extremely

---

Rowland, *Open Heaven*, 229-36.

[19]Almost the same pattern occurs in *1 Enoch* 14:14, 24.

[20]And there are other notable cases such as Gen 32:18 and Isa 6:5. And cf. Exod 33:20, in which God warns that "a person shall not see my face and live."

privileged, also experience human limitations. They know more than their audiences do. Commissioned by God to perceive secrets, visionaries stand out as persons not only of knowledge but of virtue and of pure motives as well. But visionaries are limited in terms of their knowledge, and their bodies experience exhaustion in the face of divine mysteries. While visionaries' knowledge marks them as different from the rest of humanity, their limitations invite a sense of identification from their audiences. Enhancing this sense of identification, visionaries always respond to their experiences in ways their audiences will approve.

4. Allusion to ancient *myths* is another resource for developing apocalyptic ethos. Paul D. Hanson's study of early apocalyptic eschatology in the Hebrew Bible emphasizes the prominent role the Divine Warrior myth played throughout the rise of Jewish apocalyptic eschatology.[21] Norman Cohn takes this insight so far as to make it the guiding principle for understanding "apocalyptic faith." According to Cohn, the cosmic struggle between the forces of order and those of chaos is the mythological thread that runs from ancient Egypt throughout Near Eastern history to Israel and energizes both early Judaism and Christianity.[22] Also prominent in the ancient Near East was the motif of four successive world kingdoms, which occurs not only in Dan 2 and 7 and *Sib. Or.* 4, but also in Hesiod's *Works and Days* 106-201 and the *Bahman Yasht*.[23]

To be sure, ancient myths of primordial events, cosmic conflict, and the afterlife occur frequently in Jewish apocalyptic literature. While these may not define the genre of this literature, it is appropriate to ask how they contribute to their narrators' ethos. A certain conservative effect marks these allusions. Narrators who appeal to ancient visions of order demonstrate their own awareness of a culture's roots; in doing so, they also establish their own credibility as persons who identify with order and peace. While

---

[21]*The Dawn of Apocalyptic: The Historical and Sociological Roots of Jewish Apocalyptic Eschatology*, rev. ed. (Philadelphia: Fortress, 1979) 404-405.

[22]*Cosmos, Chaos and the World to Come: The Ancient Roots of Apocalyptic Faith* (New Haven CT: Yale University Press, 1993).

[23]See Collins, *Apocalyptic Imagination*, 74-78. Cohn, *Cosmos, Chaos*, 169n.10, provides a bibliography on this subject.

this appeal does suggest conservative ideals, its potential functions are multiple. Hanson has noted that even in its early development apocalyptic eschatology, which may have risen among the dispossessed, was effectively utilized by the priestly in-groups that redacted Ezekiel and Zechariah to defend their own privilege.[24] The appeal to foundational cultural myths provides an audience something to recognize, something to identify with. That identification can be a springboard to the revolutionary.

5. The narrative framework of the ancient Jewish apocalypses enabled various modes of *address to the audience*. Sometimes the audience "overhears" discourse about itself; in other cases intermediate characters within the narrative sit in the implied audience's place.

We may observe both methods at work in *2 Baruch*. First, Baruch mentions to God that there are two groups among God's people—those moving away from the Law and those returning to it—and asks God about their disposition. God answers that evil will come to the apostates but good to those who have believed (42:1-2). Another example of this device occurs in chs. 44-47, in which Baruch calls his son along with some of the elders and tells them how to admonish the people. In both cases the audience hears about itself through Baruch's conversations with other characters in the narrative.

Second, the audience sits in the place of the people in chs. 31-34. Baruch speaks in future terms of what is for the probable

---

[24]*Dawn of Apocalyptic*, esp. 228-79. Stephen L. Cook has challenged Hanson's thesis, arguing that apocalyptic eschatology flourished in central priestly contexts from its beginnings (*Prophecy and Apocalypticism: The Postexilic Social Setting* [Minneapolis: Fortress, 1995]). Cook does not cite Jonathan Z. Smith's influential essay, which would have been helpful to his argument ("Wisdom and Apocalyptic," in *Map Is Not Territory: Studies in the History of Religions*, SJLA 23 [Leiden: Brill, 1978] 67-87). Wayne A. Meeks has also demonstrated that Paul could use apocalyptic thought for both conservative and innovative ends ("Social Functions of Apocalyptic Language in Pauline Christianity," in *Apocalypticism in the Mediterrranean World and the Near East: Proceedings of the International Colloquium on Apocalypticism, Uppsala, August 12-17, 1979*, ed. David Hellholm (Tübingen: Mohr, 1983) 687-705). Though taken somewhat out of context, John J. Collins' assessment is also appropriate here: "Apocalyptic thought allows for considerable fluidity in its mythological conceptions" (*Apocalyptic Imagination*, 85).

historical audience a past event: the Temple's destruction. But the audience also hears a message which applies in its own time:

> We should not . . . be so sad regarding the evil which has come now, but much more (distressed) regarding that which is in the future. For greater than the two evils will be the trial when the Mighty One will renew his creation. (32:5-7)

2 Baruch ends with an extended hortatory letter from Baruch to the scattered nine and a half tribes. But Baruch ties the letter around an eagle's neck and sends it away (chap. 87). Again, though the intended audience is not actually the lost tribes, they hear the letter as if it were addressed to them. They are told to read it in their assemblies and to meditate upon it during feasts (86:1).

The indirect approach of addressing an audience, though properly related to pathos (πάθος, a discourse's effect upon its audience), is also an ethical device. By gaining fictional distance from the intended audience, it avoids direct confrontation. In doing so, it "mystifies" the relationship between the historical author and the intended audience. The actual author is enabled to engage the audience without facing possible challenges to his or her authority; instead, the audience overhears authoritative figures such as God, Baruch, or Enoch. Even if the audience remains unconvinced that these persons are in fact the ones who have spoken, the person ultimately accountable still manages to linger in concealment.

6. *Crisis* rhetoric is a sixth factor in building apocalyptic ethos. As we have seen in Cicero's speeches and the rhetorical tradition, crisis rhetoric implies that the speaker is working from pure motives. So prominent is the crisis topos that until recently it was common to locate apocalyptic as a discourse of the oppressed. One scholar, David Hellholm, has taken this feature of apocalyptic discourse to be the distinguishing function of apocalypses in general.[25]

We may observe crisis rhetoric at work in *4 Ezra*. Ezra is lying in bed disturbed by Jerusalem's destruction, and he questions God:

---

[25]"The Problem of Apocalyptic Genre and the Apocalypse of John," *Semeia* 36 (1986): 27.

Why destroy Jerusalem and let Babylon (Rome) continue to prosper (3:1-3, 28-36)? Ezra learns that he is living near the end of the age, when the evil which has been sown in the world will bring forth its harvest (4:26-28). A day is coming that will bring terror and iniquity with cosmic disturbances (5:1-13). Near the end of *4 Ezra* is a warning. The last days are near, complete with multiplied evils. It is time to put away mortal concerns and dwell on heavenly things (14:10-18).

Also writing after Jerusalem's fall, *2 Baruch* acknowledges the crisis he addresses. In a sense, the distress is only temporary: "For after a short time the building of Zion will be shaken in order that it will be rebuilt" (32:2). But the present distress should not take too much attention. Worse is coming. "We should not . . . be so sad concerning the evil which has come now, but much more (distressed) regarding that which is in the future" (32:5).

Crisis rhetoric can identify with an audience's sense that it is living in particularly difficult times. It affirms the natural inclination to suppose that one is living in a period of epochal significance. But at the same time, crisis serves ethos. Crisis rhetors demonstrate their pure motivations by addressing difficult situations as of ultimate importance.

Apocalyptic Authority and Christian Origins

From the beginnings of the Jesus movement, apocalyptic visions also authorized early Christian preaching.[26] The Synoptic accounts characterize Jesus as a visionary. In Mark, the tearing open of the heavens frames his career, marking off his life as a holy time when the boundaries between heaven and earth are transcended. According to Mark 1:10, Jesus' ministry kicks off with the heavens tearing apart (σχιζομένους), a vision of the Holy Spirit, and a heavenly audition. Immediately thereafter, he enters a desert temptation by Satan and is served by angels (1:12-13). And when Jesus dies the veil of the Temple, presumably a barrier

---

[26]For a more complete discussion of this phenomenon within a broader Jewish context, see Rowland, *Open Heaven*, 351-441.

between the sacred and profane realms, is also ripped in two (ἐσχίσθη, 15:38).

The Synoptic Jesus' revelatory experiences contribute to his authority. After Jesus' disciples return from their mission and report their success over demons, Luke's Jesus announces that he has given them supernatural power. How do we know that Jesus has the authority to give this power? "I saw Satan fall like a lightning bolt from heaven," Jesus says (Luke 10:17-20).[27] Likewise, Jesus' authority is enhanced by a vision which he shares with three of his disciples, the transfiguration (Mark 9:2-13 par.).[28]

In a similar way Peter and Paul authorize their own ministries through appeals to visionary experiences. Luke particularly emphasizes this dimension of their experience, narrating the story of Peter's vision of the unclean food twice (Acts 10:9-16; 11:4-14) and that of Paul's encounter with the risen Jesus three times (Acts 9:1-9; 22:6-11; 26:12-20).[29] These visions are programmatic for

---

[27]Luke deemphasizes the fascination with Jesus' visions and his disciples' power over the demonic with Jesus statement: "But do not rejoice in this, that the spirits are subject to you; instead, rejoice that your names have been written in heaven" (10:20). Nevertheless, Luke does not erase apocalyptic elements from Jesus' words; he simply transfers present apocalyptic experience (visions, spiritual powers) into apocalyptic eschatology which has a present heavenly counterpart (having names written in a heavenly book).

[28]Peter's response ("For he did not know how he should respond, since they had become terrified" [9:6].) is consistent with those of other apocalyptic visionaries.

[29]Again, Luke does not eliminate apocalyptic elements from his narrative of Christian origins. While he may downplay the imminent eschatology often associated with apocalypticism (cf. Hans Conzelmann, *The Theology of St. Luke* [Philadelphia: Fortress, 1961] esp. 131-36), the plot of Acts is determined by visionary experiences. (We should also note in this context Stephen's vision of the coming Son of Man at 7:56.) Luke markedly associates the stories of Peter and Paul's visions. They happen almost back-to-back. Both visions feature strong apocalyptic elements. Paul is physically affected, as are many visionaries; he is blind until Ananias heals him. And Ananias is directed to Paul through a vision in which he appears as a reluctant participant (9:13-14). Peter, like Ananias, is reluctant to obey the voice in his vision (10:14). He describes his experience as coming during a trance which happened while he was praying (11:5). Just as Paul's vision required authorization from another visionary, Peter's visionary counterpart is Cornelius, who is met by an angel while he is praying, and is directed to send for Peter. His story is also narrated twice (11:3-7, 30-32). For discussions of all these motifs in Jewish apocalyptic literature (except for the pairing of visionaries), see

Luke's story of Christianity's expansion from Jerusalem to the rest of the world (1:8). Peter learns that Gentiles may receive the gospel and appeals to his vision in convincing the Jerusalem church that "to the Gentiles God has given repentance toward life as well" (10:18). Likewise, Paul's vision involves a commission to carry Christ's name to both Gentiles and Jews as well as to kings (9:15).

Luke appears to have characterized Paul accurately at least in the sense that Paul builds his apostolic ethos upon mystical experiences. Paul's most impassioned defences of his ministry—1 Cor 15, 2 Cor 10–13, and Gal 1–2—all make this connection. Defending his message of the resurrection, Paul asserts that Jesus "was revealed (ὤφθη) to me, too" (1 Cor 15:8). In 2 Corinthians and Galatians he is opposing what he considers to be "different" or "other" gospels (as if there could be any! Gal 1:7).[30] Paul claims "visions and apocalypses (ἀποκαλύψεις) of the Lord" (2 Cor 12:1), a possible response to the "superapostles" who are preaching a gospel different from his own (11:4-5).[31] And when he defends the independent authority of his message and his singular call to preach among Gentiles, Paul appeals to an "apocalypse of Jesus Christ" (ἀποκαλύψεως Ἰησοῦ Χριστοῦ, Gal 1:12). Only in his most desperate struggles does Paul invoke his apocalyptic experience to bolster his own authority.

Summary

Apocalyptic discourse provides powerful resources for building ethos. Authors almost always write in the names of prominent or enigmatic figures from Israel's past, often contributing legends that

---

the discussion above.

[30]Only here does Paul use this sort of language: εὐαγγέλιον ἕτερον (2 Cor 11:4); ἕτερον εὐαγγέλιον (Gal 1:6); and ἄλλο [εὐαγγέλιον] (Gal 1:7).

[31]See Alan F. Segal, *Paul the Convert: The Apostolate and Apostasy of Saul the Pharisee* (New Haven CT: Yale University Press, 1990) 36-37, for the possibility that both Gal 1:12 and 2 Cor 12 refer to Paul's conversion experience as well a bibliographic notes on the scholarly debate of this problem. J. Christiaan Beker (*Paul the Apostle: The Triumph of God in Life and Thought* [Philadelphia: Fortress, 1980] 42-47) associates Gal 1 with 2 Cor 10–13 on the same grounds that I do—that Paul is fighting for his authority—and argues that Gal 1:12-17 relates Paul's "conversion story" (6). My point here is that in defending his authority Paul sometimes appeals to his revelatory experiences.

characterize them as persons of extraordinary virtue and privilege. Through dreams, dialogues with heavenly figures, tours of heavenly regions, and lessons about primeval history or the fundamental elements of the cosmos, visionaries demonstrate their exclusive knowledge. These experiences often leave them terrified or exhausted, reminding the audience of their humanity. The apocalypses identify with the audience's cultural heritage and desire for stability by alluding to ancient myths in which order overcomes chaos. Using direct address, they invite the audience to share their construction of reality, which is marked by crisis. Crisis rhetoric demonstrates the visionary's goodwill while affirming the audience's sense that its struggles are of cosmic significance. From a rhetorical perspective, apocalyptic discourse is especially effective for establishing authority.

I began this section with the assumption that authority is an essential issue for apocalyptic authors. To my knowledge, O'Leary is the only author who has dealt systematically with the issue, and his work does not seriously engage Jewish apocalyptic literature. I have sketched several prominent means by which Jewish apocalyptic discourse authorized itself and shown the importance of appeals to apocalyptic experiences for early Christian claims to authority. We should expect to find echoes of these motifs in Revelation as well.

Chapter 4
John's Narrative Ethos: Self-Representation

In constructing his ethos and winning his audience's trust, John faces two related tasks. Rhetoric is the field of contention; it involves not only establishing one's own case but also winning one's audience from being persuaded by alternative positions. John must characterize himself as a person of good sense, knowledge, and goodwill; at the same time, he must provoke hostility or at least suspicion toward his opponents. As we have seen, John addresses himself to several alternative perspectives: opposing voices within the churches themselves, Jewish communities with which his audience experiences some conflict, the Empire and its claims to authority, and local affirmation of the Roman presence in Asia Minor. Though John's self-representation and his characterization of his opponents are intimately related throughout the Apocalypse, I will distinguish them for the purpose of discussion. (In doing so I follow the examples of the rhetorical handbooks.) This chapter will investigate how John portrays himself through various literary and rhetorical means.

It may be helpful to reemphasize that "John" is my own heuristic construction. Following the lead of the literary and resistance theorists, I take John seriously. Though he is my own construction, he is also a cultural product, just as "real" as any other "person" one might single out. His ethos struggles with the tensions that empower discourses of authority in popular (and critical) appropriations of Revelation. Some scholars like Burton L. Mack find it appropriate to discuss "John's fixation on slaughter" and his "loss of perspective."[1] More sympathetic readers like Wilfrid J. Harrington can describe John as a "committed Christian" who "adopted a radical stance" and "wrote to and for the like-minded."[2] Likewise, I attribute to John certain attitudes, actions, and intentions that result from my own reading of Revelation. For example, I will argue that John's allusion to several different genres, types of literature likely to be well known to his first century Christian audience, enhances his own authority. The difference between my reading and those of critics such as Mack and Harrington is that I am *self-consciously* working from a construction. I do not assume, for example, that the actual author of Revelation ever *intended* to create the effects I describe, nor do I propose that he (?) had a highly developed sense of generic distinctions. Nevertheless, this dimension of John's rhetoric might well have contributed to his ethos in the eyes of his intended audience.

I will begin with an extended reflection on John's use of *generic* allusions, particularly in Revelation's first chapter. Its first four verses hint that Revelation might be an apocalypse, a prophecy, and a letter. I devote so much attention to this problem because Revelation's genre continues to perplex its scholarly readers with proposals, including even the possibility that Revelation is the work of an "astral prophet" who sees his theology written in the sky.[3] While most scholarly readers see generic identification as a primary factor in interpreting Revelation, I suggest an "interactive paradigm." How might an ancient audience have experienced Revelation's conflicting generic clues? I propose two possibilities: (a) that they may well have experienced the clues as an invitation to participate in creating Revelation's meaning; and (b) that each clue may have enhanced John's perceived authority, with the network of generic associations being even more powerful than any particular generic location. The first option submits Revelation to

---

[1]*Who Wrote the New Testament? The Making of the Christian Myth* (San Francisco: HarperSanFrancisco, 1995) 196.

[2]Wilfrid Harrington, *Revelation*, Sacra Pagina (Collegeville MN: Michael Glazier, 1993) 12.

[3]Bruce J. Malina, *On the Genre and Message of Revelation: Star Visions and Sky Journeys* (Peabody MA: Hendrickson, 1995).

a potentially egalitarian reading; the second constructs John as a narrator extremely concerned with his own authority.

Second, I will address John's direct *claims* to narrative and religious authority. John is an unusually privileged narrator who claims extraordinary knowledge. Addressing his audience in the first person, he claims that God has called him to his revelatory task. He has seen not only past earthly events but future and heavenly ones as well. John's message is of ultimate importance: One is either blessed or cursed depending upon one's response to it. And his message derives from only one source, John's own experience, which he claims to have shared in its entirety and without mediation.

Third, Revelation's narrative rhetoric *harmonizes* several levels of discourse. While John claims to be writing in the service of God or Jesus Christ, his narrative actually incorporates the divine voices within his own discourse. Does the divine speak through John, or does John speak for the divine? Drawing from the insights of Mikhail Bakhtin, I will argue that Revelation manages to unite all voices, whether heavenly, pagan, Christian, or demonic, under John's narrative program.

A fourth factor in John's rhetoric is his complicated attempts to *identify* with his audience. In the Apocalypse, all good things function at the same level. John seeks to identify himself with things his audience would value, concepts such as endurance, faithfulness, and humility. John identifies himself as a faithful witness, linking himself to *the* faithful witness, Jesus Christ (1:5). Other faithful witnesses include the martyrs (17:6), among whom are Antipas (2:13) and the two who die for their testimony in the great city (11:3-12). In principle, any member of John's audience may become a faithful witness (12:11) as well. This network associates John with Jesus and the martyrs, but it also offers the audience an opportunity to enter the illustrious company as well.

Finally, John is aware that some aspects of his program might present problems for his audience, so he seeks to *justify* them. John envisions the devastation not only of his enemies, but of the greater part of the natural and human world. As many readers have noted, such severity threatens John's status as a person of pure motives and good sense. In order to mitigate his audience's potential revulsion, John enlists the voices of saints and heavenly beings in justifying God's global destruction. John constructs evil as a crisis, inviting his audience to perceive their neighbors and the world in dualistic terms.

In a context permeated by imperial authority and by struggles for power between Christian groups and between Christians and Jews, John creates an alternative locus of authority. Through complicated narrative patterns, John weaves a vision of absolute authority. A challenge to other voices, John's ethos reinscribes the language of ultimate dominion. By asserting his own authority above Rome and his Jewish and Christian opponents, John locates himself as the source and standard of absolute truth.

Alluding: Revelation and Genre

A primary question facing scholarly readers of Revelation is generic: "What is it?" Two paths have emerged as the most popular in this discussion. In the first, one compares Revelation to other texts which have been called apocalypses or expressions of apocalyptic. In every case that I know of, this approach leads to an easily foreseen conclusion: including Revelation among apocalyptic texts, though sometimes with reservations. The second path is to examine Revelation in its own particularity and to attempt to locate it among a broader range of ancient genres. The results of such studies do vary, but they share the common strategy of beginning with the text itself and trying to compare it to other recognized genres in terms of either form, content, or (reconstructed) function.[4] One variation on this second theme is to identify Revelation with a genre from modern literature, such as utopia or fantasy. Both paths reflect a common assumption: Genre is essential to the meaning of Revelation, and must be identified through features that reside *in* the text.

I propose a different paradigm, one that understands meaning as an event, a temporal process that includes author, text, and

[4]For a survey of various approaches to the genre of Revelation, see W. S. Vorster, "'Genre' and the Revelation of John: A Study in Text, Context and Intertext," *Neot* 22 (1988): 103-23.

reader. The question here focuses upon the rhetorical experience an informed reader might have when encountering Revelation's various generic clues, especially in chapter 1. I will proceed inductively. First, I will present the problem based upon the textual data as I understand it. Second, I will review recent scholarship on the genre of the Apocalypse in order to identify basic assumptions and procedures such studies may have in common. Third, I will reflect upon recent developments in literary and aesthetic theory that may provide clues for a different paradigm. Finally, I will sketch a proposal not only for what I call an interactive approach to genre in Revelation 1, but also for some tentative conclusions regarding the text's meaning and the problem of John's ethos.

The Textual Data

Despite scholarly efforts confusion reigns in the attempt to situate the Apocalypse. In the very first chapter of Revelation, we find hints of at least three generic codes.[5] John presents his work as an apocalypse (or revelatory literature), a prophecy, and a letter. With disorienting celerity these generic allusions confront Revelation's readers.

The early work of Stanley Fish provides one way of approaching this phenomenon.[6] Fish seeks not so much to identify phenomena in a text as to describe the process of reading it. For the early Fish, meaning is an event, the effect generated by the encounter between reader and text. The method by which Fish arrives at his conclusions is to imagine the reading process *slowed down,* to picture what happens as the reader meets textual stimuli in a temporal process.

If we read Revelation 1 this way, the results are startling. Within a mere four verses, the reader finds at least three generic allusions. The very first word, which may also serve as part of the

---

[5]Gregory Linton associates Rev 1 with at least six generic categories ("Reading the Apocalypse as an Apocalypse," *SBLSP* 30 [1991]: 174-77).

[6]"Literature in the Reader: Affective Stylistics," in *Reader-Response Criticism: From Formalism to Post-Structuralism,* ed. Jane P. Tompkins (Baltimore: Johns Hopkins, 1980) 70-100.

title, is 'Αποκάλυψις, or revelation. Though scholars often assume that Revelation fits the generic category of apocalyptic literature, it is important to note that in no earlier text does the word ἀποκάλυψις or its verbal form ἀποκαλύπτω describe the whole of the revelation; in fact, these words are surprisingly rare in ancient revelatory literature.[7] In other words, the category "apocalypse" may merely be a modern code for reading this family of ancient texts, though ἀποκάλυψις and its cognate terms do appear often enough to discourage such an assessment.[8] Ancient apocalyptic texts share several common features, enough that one team of scholars has reached a consensus definition of the genre:

> a genre of revelatory literature with a narrative framework, in which a revelation is mediated by an otherworldly being to a human recipient, disclosing a transcendent reality which is both temporal, insofar as it envisages eschatological salvation, and spatial insofar as it involves another, supernatural world.[9]

Read as an apocalypse or revelation, Revelation offers an "insider's look" into ultimate things.[10]

The reader scarcely has time to settle into a seat before being confronted by the next generic allusion: "Blessed is the one who reads and those who hear the words of the *prophecy* and keep the things which are written in it, for the time is near" (1:3). The essential claim seems to be that John is presenting an authentic message from God (or from Jesus Christ) involving immanent eschatological judgment and salvation.[11] As opposed to apocalyptic, prophecy has a more established history among ancient Hebrew and Christian

---

[7]Morton Smith, "On the History of ΑΠΟΚΑΛΥΠΤΩ and ΑΠΟΚΑΛΥΨΙΣ," in *Apocalypticism in the Mediterranean World and the Near East: Proceedings of the International Colloquium on Apocalypticism, Uppsala, August 12-17, 1979*, ed. David Hellholm (Tübingen: Mohr, 1983) 14.

[8]John J. Collins, *The Apocalyptic Imagination: An Introduction to the Jewish Matrix of Christianity* (New York: Crossroad, 1984) 3.

[9]John J. Collins, "Introduction: Towards the Morphology of a Genre," *Semeia* 14 (1979): 9.

[10]Markus Bockmuehl, *Revelation and Mystery in Ancient Judaism and Pauline Christianity* (Grand Rapids MI: Eerdmans, 1997) 1.

[11]Elisabeth Schüssler Fiorenza, *Revelation: Vision of a Just World*, Proclamation Commentaries (Minneapolis: Fortress, 1991) 40.

texts. Though prophecy was a varied phenomenon and defies definition, prophets did play an established role in ancient Israel and Judah, and prophetic texts gained a prominent spot in the Jewish canon. Prophecy was a respected form among early Christians as well, and prophets appear to have performed some leadership functions in their communities.[12] One way to distinguish prophecy from apocalyptic is to view prophecy as less radical in terms of its worldview. While apocalyptic separates the wicked from the righteous absolutely (in terms of both their natures and their fates), prophecy continues to hope for the repentance of the wicked and to admonish the righteous.

Again things change quickly. With the next verse (1:4) the reader encounters the marks of an early Christian letter. This epistolary prescript, with its wish for grace and peace, is an early Christian adaptation of ancient letter writing practice.[13] The "grace and peace" formula appears in all of Paul's letters, and it is further developed in 1 and 2 Timothy, 1 and 2 Peter, 2 John, and possibly Jude. The greeting in Paul's earliest letter, 1 Thessalonians, is the simplest—"Grace to you and peace" (1:1)—and may indicate that Paul developed the greeting himself and modified it over time. The exact same words occur in Rev 1:4, but with development in terms of the agents who may bestow the blessing.

Two things tie these generic allusions together: (1) they all include direct address to the audience and (2) they all increase the rhetorical authority (ethos) of the narrator, John. The first point is easily demonstrated: each verse in 1:1-4 mentions the audience intended for the revelation, prophecy, or letter. The second point is just as important. In the allusions to apocalyptic and prophecy, John claims direct divine revelation. The letter form, on the other hand, identifies John both with early Christian leaders such as Paul

---

[12]The most exhaustive study of Jewish and early Christian prophecy and their many forms and functions may be David E. Aune, *Prophecy in Early Christianity and the Ancient Mediterranean World* (Grand Rapids MI: Eerdmans, 1983). Aune maintains that Jewish attitudes toward prophecy during the Second Temple period varied greatly (103-106). Aune also argues that Christian prophets were influential, though not dominant, leaders in their communities (201-11).

[13]David E. Aune, "Intertextuality and the Genre of the Apocalypse," *SBLSP* 30 (1991): 146.

(who made the "grace and peace" formula famous) and with his audience. (In 1:5 John shifts to first person plural to identify himself with his audience.)

The Case of the Apocalyptic Detectives: Scholars Seek a Solution

Scholarship on Revelation has generally attempted to develop *solutions* to its genre problem. We might characterize such proposals as positivistic, not in the sense that they claim absolute certainty, but with relation to their basic assumption: Once the genre of Revelation has been identified, a basic problem is solved, and readers may begin the work of interpretation. I find it helpful to gather these approaches in two main groups.

This classification excludes those who regard the generic confusion of Revelation as essentially an accident of writing. The tendency here is to view John not as a literary figure who knows and appropriates generic conventions, but as a relatively unskilled writer who does not think in terms of designing a rhetorical effect through genre: "The Apocalypse is far from a finished, unified composition."[14] This perspective does assign genres to Revelation, but only by dividing it into "apocalyptic" and "epistolary" parts and seeking to identify the traditions and sources that determined John's options.[15] John may be a visionary, or even heir to a tradition, but the Apocalypse is by no means a polished literary work. His visions and auditions are the stuff of primal religious experience more than learned reflection.[16]

Among those who take Revelation's literary qualities seriously, by far the most popular path is to name a single genre which may serve as the primary code for reading Revelation. Generally this is done by finding the ancient genre which best explains the data in Revelation, be it prophecy, apocalyptic, or epistolography. One

---

[14]Ibid., 145.

[15]Cf. Philipp Vielhauer and Georg Strecker, "Apocalypses and Related Subjects," in *New Testament Apocrypha*, 2 vols., rev. ed., ed. Wilhelm Schneemelcher (Louisville: Westminster/John Knox, 1992) 2:542-602, esp. 583-89.

[16]Thus, Otto Böcher: "sind diese Visionen und Auditionen offenbar weitgehend 'erlebnisecht,' nicht oder doch nur teilweise gelehrte Schreibtischarbeit" ("Die Johannes-Apokalypse in der neueren Forschung," *ANRW* 2.25.3851).

work in particular, that of W. S. Vorster, stands out from this crowd by offering a metacritical perspective. Vorster argues that scholars have placed too much emphasis upon the form, content, and (hypothesized) function of Revelation, ignoring its most obvious characteristic, the narrative mode of presentation. The Apocalypse belongs to a subgenre of narrative; it is "a circular letter in narrative form."[17] Even Vorster, one notices, privileges one dimension of Revelation—narrative—above other possibilities.

One variation of the single-genre approach would assign Revelation not so much to an ancient genre, but to a more recent category. Randall C. Webber recently proposed reading Revelation as a utopia, a work "concerned primarily with an ideal or perfect polity."[18] Webber suggests that, while the category utopia may not provide a natural setting for Revelation, it may provide an informative comparison for contemporary readers.[19] On a different trajectory is Tina Pippin, who compares the Apocalypse to ancient and contemporary fantasy literature, "a subversive literature of the supernatural."[20] According to Pippin, though Revelation may envision the destruction of oppressive structures, its fantasy is by no means liberating for women.[21]

A second general approach accepts that Revelation features aspects of multiple genres, and then ties them together in one comprehensive package. Barbara Wooten Snyder notes the triple form of apocalypse, prophecy, and epistle in Revelation, and argues that the three genres function as a unified whole. As prophecy, the text informs its audience *from whom* the message comes—God. As letter, it reveals *for whom* the message is intended, the churches in Asia Minor. And, as apocalypse, the text reveals *what* it is, "an

---

[17]"Genre." Vorster is by no means the only scholar who makes metacritical analyses, but his work is unique in that it renders explicit the distinctions among generic studies which focus upon form, content, and function, and then proposes a fourth category—mode of discourse (103-104).

[18]"The Apocalypse as Utopia: Ancient and Modern Subjectivity," *SBLSP* 32 (1993): 114.

[19]Ibid., 115.

[20]*Death and Desire: The Rhetoric of Gender in the Apocalypse of John*, Literary Currents in Biblical Interpretation (Louisville: Westminster/John Knox, 1992) 27.

[21]Ibid., 80.

apocalypse or revelation concerning the consummation of all things."[22]

One might also choose to live with the many generic allusions and hold them in tension. Though I quoted David E. Aune above as evidence of a historicizing approach that deemphasizes Revelation's literary character, his proposal does allow for the complex assessment of multiple generic influences through the method of intertextuality. The goal is "understanding the impact and function of both earlier and contemporary texts in a given text."[23] Not only does Aune assess the impact of various literary forms (and he proposes many for Revelation), but he includes allusions to the Hebrew Bible and to stock apocalyptic imagery as well.[24] Two of Aune's conclusions are that the complexity of intertextual allusions in Revelation might even have confused its ancient audience, and that Revelation synthesizes apocalyptic and prophetic literary traditions by juxtaposing them.[25]

Each of these approaches uses genre as a category for unlocking the meaning of Revelation. The analyses of form, content, function, and even mode of discourse, however, limit the discussion of meaning to static categories: meaning is seen to reside in the formal features of the text. Some studies give lip service to the role of the reader in creating generic expectations,[26] and some may even note the temporal dynamic when a reader successively encounters diverse generic clues.[27]

---

[22]"Triple-Form and Space/Time Transitions: Literary Structuring Devices in the Apocalypse," *SBLSP* 30 (1991): 443. Like Vorster and many others, Wooten Snyder's proposal does seem to foreground one particular genre—in her case apocalyptic is most prominent. But her proposal stands apart from those which seek *one* basic genre to explain Revelation in that she seeks to maintain the significant contribution of each of the three genres in their particularity to the meaning of the whole.

[23]"Intertextuality," 142.

[24]Ibid., 145.

[25]Ibid., 159. Aune barely touches the question of Revelation's effect upon its audience.

[26]Such discussion is generally limited to the theoretical sections of their articles, and plays little or no part in the actual working out of their conclusions.

[27]Aune, for example, mentions the confusion ancient audiences may have felt when encountering this dynamic ("Intertextuality," 159). Linton calls attention to it by means of a critique of actual scholarly readers ("Reading," 178-86).

In the final analysis, however, none of the studies consistently explores Revelation through interactive rhetorical lenses. It remains to be seen how a study of the generic clues in Revelation might proceed when it consistently includes author, text, and audience in a temporal reading process, and when meaning is viewed in terms of a description of that process rather than of an analysis of formal textual features.

Trackings: Toward an Interactive Paradigm

It is not as if the hunt for a fresh approach to Revelation's generic problems has to proceed without markers. The tracks of several thinkers open new paths for reflection upon genre, art, and the reading event. By tracking these various paths, we may find ourselves at a new place, a site from which we may glimpse a richer experience of the Apocalypse.

One such thinker is Mikhail Bakhtin, who has argued that an author can express multiple voices in one narrative by incorporating diverse genres within the narrative.[28] His idea is that different genres embody various social points of view in distinct kinds of language.[29] Bakhtin's proposal opens the way for a different approach to Revelation's generic clues, but one must be careful. I will argue below that the last thing John desires is to represent multiple voices as legitimate, which is what Bakhtin has in mind. Nevertheless, Bakhtin has introduced a provocative concept: the power of conflicting generic clues to influence an audience.

The Author. Perhaps John is smarter than we have thought. Perhaps he has embedded multiple and conflicting generic clues at the very beginning of his text in order to create something different. If so, John is a creator of what Gary Saul Morson might call a "boundary work," in which "it is uncertain which of two [in

---

[28]Mikhail Bakhtin, *The Dialogic Imagination: Four Essays*, ed. and trans. Michael Holquist and Caryl Emerson, Slavic Series 1 (Austin: University of Texas Press, 1981) 324, 355.

[29]This is an assumption shared by early form critics, and perhaps by more recent "rhetorical critics" such as Burton Mack (*A Myth of Innocence: Mark and Christian Origins* [Philadelphia: Fortress, 1988]; *The Lost Gospel: The Book of Q and Christian Origins* [San Francisco: HarperSanFrancisco, 1993]; and *Who Wrote the New Testament?*).

our case, more] mutually exclusive sets of conventions governs a work." More specifically, John has created "threshold art" of a particular variety by intentionally "embedding or juxtaposing sections of radically heterogenous material."[30] Like all threshold art, John's Apocalypse "foregrounds its thresholds."[31]

In this case the act is conspicuous. Within the very first verses John has presented the reader with at least three options. And which is more convincing, to view this densely packed introduction to an intricately structured work as a literary accident, or to conclude that John is up to something creative? Is John randomly scattering traces of apocalyptic, prophecy, and epistolography from his literary subconscious, or is he intentionally transgressing conventions of writing and reading with which he is familiar? Because the threshold artist knows the boundaries of literature, it is no accident when he or she confounds them.

The Text. The categories of apocalypse, prophecy, and letter in Rev 1:1-4 are not static but engage the reader all at once. John Briggs's concept of the "reflectaphor" offers a perspective which may be helpful in tracking these features. Briggs' project is much broader than what I am representing here, but it offers a creative way of approaching the "irreconcilable differences" that occur in texts like Revelation. Briggs never provides a clear definition of the reflectaphor, but the concept involves at least two important dynamics. The reflectaphor is like a metaphor in that it involves both comparison and contrast of elements within and/or implied by the text. Thus, the reflectaphor functions as one part of a larger artistic system. And the reflectaphor resembles a mirror in its capacity to provoke its apprehender, to reveal and involve the observer of the work in the production of meaning.[32]

Both dynamics are kinetic, not static. The reflectaphoric elements of the text are in mutual interrelationship; there is no way to freeze the process of their interaction. At the same time, the reader is also in mutual relationship with the text. Though "Our

---

[30]*The Boundaries of Genre* (Austin: University of Texas Press, 1981) 48-50.

[31]Ibid., 65.

[32]"Reflectaphors: The (Implicate) Universe as a Work of Art," in *Quantum Implications: Essays in Honour of David Bohm*, ed. B. J. Hiley and F. David Peat (London/New York: Routledge & Keegan Paul, 1987) 414-35.

minds prefer to see one side or the other" of the reflectaphoric system, "The power of a great work of art is that it gives both [or all three?] sides simultaneously."[33] The truth that emerges in this encounter is also kinetic, moving both in the productive energy of the artist and in the consciousness of the viewer.[34]

With respect to Revelation it may be possible to view its generic codes as a reflectaphoric system. Seen this way, Revelation proclaims itself as *like* an apocalypse, *like* prophecy, and *like* an early Christian letter, but not limited to any category. All three of these dynamics inform each other. The problem for the reader is to decide whether to emphasize one of the three above the others, or to wrestle to perceive all three working at once.

The Readers. Both Morson's concept of threshold art and Briggs's model of the reflectaphor have implications for the role of the reader. I would like to add two other proposals, Umberto Eco's "work in movement" and John McCumber's "poetic interaction," to reflect further upon those implications.[35]

Eco identifies works in movement as those which "though organically completed, are 'open' to a continuous generation of internal relations which the addressee must uncover and select in his act of perceiving the totality of incoming stimuli."[36] By authorial design and by textual property, it is necessary for the reader to contribute to the definition of the work. Though the author has supplied parameters for appropriation, it is up to the reader to decide how to appropriate the text within those boundaries.

What happens here can be profoundly liberating. It is when the reader finds specific options delimited—apocalypse, prophecy, letter—that potentials for interpretation become realistic. Those enclosed options create the space for multiple experiences and appropriations. The multiple generic codes available to the reader encourage interaction. After all, a blank page encourages nothing;

---

[33]Ibid., 429.

[34]Ibid.

[35]Eco, "The Poetics of the Open Work," in *The Role of the Reader: Explorations in the Semiotics of Texts* (Bloomington: Indiana University Press, 1984) 47-66; McCumber, *Poetic Interaction: Language, Freedom, Reason* (Chicago: University of Chicago Press, 1989).

[36]"Open Work," 63.

it is only when space is closed through specific letters, sentences, and so forth that the world of communication opens to the reader: "Occlusion, the release of spacings, leads from reason to imagination."[37]

McCumber argues that such communication, what he calls "poetic interaction," can be liberating. Poetic interaction "takes as its material ambiguous, vague, and otherwise 'strange' utterances, and seeks to understand them by looking to the life-world structuring properties of the words they contain."[38] The key to poetic interaction is its effect upon the reader, who is called upon to either select from among several possible interpretations or extrapolate one of an entirely new type. When a form of communication *intentionally* leaves room for multiple interpretations, the reader "plays a productive role with respect to the utterance's meaning."[39]

For McCumber, emancipation occurs not through a text's content, but through "the interaction it provokes among its spectators."[40] In poetic interaction, reason is free to situate itself, to happen. It is in the freedom to choose *how* to hear the Apocalypse that the reader must reflect upon the Apocalypse he or she wants to read. The text provides both stimulus and resource for such reflection, as does the reader's actual and hoped-for world, and the reader is both challenged and set free to produce the apocalyptic world.

Assessment

What William Franke says of Dante's *Commedia* could also be said of Revelation:

> What we have, then, is a text that announces itself as not just a text. Dante's text projects itself as a discursive event, as situated enunciation. The addresses [to the reader] speak up for the fact

---

[37]John Sallis, *Spacings—of Reason and Imagination in Texts of Kant, Fichte, Hegel* (Chicago: University of Chicago Press, 1987) xv.

[38]*Poetic Interaction*, 379.

[39]Ibid., 383-89.

[40]Ibid., 371.

that poetic discourse exists as enunciation as well as in textual form.[41]

Just as does the *Commedia*, Revelation addresses its audience directly: "Blessed is the one who reads and those who hear the words of the *prophecy* and keep the things which are written in it, for the time is near" (1:3). By responding to this address, "the reader qua reader gains self-awareness of her own reality only insofar as this is disclosed in, and in responding to, the text."[42]

The tracks we have followed have led to a different paradigm for approaching the generic clues of Revelation. By exploring the succession of those clues as a development which requires the participation of the reader, it may be possible to envision fresh readings. At present, I can propose two possibilities.

According to the first, Revelation's calls to the reader extend beyond the direct addresses in 1:3-5d, 13:10, 14:12, and 22:18-19. The succession of conflicting generic clues also invites John's audience to participate in the event of meaning: "How will we hear this? Shall we hear it with eschatological urgency and hope? Shall we respond to it as prophecy, with its claim upon our lives in the present? Shall we consider it a message to our communities, one word among others but specifically addressed to us? Shall we try to do all at once?"

All of the above become possible and legitimate as the clues follow one after the other. By choosing one option and closing off others, the reader is free to follow the implications of the way chosen, however provisionally. In such a case, closing actually becomes an opening. On the other hand, the reader may find it useful to hold the options in tension for a while, or even to shift back and forth. That strategy might hold its own advantages. With respect to Revelation's authority problem, this reading has egalitarian implications: The audience may share John's status as cocreators of Revelation's meaning. As we have seen, both strategies are reflected in the scholarly literature.

---

[41]*Dante's Interpretive Journey*, Religion and Postmodernism (Chicago: University of Chicago Press, 1996) 40.

[42]Ibid., 43.

A second, less open, possibility for interpreting these clues lies in the realm of rhetoric, particularly the domain of ethos. The rapid succession of allusions to apocalypses, prophecies, and epistles enhances John's authority. At issue here is the cumulative effect those allusions have in succession. The reader experiences the text as an urgent word about the end, as a message from God, and as a pastoral letter with his or her interests at heart. Each of these options may be important for John, who was struggling to ensure that his voice would be heard over that of others.

These two readings sketch the potential for a fresh paradigm. Attempts to classify the genre of Revelation may be neglecting the key ingredient—the experiences of readers as they read. I propose that meaning is an event which involves reader as well as author and text in the construction of meaning. What is more, the tension among multiple possibilities can be liberating or onerous: How free is the audience to choose the sort of text and world they want to inhabit?

Claiming: Overt Claims to Authority

John can be passably subtle in establishing his own credibility. But sometimes he makes overt claims for his own status as God's messenger to the churches. These claims typically involve his status as a person who has received revelation directly from God, someone whose message commands absolute obedience, and whose authority even includes the power to bless and to curse (1:3; 22:18, 19). The result for those who do not obey, even for those who would alter a single word of the prophecy, is that they will experience "the plagues which are written in this book" (22:18).

Like all apocalyptic visionaries, John claims special privilege. He has received the revelation of Jesus Christ, a message given by God through an angel. And while John stands relatively low on the ladder of knowledge—beneath God, Jesus Christ, and the angel—his privilege is extraordinary from a literary perspective.[43]

---

[43]Wayne C. Booth, *The Rhetoric of Fiction*, 2nd ed. (Chicago: University of Chicago Press, 1983; [1]1961) 160-63; Susan Snaider Lanser, *The Narrative Act: Point of View in Prose Fiction* (Princeton NJ: Princeton University Press, 1981) 161-63.

Among narrators who participate in their stories the visionary is the most privileged. One recalls here the words spoken by Luke's apocalyptic Jesus: "I saw Satan fall like a lightning bolt from heaven" (10:18). This statement establishes Jesus' ethos, for in the very next verse Jesus gives *authority* to his disciples. Or we might remember Paul's appeal to his trip to the third heaven (2 Cor 12:1-10). Apocalyptic knowledge implies authority.

What John sees and hears is important. The form εἶδον ("I saw"), which occurs forty-seven times in the Apocalypse,[44] emphasizes his continuing mediation of the narrative. John sees the risen Christ, the throne of God, future and eschatological events, and scenes from heaven. In addition, he participates in the drama himself, writing letters to the churches, being taken up into heaven, conversing with angels (and sometimes worshiping them), eating a scroll, and measuring the temple.

John, then, is a self-conscious narrator.[45] He constantly foregrounds how he acquired his special knowledge and how he is sharing it with his audience. Though it is not pseudonymous like almost every other apocalypse, Revelation does offer a narrative of its origins, including John's prophetic call. The Apocalypse begins with an overt claim: John has received his revelation from God through an angel. And he claims that he is relating "all that he saw" (1:2) to his audience, an offer of maximal information.[46] Several times John reminds his audience that he is specially commissioned to write. His initial vision of the risen Christ is framed by commands to record what he sees and forward it to the seven churches (1:11, 19). Each of the letters to the churches begins with the simple command: "To the angel of the church in . . . write." Other explicit commands to write appear at 14:13 and 19:9, both of which precede potential blessings for the audience, and at 21:5.[47]

John may be self-conscious, but his ethos also presents a more humble dimension. Stephen D. O'Leary would identify John as a

---

[44]The form ἤκουσα ("I heard") occurs twenty-seven times.
[45]Booth, *Rhetoric of Fiction*, 155; Lanser, *Narrative Act*, 176-78.
[46]Lanser, *Narrative Act*, 203-206.
[47]As we shall see, John does not in fact write all that he sees.

"self-effacing interpreter."[48] By denying his mediation of the story he is telling, John seeks to remove himself from the audience's consciousness. The story is not John's; it is the "revelation of Jesus Christ." O'Leary points out that popular North American prophecy teachers such as William Miller and Hal Lindsey have adopted the same technique. By presenting their eschatological systems as "literal" interpretations of what the Bible teaches, systems which any reasonable reader could verify,[49] they camouflage the fact that their systems are their own interpretive constructions.

Contemporary ideological critics have sharply contested the possibility of such objective reporting. However much John might protest that he is describing "all that he saw," he adopts what Edward Said would call a "strategic location."[50] He represents not only himself and the heavenly realms but also humankind in general and his opponents—Rome, Jews, and other Christians—in particular. John's characterization looks "down" upon humanity, which he regards only as masses, as strategic topoi to be fitted into his larger project. His superiority to other persons relates intimately with his exteriority to them.[51] His superhuman point of view claims power, the power of an eyewitness, of "being able to" narrate the final telos for all persons.[52]

John frames the Apocalypse with blessing and cursing, a device that reflects his status as the mediator of heavenly truth. Indeed, one prophecy teacher notes that "The Apocalypse is the only book that contains a promise of blessing for those who read it."[53] Many commentators have noted that Revelation's first and last chapters form a grand *inclusio*. Perhaps most striking are the parallel blessings at 1:3 and 22:7.[54] In both verses John blesses those who

---

[48]*Arguing the Apocalypse: A Theory of Millennial Rhetoric* (New York and Oxford: Oxford University Press, 1994) 77-78.

[49]At this point Miller and Lindsey are more democratic than John would be.

[50]*Orientalism* (New York: Random House, 1978) 20.

[51]Cf. ibid., 21.

[52]Ibid., 32.

[53]Jeffrey, *Apocalypse*, 3.

[54]Close verbal parallels appear between 1:3 (Μακάριος ὁ ἀναγινώσκων καὶ οἱ ἀκούοντες τοὺς λόγους τῆς προφητείας καὶ τηροῦντες τὰ ἐν αὐτῇ γεγραμμένα, ὁ γὰρ καιρὸς ἐγγύς) and 22:7 (καὶ ἰδοὺ ἔρχομαι ταχύ. μακάριος ὁ τηρῶν τοὺς λόγους τῆς προφητείας τοῦ βιβλίου τούτου).

keep the words of the prophecy in light of the imminent eschaton. In 22:18-19 John reinforces his blessing by adding a threat: whoever would add to or subtract from the message should expect damnation.[55]

While John blesses and curses in general terms at the beginning and end of the Apocalypse, the device becomes both more personal and more authoritative in the letters to the seven churches. Each letter concludes with a promise: "whoever conquers" will receive an eschatological or heavenly reward.[56] John shrouds the seven letters with the authority of the risen Jesus, indicating an extraordinary *status* for them. They are words of the Lord given through John's transcription. This device invites the audience to dissociate the letters from their own impressions of the narrator. At the same time, John creates a more direct *contact* with the churches by addressing particulars of each local situation. The overall rhetorical effect is stunning if not subtle: The churches are to hear the letters as direct address from the risen Christ to their own communities. Their agenda seems to be not John's so much as that of Jesus.

That John begins and ends his message with blessing and cursing is consistent with the classical rhetorical tradition, in which beginnings and endings were particularly important for ethos. Beginnings and endings served as opportunities to stress how important were the issues at hand, what the *Rhetorica ad Herennium* calls "amplification."[57] John has chosen to frame his own message as one which requires his audience's obedience—or else. Blessing and cursing work throughout the Apocalypse. Those are blessed who "die in the Lord" (14:13), who are awake and clothed at Jesus' return (16:15), who are called to the wedding feast (19:9), and who participate in the first resurrection (20:6). But John's authority to

---

[55]According to the tradition of *Ep. Arist.* 310-11 (second century BCE), a curse was applied to anyone who altered the LXX. According to Caird, who also cites *Ep. Arist.*, this was a common literary and theological convention in ancient Jewish and Greek sacred literature (*Revelation*, 287-88).

[56]Conquering presumably implies meeting the requirements spelled out in the letters.

[57]*Ad Her.* 2.47-50; cf. 1.7; Aristotle, *Rhet.* 3.14.7; 3.19.2.

bless and curse receive special emphasis at the beginning and end of the Apocalypse.

In Lanser's terms, what is at stake in John's claims is status, his qualifications to win his audience's trust. He is the one who knows the ultimate truth, whose message compels obedience. Those who dismiss or alter his message insure their destruction; those who respond positively may expect blessing.

Revelation may go farther than any apocalyptic literature of the period in claiming that the fate of its audience depends upon their reception of its particular message. Certainly apocalypses, such as *2 Baruch, 3 Baruch,* and *4 Ezra,* depicted ultimate bliss or punishment for those who conform to or resist their perspectives. But John's focus is different. John claims that blessing or punishment depends not merely upon his audience's disposition toward good or evil, but upon their *literal preservation* of his message. While it was standard rhetorical practice to emphasize the importance of a message, John's rhetoric goes much farther: John claims that his message itself conveys blessing or a curse. In Bakhtin's terms, there is no room for the dialogic imagination in John's vision. There is no space for comment; one does not "talk back." One either obeys or suffers.

But why would John go so far in claiming absolute authority? What could cause an author to resort to promises and threats? The traditional answer might be that John regards his message as absolutely important, so important that his audience must fully appreciate the crisis in which they live. To accommodate zeal for Christ to the demands of empire and local culture would be to abandon Christ altogether, and thus to earn one's own doom.

Revelation's popular and academic readers adopt John's urgency. As some contemporary fundamentalists may transfer Revelation's eschatological urgency into a daily "motivational factor,"[58] John's rhetoric serves to raise the stakes. Using Matthew's Jesus to elucidate Rev. 20:4-11, Grant R. Jeffrey insists that "those who reject God's mercy will possess both their soul and body in

---

[58]Charles B. Strozier, *Apocalypse: On the Psychology of Fundamentalism in America* (Boston: Beacon, 1994) 77.

hell forever."[59] And in his concluding comments on Revelation Billy Graham "reflect[s] exactly the way the ancient apostle John felt" by inviting his readers "to be absolutely sure that you are Christ's."[60] Not only do conversionist readings reflect John's urgency, but social activist readings do as well. Allen Boesak, who indeed wrote in a time of crisis, argues that his is "a situation the clarity of which no one can deny."[61] Dale Aukerman charges the United States and other world powers with exercising imperial ambitions. They overlook "the most ominous worst-case scenario," God's imminent judgment, which may be averted only by repentance.[62]

Critical biblical scholars, who routinely ridicule Revelation's popular readers, often follow the same pattern.[63] They assume that John wanted "to motivate the audience to pursue a life of faithfulness and purity in order to avoid the punishments awaiting those who follow the wrong path."[64] Revelation's first audience represented an uncompromising minority view, one which made conflict with the imperial structures almost unavoidable.[65] And Revelation presents an urgent message for today. According to R. H. Charles, Revelation depicts a continuing cosmic struggle and calls upon contemporary believers to participate.[66] Revelation's contemporary readers may understand the crisis John's original audience faced if they can share John's resistance to injustice. Elisabeth Schüssler Fiorenza offers a strategy for hearing the Apocalypse in the present:

---

[59]*Apocalypse*, 319.

[60]*Approaching Hoofbeats* (Dallas: Word, 1983) 231.

[61]*Comfort and Protest: Reflections on the Apocalypse of John of Patmos* (Philadelphia: Westminster, 1987) 36.

[62]*Reckoning with Apocalypse: Terminal Politics and Christian Hope* (New York: Crossroad, 1993) 112.

[63]Leonard L. Thompson, *The Book of Revelation: Apocalypse and Empire* (New York: Oxford University Press, 1990), and Adela Yarbro Collins, *Crisis and Catharsis: The Power of the Apocalypse* (Philadelphia: Westminster, 1984), are among the scholars who identify Revelation's crisis rhetoric as an attention-seeking device.

[64]Aune, "The Apocalypse of John," *Semeia* 36 (1986): 91.

[65]Cf. Harrington, *Revelation*, 10-12.

[66]Charles, *Revelation*, 1:xv.

> John's attempt to formulate the reality and meaning of eschatological salvation in sociopolitical language gains greater significance again at a time when those who share the author's stance toward sociopolitical oppression and exploitation attempt to formulate their own theology of liberation and to stake their life on it.[67]

Readings that buy into John's crisis rhetoric exempt the Apocalypse from rhetorical suspicion: surely there was another way in which John could have voiced his intense concern. As we have seen, speakers who go to tremendous lengths to assert their qualifications are often concerned that their audiences may be resistant.[68] Not only does John consider his message to be urgent, he is also unsure of its reception. That is why he must continually reinforce it.

Harmonizing: Many Voices, All Working Together

Mikhail Bakhtin's problematization of plurivocality offers one means by which to assess John's narrative ethos. I have argued that John seeks to elevate his own voice to absolute authority by making overt claims to privilege, knowledge, and power. I would like to move on to John's attempt to write an apocalypse with one voice, the perfect monological work.

Revelation resounds with voices divine, heavenly, human, and mythological. The fascinating thing is that John seeks to remove all traces of conflict among these multiple speakers. Those voices that oppose John's central point of view must accommodate themselves to the dominant perspective. Even Babylon, the great city which John opposes, names itself according to John's point of view: "Babylon the great, the mother of harlots and of earth's abominations" (17:5).

---

[67]*Revelation*, 128.

[68]Lanser, *Narrative Act*, 178; Booth, *Rhetoric of Fiction*, 179.

Bakhtin's research on the novel raises questions about John's own narrative rhetoric.[69] For Bakhtin the novel is unique in that it includes subordinated but autonomous voices:

> The novel can be defined as a diversity of social speech types (sometimes even diversity of languages) and a diversity of individual voices, artistically organized.[70]

But Bakhtin's novel does not eliminate the differences among its various voices. The ideal novel "refuses to acknowledge its own language as the sole verbal and semantic center of the ideological world."[71]

The possibility Bakhtin envisions is true polyvocality, a dialogic discourse that can express diverse and even conflicting voices on their own terms.

> A character's word about himself and his world is just as fully weighted as the author's word usually is; it is not subjected to the character's objectified image as merely one of his characteristics, nor does it serve as a mouthpiece for the author's voice.[72]

John inscribes his authority by his skillful use of levels of discourse, making his characters serve as mouthpieces for his own point of view. Lanser imagines levels of narrative authority in terms of Chinese boxes. One level fits within another which is contained by a greater level, and so forth. The greater the level of discourse, the more a speaker knows and the more power and responsibility she has for what is said. The narrator/implied author knows more than a speaking character, who knows more than the other characters whom she describes, and so forth.[73]

For example, we have seen that John claims the power to bless and curse his audience. Especially interesting is how this motif is

---

[69]Of course, John is not writing a novel. But Bakhtin's questions offer avenues for investigating John's manipulation of narrative voice.

[70]*Dialogic Imagination*, 262.

[71]Ibid., 366.

[72]Mikhail Bakhtin, *Problems of Dostoevsky's Poetics*, ed. and trans. Caryl Emerson, Theory and History of Literature 8 (Minneapolis: University of Minnesota Press, 1984) 7.

[73]*Narrative Act*, 132-47.

expressed in terms of levels of discourse. John himself gives blessings and curses at the beginning and end of Revelation, but in 14:9-13 several voices contribute to the blessing and cursing. First, an angel curses those who receive the beast's mark (14:9-11), then a heavenly voice, certified by the voice of the Spirit, blesses those who will die for their testimony (14:13). But it is John's voice that mediates between the cursing and blessing voices: "Here is the endurance of the saints, those who keep God's commandments and Jesus' faith" (14:12).[74] In other words, while heavenly voices bless and curse, John is the one who gives meaning to those voices by joining them.

Sometimes Revelation's levels of discourse are not clearly marked; at other times they are simply confusing. In Rev 14:3 John hears the mysterious crowd of 144,000 singing:

> a new song before the throne and before the four living creatures and the elders. But no one could learn the song except the 144,000 who have been redeemed from the earth.

One wonders: John has heard the song, but is he able to learn it? He alludes to the song, but he indicates that few can know it. John does not indicate that he knows the song, yet the narrative implies that he has heard it. Or consider the scene in 15:8. No one can enter the temple, but John somehow knows that God's glory has filled it with smoke. John knows a mystery is here, but it doesn't appear that he has full access.

Such tension among levels of discourse is universal in Revelation and other apocalyptic literature. The narrator, usually the visionary himself, stands at the highest level of knowledge and responsibility. Yet he claims to represent even higher realms, particularly heavenly beings. In a sense God, Christ, and the other heavenly beings are simply speaking characters within the world John constructs. They know and say only what he allows them. But in another sense—and this is a frequent topos of apocalyptic

---

[74]I would maintain that the voice in 14:12 is John's own, though the immediate context does not make this obvious. However, a similar formula ("Here is the endurance and faithfulness of the saints.") occurs in 13:10, in which it is more clear that John is the one speaking.

literature—John represents himself as limited in both knowledge and perception. He needs things explained to him and sometimes even needs correction.

Perhaps the most stunning example of this tension is the letters to the churches. As John tells the story, these letters are verbatim messages from the risen Christ. But from a literary-rhetorical perspective, these letters actually use Christ's authority to convey a message that is ultimately John's own. For example, "Jezebel," like Balaam and the Nicolaitans, is John's enemy. In the letter to Thyatira, the risen Jesus chides, "I gave her time to repent" (2:21). But, inquiring readers want to know, how did Jesus speak to Jezebel, if not through John? The mingling of levels of narration establishes John's voice above those of the heavenly figures, even above God and Christ. This problem is endemic to any claim to represent the divine perspective, and people do it all the time. Nevertheless, it is critical for an analysis of John's ethos to recognize these effects of his apocalyptic vision.

Since Revelation is a form of resistance literature, it should not surprise us how important the representing voice is to its narrative rhetoric. The authority to represent promises the power to endure, to resist colonial domination through an alternative vision. While claims to such authority can serve liberation, they can also turn back on themselves. John seeks to provide his audience with the resources to endure; at the same time, he denies them the freedom to do their own imagining. Resistance must be on John's terms, and his terms only. John cannot escape a problem fundamental to the act of resistance: One tends to reinscribe the very practices one opposes. His message is in a profound sense no different from that of the Empire: Neither allows dissent.[75]

---

[75]Many theorists of postcolonial and resistance literature argue that such literatures often mirror the practices of those they resist. This is the thesis of Richard Terdiman, *Discourse/Counter-Discourse: The Theory and Practice of Symbolic Resistance in Nineteenth-Century France* (Ithaca NY: Cornell University Press, 1985). Averil Cameron uses this pattern to analyze the history of early Christianity (*Christianity and the Rhetoric of Empire: The Development of Christian Discourse*, Sather Classical Lectures 55, [Berkeley: University of California Press, 1991]). Cf. also Bill Ashcroft, Gareth Griffiths, and Helen Tiffin, *The Empire Writes Back: Theory and Practice in Post-Colonial Literatures*, New Accents (New York: Routledge, 1989) 170; Barbara Harlow, *Resistance Literature* (New York: Methuen, 1987) 29; and Neil ten

Identifying: Making Associations

Among Kenneth Burke's most provocative insights is his argument that identification is at the heart of rhetoric. Theorists have always advised speakers to align themselves with their audiences' sympathies; Burke's contribution has been to locate identification as a determinative feature of rhetoric. Whether consciously or unconsciously rhetoric persuades by means of identification.[76] Wise speakers identify with their audiences, inviting them into a partnership of status and disposition.[77] By associating themselves with concepts, persons, or things valued by the audience, rhetors win attention, credibility, and goodwill. In contrast, successful speakers identify their opponents with things their audience loathes.

At first sight John's contact with the audience offers what we might call an egalitarian vision. He addresses them as their "partner" (1:9), one who shares a divinely given status as "kings, priests to God" (1:6). In other words, John identifies himself with his audience in experience, conviction, and status, striking a note of intimacy by seeking a coincidence of ideological point of view.[78] Like them, he has been freed from his sins (1:5), and like them, he has experienced distress as a side effect (1:9). Just like his real audience, his apparent condition as one who is an outcast for "the testimony of Jesus" (1:9) means nothing beside his real status among those who will conquer and reign with God (2:26-28).

One means by which John reaches out to his audience is by describing his own behavior. We have seen that John is not only Revelation's narrator, he is an important character as well. Some of his actions reflect his singular privilege. He measures the temple, ingests the heavenly scroll, hears things other mortals cannot hear. But John is also quick to represent his own humanity. Like other visionaries, he narrates the physical effects of his

---

Kortenaar, "Beyond Authenticity and Creolization: Reading Achebe Writing Culture," *PMLA* 110 (1995): 41.

[76]Kenneth Burke, *A Rhetoric of Motives* (repr.: Berkeley: University of California, 1969; [1]1950) 35, 46.

[77]Ibid., 55, 67.

[78]Lanser, *Narrative Act*, 179, 219.

experience. Confronted by his vision of the risen Christ, he "fell at [Christ's] feet as though I were dead" (1:17). Unfortunately, John does not only fall when it is appropriate. Sometimes he falls at the feet of angels, who gently correct him (19:10; 22:8). This motif presents John as a person who is pious, and though not always perfect, one who is humble enough to report his own mistakes.

John also describes his lack of knowledge, a device common among apocalypses like Daniel, *3 Baruch*, and *4 Ezra*. As John learns that no one is able to open the heavenly scroll, he reveals his piety and ignorance by weeping greatly (πολύ). An elder tells him not to weep, for the Lion of Judah has prevailed to open the scroll (5:4-5). Then, when quizzed about the identity of those who are robed in white, John admits that he is ignorant. The inquiring elder then interprets his vision (7:13-17). And when he is confused by the vision of Babylon, an angel explains it to him (17:7-8). Again, John represents himself as a person who desires to know heavenly things even as he identifies with his audience's possible confusion.

Revelation presents its audiences with a perplexing tapestry of associations. While the next chapter will discuss how John characterizes his opponents, it is enough for now simply to trace John's own self-identification. In this rich fabric everything good functions at the same level. Even the saints share dominion with Christ in the millennium:

> Then I saw thrones, and they sat upon them, those to whom judgment had been given and the souls of those who had been beheaded on account of the testimony of Jesus and the word of God, even those who worshiped neither the beast nor its image and who did not receive its mark upon their foreheads or their hands. Now they were alive and reigned with Christ for one thousand years. (20:4)

Here we observe several critical dimensions of how John weaves associations. Those who testify in Revelation, the witnesses, include Jesus, John, Christian prophets, and the martyrs, in addition to the members of John's audience who do as he says. The witnesses are highly valued for their trustworthiness and faithful endurance, since all participate in the testimony of *the* faithful witness, Jesus.

Because John's web of identification is so complex, an orderly assessment eludes our grasp. Before reflecting on Rev 1:9, the most obvious example of John's audience identification, I will emphasize three prominent motifs by which John enhances his own status: witness, slavery, and prophecy. These are not discrete categories in the Apocalypse. One cannot discuss John's use of the witness motif, for example, without dealing with how he adapts metaphors such as slavery and prophecy. Sometimes we must retrace our steps. The reward promises to be worth the wandering.

To witness is, along with to endure and to conquer, among the most positive things a person can do in Revelation. It implies seriously risking one's life.[79] The primary reference points for witness are Jesus and John himself; it is extremely difficult to discern whether one is more prominent than the other. Jesus is the "faithful and true witness" (3:14; cf. 1:5). In a sense so is John, who "testified to the word of God and the testimony of Jesus all that he saw" (1:2), and who finds himself on Patmos "on account of the word of God and the testimony of Jesus" (1:9). And since the words John writes are Christ's revelation, they also are "faithful and true" (22:6; cf. 1:1, 5).[80]

---

[79]Allison A. Trites has traced the semantics of μάρτυς and its cognates in Revelation, concluding that death has not yet developed into their primary implication ("Μάρτυς and Martyrdom in the Apocalypse: A Semantic Study," *NovT* 15 [1973]: 72-80). Trites assumes that explicit statements that a witness dies indicate that death is not itself part of *martys*' semantic meaning. Trites may be correct from the standpoint of semantic methodology; however, for our purposes it is important to note that, in Revelation, to witness is to risk one's life. See also B. Dehandschutter, "The Meaning of Witness in the Apocalypse," in *L'Apocalypse johannique et l'Apocalyptique dans le Nouveau Testament*, ed. J. Lambrecht, BETL 53 (Leuven: Leuven University, 1980) 283-88.

[80]Scholars disagree as to who is speaking in 22:6. Charles attributes 22:6-7 to Christ's voice on the basis of καὶ ἰδοῦ ἔρχομαι ταχύ in 22:7 (*Revelation*, 2:217). Schüssler Fiorenza agrees but notes that most critics ascribe these verses to the bowl angel (*Revelation*, 114). Though I agree with Charles and Schüssler Fiorenza on this point, the context is more difficult than either admits. The speaker in the preceding verses is the angel, and John provides no clear transition to another speaking voice. Collins notes that it would be awkward for the speaker of 22:6-7 to be the angel, since 22:6 refers to an angel in the third person, then suggests that, "The speaker's identity is unimportant" (*Apocalypse*, 152).

The witness motif functions to identify John and his words with Jesus and his words. John receives the revelation from Jesus (1:1); he testifies to all that he sees. Jesus is called the faithful witness; John is a witness who is faithful as well. Without applying to himself the title he reserves for Jesus, John has characterized himself in the same terms.

But John is willing to share Jesus' title with another character, Antipas. This "faithful witness" lived among the church in Pergamum (2:13); evidently he died as a result of his testimony. Antipas is not the only such case. In his heavenly ascent John sees the souls of witnesses who have died on account of their testimony (6:9-11). Clearly, John associates testimony with risk:

> Now these are they who have conquered [Satan]
> through the blood of the Lamb
> and the word of their testimony,
> for they did not love their souls
> even to the point of death. (12:11)

More difficult to assess is the significance of the mysterious two witnesses in Rev 11. The majority of commentators today identify these figures as models for John's audience. They are exemplary witnesses, or perhaps Christian prophets, who not only endure martyrdom but also experience eschatological reward.[81] But Charles points out that the witnesses have the powers of Elijah (shutting off rain) and Moses (turning water into blood), the two figures who accompany Jesus at the transfiguration in Luke.[82] The trouble with Charles' suggestion is that it makes no sense of the passage; Charles himself is forced to label it a "backwater" in John's narrative.[83]

If one adopts the majority reading, the dramatically democratic potential of John's vision leaps forward. All believers are faithful witnesses; all are prophets. After all, "the testimony of Jesus is the

---

[81]E.g., Caird, *Revelation*, 134; Collins, *Apocalypse*, 69-72; Harrington, *Revelation*, 123; Krodel, *Revelation*, 222-24; Jürgen Roloff, *The Revelation of John*, trans. John E. Alsup, Continental Commentaries (Minneapolis: Fortress, 1993) 131; Schüssler Fiorenza, *Revelation*, 77; and Wall, *Revelation*, 143-45.

[82]*Revelation*, 1:282-85.

[83]Ibid., 1:282.

spirit of prophecy" (19:10; cf. 11:6). And sure enough, John also associates himself with the prophets.[84] His text is a prophecy (1:3; 22:7, 10, 18-19), and he receives a prophet's commission: "You must prophesy again concerning many peoples and nations and tongues and dominions" (10:9).

By implication any member of the seven churches may become a witness or a prophet. What is required is that one maintain one's confession in the face of danger. So the concept of witness plays a complicated function in Revelation. At one level it legitimates John and his message. Like Antipas and other respected saints who die for their testimony, John is a persistent witness. Like the "faithful and true witness" Jesus, John's words are "faithful and true." So John is identified not only with saints of the highest status, his discourse assumes the authority of Christ. But at another level, the witness motif can be stunningly democratic: Anyone can be a witness or a prophet *if she or he lives as John says*. While the highest status is in principle open to members of John's audience, they must subordinate themselves in order to achieve it. Though John associates testimony with prophecy, it is clear that *his* prophecy is uniquely authoritative. Whoever heeds its words will be blessed; whoever modifies or neglects it faces a curse.

There are prophets and then there are prophets. John identifies himself with the audience by revealing secrets to them, claiming to share "all that he saw" (1:2). He shares heavenly mysteries that are otherwise inaccessible (1:20; 10:7; 17:5, 7), and he even clues his audience to difficult parts of the message.

> Now here is wisdom: let the one who has wisdom count the number of the beast, for it is a mortal's number, its number is six hundred sixty-six. (13:18)

Like other apocalyptic narrators John addresses his audience directly. By disclosing eschatological secrets and by calling upon his audience to fill in his message, John invites his audience to

---

[84]So commentators frequently identify John as a prophet known to the communities he addresses. Caird may be the most certain of John's reputation, claiming that for Revelation's audience "John was their personal friend" (*Revelation*, 7).

draw closer. Twice John invites the audience to discern the saints' endurance (13:10; 14:12), and twice he provides clues for them to identify the beast and the harlot (13:18; 17:9). In addition, John also calls upon the audience to demonstrate their wisdom by understanding what he is saying: ὁ ἔχων οὖς ἀκουσάτω.[85] If they respond to these invitations, the audience enjoys two benefits. First, their participation in the drama increases, as they fill in the hints John leaves for them. Second, they participate in John's status as well. Just as John hears the heavenly voice say, "Come up here" (4:1; 11:12), so do they.

But John does *not* share all that he sees. In Rev 10:4 John hears the voices of seven thunders. Though he starts to write down what he has heard, another heavenly voice stops him: "Seal up the things the seven thunders said; do not write them." John is willing to record what he hears, but a higher authority prevents him. Later in the same scene, John is ordered to ingest a scroll, the contents of which are not disclosed (10:8-10). Immediately multiple voices recommission John as a prophet: "You must prophesy again concerning many peoples and nations and languages and dominions" (10:11).

How does one evaluate John's obedience in not revealing what he has heard, then in eating the scroll? One might argue that John appears the perfect narrator. He wants to tell his audience everything; he even lets them know when some things are secret. But John maintains the knowledge gap between himself and his audience. Read rhetorically, John's story is not simply a narration of a given experience; instead, John is a speaker, someone who shapes the message he delivers.[86] He chooses to maintain secrets

---

[85]The clause occurs in each of the letters to the churches as well as at 13:9.

[86]Before literary criticism became popular in New Testament studies, Austin Farrer wrestled with this problem in a profound way. Farrer distinguished between revelatory and literary activity, noted that Revelation featured characteristics of both, and suggested that John's vision occurred in the context of scriptural meditation, that his vision occurred with pen in hand (*The Revelation of St. John the Divine* [Oxford: Clarendon, 1964] 23-29). Farrer's argument is congenial to the later work of Christopher Rowland, who argues that early Jewish and Christian apocalyptic visions resulted from mystical reflection on sacred mysteries (*The Open Heaven: A Study of Apocalyptic in Judaism and Early Christianity* [New York: Crossroad, 1982]).

from his audience. In this case one result is that John reinscribes his superiority to them. He knows more than they do, and his ingestion of the scroll internalizes his privilege.

A recent paper by Jean Pierre Ruiz reveals the distinction between a rhetorically oriented reading of Rev 10:4 and a more trusting exegesis.[87] Ruiz takes issue with Jürgen Roloff. Roloff asserts that Rev 10:4 ought not be compared with Paul's "inexpressible words which are not possible for a mortal to utter" (ἄρρητα ῥήματα ἃ οὐκ ἐξὸν ἀνθρώπῳ λαλῆσαι) in 2 Cor 12:4, since John's secrecy serves a different purpose: it enables eschatological mysteries to be sealed until the eschatological generation.[88] Instead, Ruiz maintains that John's secrecy contributes to his ethos. By *not writing* what the thunders said and by swallowing the scroll, John creates a tension between his text and his person. John, who faces challenges to his authority from the churches he is addressing, refuses to share his knowledge through his text. Instead, he "becomes an embodied prophetic document" by eating the scroll.[89]

While I am not convinced that Rev 10 sets up a play between textuality and John's embodied authority, John's ethos is certainly at issue. First, John becomes a character in the heavenly and eschatological drama. He is invited to see mysteries, and he participates in their mediation by eating the scroll. Second, John presents himself as a prophet of good will, someone who would disclose these mysteries if only he were allowed. Third, John maintains the distance in his contact with his audience.[90] He alone knows what the thunders have said, and he is the one who has ingested the scroll. Both the secrets he keeps and the scroll he has eaten remind the audience that they depend on John for whatever revelation they may receive. What we have is a narrator who

---

[87]"Hearing and Seeing but Not Saying: A Look at Revelation 10:4 and 2 Corinthians 12:4," *SBLSP* 33 (1994): 182-202.

[88]*Revelation*, 124.

[89]"Hearing and Seeing," 201.

[90]Lanser's terms "deference" and "contempt" (*Narrative Act*, 179) do not adequately express what John is about here. He is superior to his audience, but also goes to great lengths to identify with them.

claims to share all he knows with his audience, but who maintains distinctions in knowledge and status between himself and them.

In addition to witness and prophet, the topos of slavery also links John to his audience. John is God's slave (1:1), as are the prophets and even the angelic interpreter (10:7; 22:9). The message itself addresses God's slaves (1:1; 22:6), with whom the prophets are somehow related.[91] But slavehood is not restricted to John and his fellow prophets. God's slaves are "all who fear [God], the small and the great" (19:5).[92] Those who worship God in the new city—potentially anyone in the audience—will be slaves (22:3). Even those who are following "Jezebel" are reckoned among the slaves (2:20). So who is a prophet, and who is a slave? The answer seems to be that while anyone may be a prophet or a slave, John is preeminent among equals. John is *the* slave who mediates the vision, and the prophets are specially set apart as slaves (10:7; 22:9). Any member of his audience may receive these titles, but only in a derivative sense. The prophets define slavehood, John is first among them, and the rest of the community participates in that status.

We might get the impression that John is confused. Perhaps he is muddling his categories, confusing slaves, prophets, and witnesses. But Dale B. Martin has demonstrated that the slavery metaphor was a common and effective political device in the ancient Mediterranean. People who sought status as populist leaders, whatever their own social status, characterized themselves as enslaved leaders, what we might call servants of the people.[93]

---

[91]According to Charles, "the servants, who are God's servants (αὐτοῦ), are the Christian prophets" (*Revelation*, 1:6; but cf. Krodel, *Revelation*, 78).

[92]There is a textual problem here. The majority reading (πάντες οἱ δοῦλοι αὐτοῦ, καὶ οἱ φοβούμενοι αὐτόν . . .) could—the syntax remains ambiguous—suggest a distinction between the slaves and those who fear God. According to Bruce M. Metzger, the transcription possibilities are too evenly matched for a clear determination (*TCGNT*, 759-60). However, the majority reading is awkward at best, as the qualifier οἱ μικροὶ καὶ οἱ μεγάλοι would apply only to those who fear God. The literary structure of the proclamation reflects more balance if the καί is omitted, enabling a double qualification: "all [God's] slaves" fear God, whether small or great. David Aune notes that most instances of δοῦλος in Revelation refer to Christians in general (*Revelation 1-5*, 13).

[93]*Slavery as Salvation: The Metaphor of Slavery in Pauline Christianity* (New Haven CT: Yale University, 1990) 86-115.

Paul, to whom John alludes (1:4), drew upon this metaphor to empower his own ethos. Some Christians even attributed it to Jesus, who named slavery as the path to status among his disciples (Mark 10:44 par.). In other words, John's ambiguity regarding motifs such as slavery (along with witness and prophet) serves a definite rhetorical purpose. It enhances his ethos by identifying him with his audience even as it locates him as an authoritative person.

One wonders: Perhaps John's vision is conflicted at its core. It is at once radically democratic and fundamentally authoritarian. John is one with his audience, a witness, slave, prophet who would share everything he knows. But he differs from them in both knowledge and status. He is a witness who cannot relate everything he has seen. He is a slave, but one who performs special services in the heavenly realms. He is a prophet, the one upon whom all other prophets rely for knowledge.

No wonder readings of the apocalypse range from the authoritarian to the egalitarian, from the dogmatic to the dialogic. Revelation envisions egalitarian community even as John identifies himself with absolute authority. John F. Walvoord can promise "a sure word from God Himself,"[94] while Hal Lindsey can look forward to telling people "I told you so" at the Rapture.[95] But a Dale Aukerman might confess, "Disciples are hardly ever free from elements of complicity in the worst that is being perpetrated by the society."[96] John's identification *with* his audience provides the rhetorical means by which readers who identify themselves *as* his audience may characterize themselves among or above their peers.

Not surprisingly, professional readers of Revelation mimic popular readers. Surely John, servant of God, of his apocalypse, and of his audience, tells what he has seen without guile. According to David E. Aune,

> The Apocalypse of John is a literary replication of the original and unique revelatory experience of John the Seer which . . .

---

[94]John F. Walvoord, *Armageddon, Oil, and the Middle East Crisis*, rev. ed. (Grand Rapids MI: Zondervan, 1990; [1]1974) 14.

[95]*The Late Great Planet Earth* (Grand Rapids MI: Zondervan, 1970) 143.

[96]*Reckoning with Apocalypse*, 177.

> communicates the author's paraenetic message with divine authority.[97]

Most commonly, scholars emphasize the egalitarian dimensions of John's rhetoric, arguing that John is simply sharing an urgent message with his equals. Aune argues that John "democratizes" his message, viewing all Christians as kings and priests.[98] Critical scholarship can be trusting in the extreme: "John withdraws himself completely; he wishes to be nothing more than an effective tool."[99] And we may be sure that John's authority relies on no criteria external to his divinely authenticated message:

> Since the only predicate that he claims for himself is that of being a servant of Jesus Christ, which is none other than that attributed to all members of the church, we must conclude that John consciously and adamantly rejects a claim to authority on the basis of his office or position.[100]

Our study of John's rhetoric of identification may conclude with Rev 1:9, his most overt attempt to identify with his audience:

> I John, your brother and partner in the distress and dominion and endurance [which are] in Jesus, arrived on the island called Patmos on account of the word of God and the testimony of Jesus.

Among the things John claims to share with his audience are status, suffering, and hope. Trusting readers will agree with Gerhard A. Krodel, who perceives that 1:9 establishes John's ethos "from below."[101]

According to this (majority) reading, John is a people's prophet, a person who puts his life where his mouth is. But like the terms witness, prophet, and slave, John's status as a brother and partner

---

[97]"The Apocalypse of John and the Problem of Genre," *Semeia* 36 (1986): 91.

[98]Cf. esp. "The Social Matrix of the Apocalypse of John," *BR* 26 (1981): 19; *Prophecy*, 206.

[99]Roloff, *Revelation*, 19, buying into the technique of the self-effacing interpreter.

[100]Ibid., 20.

[101]*Revelation*, 54.

are ambiguous. "Brother" occurs in four other contexts in Revelation: once to refer technically to those who suffer martyrdom (6:11); once in relation to those saints whom Satan accuses (12:10); and twice when the angelic mediator shares his status as brother and [fellow slave] with John (19:10; 22:9). By calling himself "brother" to his audience, John is not so much lowering himself to their status and inviting them "up" to his level. And though John shares certain fundamental convictions or experiences with his audience, his are particularly privileged. Only John is on Patmos, presumably as a punishment for his testimony,[102] and he alone mediates the vision which begins in the next verse, 1:10. Even when John "shares" with his audience, he is not giving away his unique claim to authority.

Justifying: How John Cuts Off Objections

As Lanser and Booth point out, some narrators worry about how they will be received.[103] A telltale sign of such anxiety is a narrator's repeated attempt to justify her point of view. The narrator may address the audience directly, explaining why it is necessary that things be the way they are.[104] Another option is to have reliable characters perform similar functions, addressing either other characters or the intended audience.

---

[102]Why John is on Patmos has been an occasion for a great deal of scholarly debate. Christian sources such as Tertullian (*De Praescr.*, 36) and Jerome (*De Vir. Ill.*, 9) maintain that John had been banished for life to the island, and Adela Yarbro Collins judges that their explanation is probably accurate (*Crisis and Catharsis*, 102-104). Leonard L. Thompson is less convinced (*Revelation*, 172-73). Some scholars inaccurately claim that Pliny the Elder's *Natural History* (4.23; cf. 4.69) locates Patmos as a penal colony (e.g., J. N. Sanders, "John on Patmos," *NTS* 9 [1963]: 76; Charles, *Revelation*, 1:21), but no clear evidence exists that Patmos functioned as a penal colony in the first century CE (cf. Caird, *Revelation*, 21). The best evidence that John is alluding to his banishment is his claim to be on the island "on account of . . . the testimony of Jesus." Other occurrences of μαρτυρία and its cognates in Revelation imply personal risk for those who testify. However, for a full argument that Patmos, which was well populated, was not known as a penal colony in antiquity, see H. D. Saffrey, "Relire l'Apocalypse Patmos," *RB* 82 (1975): 385-417, esp. 398.

[103]Lanser, *Narrative Act*, 178; Booth, *Rhetoric of Fiction*, 179.

[104]Direct address for moral purposes is rare in modern fiction.

Jewish apocalyptic literature often used human or heavenly voices to justify God's judgments. In 2 *Baruch* the visionary warns the people of a coming tribulation, then leaves them. The people respond with grief: "Where are you going from us, Baruch, and do you leave us as a father who leaves his children as orphans and goes away from them" (32:9)? Baruch does not promise relief from the coming calamities, but he does promise to return to the people (34:1). Later Baruch exhorts the people to make their ways straight (77:5). When he finishes the speech, the people ask him to send his message to the Diaspora, since they lack sources of authority (77:11-14). Though Baruch points to the Law as proper authority, he agrees to write the letter. In these cases the people and Baruch authenticate one another. The people testify that Baruch is a worthy prophet; by fulfilling their requests Baruch affirms their witness to himself.

Multiple voices also defend God's judgments in *Fourth Ezra* and 3 *Baruch*. The problem 4 *Ezra* addresses is theodicy, why Zion faces desolation while "Babylon" (i.e. Rome) prospers. The theodicy is frustrated, with Ezra repeatedly learning that God's judgment is beyond his own reckoning. When Ezra asks the angel why Israel has suffered defeat, the angel offers justification: "unless the living pass through the difficult and vain experiences, they can never experience those things which have been reserved for them" (6:14). *Third Baruch* (Greek) begins with a similar problem: "Lord, why have you set fire to your vineyard and laid it waste" (1:2)? Baruch converses with angelic interpreters, some of whom condemn the world for its wickedness. Eventually the angel Michael pronounces suffering upon humanity, a verdict justified by human refusal to obey God's voice. The voices of several angels prepare for this judgment: "We are unable to remain with evil and foolish men. For there is no goodness in them, but only every unrighteousness and greediness" (13:3).

A prime example of John's attempt to defuse objections to his message occurs as the seven bowls of God's wrath are being poured out upon the earth (15:1–16:21). The bowls are devastating. David Barr aptly characterizes them as "a successive bombardment upon the earth."[105] John sees the seven angels with the final plagues, but before the plagues are scattered there is an interruption in which several voices join in justifying the plagues. Those who have conquered the Beast sing a song:

> Great and marvelous are your works,
> O Lord God the Pantocrator;
> Righteous and true are your ways,
> O ruler of the nations.
> Who will not fear, O Lord,
> and glorify your name?
> For you alone are holy:
> All nations will come
> and prostrate themselves before you,
> Because your judgments have been revealed. (15:3b-4)

Which of God's ways are "righteous and true"? We learn when those who have worshiped the Beast suffer from sores amid global catastrophes. Let us suspend the question of whether John's program is "great and marvelous" in order to view his rhetorical strategy. John might suspect that his audience is likely to respond ambivalently at best to this gory spectacle. His solution is to place the justification for these judgments in the mouths of his most respected human characters—the conquerors. If they, who suffered greatly for their testimony, perceived the justice in God's action, perhaps the audience will identify with them.

The third bowl causes the earth's fresh water to turn into blood. As the bowl is poured out, John introduces another voice. The angel of the waters sings a song similar that of the conquerors, one sure to appeal to the audience's pathos:

> You are righteous,
> the one who is and who was, the Holy One,
> for you judged these things,
> Because the blood of saints and prophets they poured out,
> and now you have given them blood to drink:
> They deserve it. (16:5b-6)

---

[105] *Tales of the End*, 131.

Then John hears another voice as the heavenly altar speaks:

> Yes, O Lord God the Pantocrator,
> True and Righteous are your judgments. (16:7)

Similar voices praise God for the destruction of Babylon/Rome (19:2-5). A heavenly multitude echoes that God's judgments are "true and righteous," a verdict confirmed by the twenty-four elders and the four living creatures. Even from the throne itself comes the call for God's slaves to praise God. "In righteousness" Christ, the rider of the white horse, "judges and makes war"; he is "faithful and true" (19:11; cf. 1:5; 3:14). And what about those who are condemned? "Let the evildoer still do evil, and let the degenerate remain degenerate; but let the righteous still do right, and let the holy still be holy" (22:11).

John also employs crisis rhetoric to justify his version of God's vengeance. His vision concerns things which are about to happen (1:1, 3, 19; 2:16; 6:11; 22:6). It grows from contexts of distress, probably sporadic local persecution (1:9; 2:10, 13; 6:9-11; 12:17; 13:15; 17:6; 18:24; 20:4). To endure is to conquer, reaping eschatological rewards.

Crisis rhetoric is so much a feature of ancient and contemporary apocalyptic discourse that prominent scholars such as David Hellholm and Paul D. Hanson identify crisis as one of its defining characteristics.[106] But a rhetorically sensitive understanding of crisis rhetoric in apocalyptic discourse would emphasize that crisis is an extremely effective topos, one often employed by Cicero. By persuading his audience to adopt his crisis perspective, John has a chance of justifying the severity of his vision.

Scholars sometimes follow John's lead in dealing with his violent vision. In addressing the question of vengeance in the Apocalypse, William Klassen asked whether Revelation's thirst for vengeance should be "embarrassing" to Christians, or whether it

---

[106]Hellholm, "The Problem of Apocalyptic Genre and the Apocalypse of John," 27; Hanson, *Dawn of Apocalyptic*, esp. 232, 408-409, 430. Cf. O'Leary, *Arguing the Apocalypse*, 33, 64.

violates "the heart of the Gospel." How does Klassen respond? Through justification!

> It is tempting for those who have never had to wrestle with major injustices to criticize these intense longings for justice as sub-Christian or a reversion to Judaism.[107]

After all, Klassen argues, in Revelation the saints themselves do not execute their desires, nor is their joy in others' suffering eternal.[108]

Before John's audience has the chance to formulate its objections, John interjects authoritative voices to stifle them. It is not so much that John has the conquerors and heavenly representatives back him up that is significant. What is impressive is John's timing: The voices step in precisely when John is open to examination. Just when we begin to wonder whether John might be a little too vengeful, he tells us why he is right. Moreover, John permeates his vision with crisis rhetoric, suggesting that the violence has begun not with him but with those who oppress his audience. John "knows" his program is suspect.[109] As David Spurr says of postcolonial rhetoric, the seeds of resistance to John's discourse lie within the discourse itself.[110] John's anxiety surfaces as he asserts his own righteousness most loudly.

Conclusion

We have reviewed five ways in which John has constructed his own narrative ethos: generic allusions, overt claims, harmonized levels of discourse, attempts to identify with his audience, and efforts to justify potentially objectionable aspects of his vision. Each of these elements could contribute to John's self-characterization as a person of good sense, knowledge, and goodwill. John desires justice for those who have suffered martyrdom and is willing to suffer himself for the testimony of Jesus. At the same time, John is

---

[107]"Vengeance in the Apocalypse of John," *CBQ* 28 (1966): 303.

[108]Ibid., 305-308.

[109]By saying that John "knows" something, I am personifying my own reconstruction of the narrator.

[110]*Rhetoric of Empire*, 178.

a person of extraordinary privilege and experience. He knows heavenly secrets of ultimate importance, and he is willing to share them in their entirety. Despite his remarkable qualifications, John displays some of the caution the rhetorical handbooks advise, going to great lengths to identify with his audience. He is a "brother" to his audience, one who shares their hardship and endurance, and even to a degree their lack of knowledge.

But a tension tightens John's rhetoric. John often ignores the theorists' canon of ethical modesty, sounding as self-important as Cicero in his political speeches, Enoch in the *Dream Visions*,[111] and Ezra in *4 Ezra*. How can John be so superior in knowledge and privilege, yet claim to be equal to his audience? If they are all members of a "priestly dominion for God" (1:6), why does he alone possess the authority to bless and to curse? Why is his message the only revelation of Jesus Christ (1:1), and not to be tampered with (22:18-19)? And for the theologically inclined, how does one respond to a narrator who inscribes heavenly beings, including God and Christ, within his own discourse, effectively reducing them to characters of his own construction? For that matter, how does one talk about the divine realm without doing the very same thing?

These tensions lie close to the heart of the Apocalypse, and perhaps to Christian discourse in general. They certainly feed into how people read Revelation. How does one speak of ultimacy in an effort to resist other and oppressive voices? Is it possible to use such intense rhetoric or to make such grand claims without replicating oppression?

---

[111]Cf. *1 Enoch* 84:5-6. John does not exalt himself quite as much as Enoch does in the *Similitudes*. In *1 Enoch* 70:1-4 and 71:14-17, Enoch becomes the model of the righteous mortal. Perhaps *1 Enoch's* almost obvious pseudonymity enables this sort of freedom. Because many members of his audience probably knew John, his literary freedom was more restricted.

Chapter 5
John's Narrative Ethos: Representation of Opponents

John's struggle for authority does not happen in a vacuum. While he calls his book "The Revelation of Jesus Christ," John pays almost as much attention to those who oppose his vision. Revelation is full of allusions to a range of opponents, within and without the churches he addresses, individual, institutional, and corporate.[1] The Apocalypse attacks competing Christian preachers and their followers, Jewish communities, the Empire and its partners, and humanity in general, linking all of them to the demonic realm.

According to John, each of these groups threatens his audience. The Empire's cultic and commercial systems oppress humanity, and its functionaries will execute believers who refuse to participate in those institutions. Jews slander Christians, exposing them to danger from the civil authorities. People in general are indifferent to John's churches, but their participation in the larger culture contributes to Christians' marginalization. And by accommodating themselves to the rest of society, John's Christian opponents are unfaithful to Jesus and may place added pressure upon the "true" believers who refuse to compromise. All of these groups are either identified with, motivated by, or complicitous with the realm of Satan, the Dragon.

John's oppositional characterizations should help us understand the polemics we find among Revelation's contemporary readers. John's readers—liberationist, millenarian, or critical—are

---

[1]To my knowledge, Adela Yarbro Collins, *Crisis and Catharsis: The Power of the Apocalypse* (Philadelphia: Westminster, 1984) 145-52, offers the most rhetorically sensitive analysis of John's polemic to date.

given to the discourses of opposition and jeopardy. Liberationist readers condemn other readings as ideological if not dangerous, while prophecy students dwell on the perils of failing to take literally the Bible's end-time message. And scholars are no exception when they represent millenarian readings as practical and theological threats to both society and church.

From John's perspective there are no other perspectives. All voices who might utter a contrary word must be silenced, a crucial dimension of his rhetorical task. That they may be relatively close to John's own point of view or diametrically opposed is of no consequence: John rejects such distinctions. Only a few have their names in the Book of Life (13:8; 17:8; 21:27), while the rest of the world faces destruction.

John is not unique in this regard. Many ancient speakers used highly charged rhetoric against their opponents. Our task, at least at this stage, is not to justify or condemn John, but familiarity with John's broader cultural and discursive context should enhance our understanding of his program. According to Aristotle, invective was one of the earliest forms of Greek literature (*Poet.* 4.8-12). From his advice that the object of one's blame should appear shameful (*Rhet.* 1.9.9), to 1 Maccabees' characterization of "illegitimate sons" or "unlawful persons" from Israel (1:11), and from 4 *Ezra's* prediction of torment for those who disregard to law (9:10-12) to Juvenal's portrayal of Rome's declining masculinity (*Satire* 2.51-63), intense language was a prime characteristic of ancient polemic.[2] As we have seen, Cicero could go to extremes in debasing antagonists such as Catalina, blaming him for every evil in Rome.

---

[2]For a review of the conventions of ancient polemic, especially as they apply to early Christian texts, see Luke T. Johnson, "The New Testament's Anti-Jewish Slander and the Conventions of Ancient Polemic," *JBL* 108 (1989): 419-41; Sean Freyne, "Vilifying the Other and Defining the Self: Matthew's and John's Anti-Jewish Polemic in Focus," in *"To See Ourselves as Others See Us": Christians, Jews, "Others" in Late Antiquity*, ed. Jacob Neusner and Ernest Frerichs, Scholars Press Studies in the Humanities (Chico CA: Scholars Press, 1985) 117-43; and Peder Borgen, "Polemic in the Book of Revelation," in *Anti-Semitism and Early Christianity*, ed. Craig Evans and Donald Hagner (Minneapolis: Fortress, 1993) 199-211.

How should we analyze John's rhetorical attack? Rhetorical categories structured the discussion of John's self-characterization in the last chapter, but that strategy may be more problematic here. John is concerned with many perceived enemies, and he uses several common techniques against them. To identify prominent rhetorical motifs as they apply to each group of opponents runs the risk of being overly repetitive, but the same risk occurs if we begin with the opponents themselves. Because I am more interested in John's rhetoric than in his historical context, I have again chosen to shape this chapter according to John's devices. This strategy promises two advantages. First, it allows us to see how John's devices apply against all his opponents, thus demonstrating that for John all opponents are of the same status. Second, it reveals the pervasiveness of these categories in John's argument.

John's polemic resources are impressive. He employs multiple levels of voice and characterization to complement his own narration. This technique allows condemnations of his opponents to come from heavenly beings and heroes such as the martyrs, rather than from John himself. Through the rhetoric of (dis)identification and remythologization, John links his opponents to villains from biblical tradition and to destructive mythological forces. John subverts imperial discourse from within through parody and satire, while taunting and debasement offer a more direct means of deprecating his opponents. Finally, John cuts off his audience's sympathy for his opponents through dehumanization and negation, stripping them of their human identity.

Voice

The most basic means by which John attacks his opponents is through his use of narrative voice. Whether the speaking voice is the risen Christ or another heavenly figure, perhaps even a human martyr, John often employs a more authoritative persona when taking on his enemies. In our study of how multiple levels of discourse serve to justify the harshness of John's vision, we observed that other apocalyptic authors frequently used narrative voice for similar effects. But John's use of narrative voice serves not only to build his own ethos, it is also an effective weapon. We have also noted Aristotle's advice that sometimes "we must make another speak in our place" (*Rhet.* 3.17.16), counsel that applies to attack as well as to self-defense. It is this dimension of Revelation that I investigate here.

The most obvious cases are the letters to the seven churches (Rev 2–3) and Rev 22:12-20, in which the risen Christ provides the speaking voice. Those passages represent John's entire characterization of his Christian opponents and, with the possible exception of Rev 11, of neighboring Jewish communities as well. These are not coincidences. John likely knows that his audience may resist these censures. After all, it is extremely likely that the churches include the Christians he is denouncing, and it is also probable that some members were on friendly terms with their Jewish neighbors.[3] So John assigns these most problematic of his conflicts to his most authoritative witness.

In the letters and in the Apocalypse's concluding verses, John's enemies are Christ's enemies (2:2, 6, 9, 14-15, 20-24; 3:9). John's primary charge against them is that they are involved in some sort of falsehood, whether they misrepresent themselves (2:2, 9, 20; 3:9), falsely accuse believers (2:9; 3:9) or deceive church members (2:14, 20).[4] John's curses for those who would alter the vision (22:18-19) participate in this motif. In contrast to these deceivers John places Antipas, the "faithful witness" (2:13), and Christ himself, "the faithful and true witness" (3:14), "the true one" (3:7), and "the one who searches minds and hearts" (2:23). By speaking through Christ's voice, and by juxtaposing these opponents against Christ, John's renders his accusations more palatable.

John's heavenly interpreters also lend authority to his accusations. It is through angels that the seal, trumpet, and bowl judg-

---

[3]As I argued in chap. 1, the trouble between Jews and Christians reflected in Rev 2:9 and 3:9 probably resulted from some Christians claiming Jewish identity–whether Jew or Gentile we can only guess–seeking to be members of local Jewish communities. Jewish responses are likely to have varied.

[4]John J. Pilch, "Lying and Deceit in the Letters to the Seven Churches," *BTB* 22 (1992): 126-34. Unfortunately, Pilch crunches these charges into the familiar honor-shame framework, which, though often helpful heuristically, merely obscures John's concerns with his opponents here. Certainly John seeks to bring shame upon his enemies, but he is primarily concerned that they are threatening himself and his audience or that their teaching is contrary to his own, not because they are violating honor/shame conventions.

ments are administered; even more significant for our purposes is the role of heavenly figures in interpreting these horrific happenings. As the final three trumpet judgments bring a new ferocity to the world's suffering, an eagle flying in middle heaven announces, "Woe, woe, woe to the inhabitants of the earth, from the noise of the trumpets that the three angels are about to blow!" (8:13).[5] The twenty-four elders praise God for executing the divine wrath (11:16-18), and unnamed heavenly voices direct John (14:13) and announce the Lamb's victory (12:10-12; 18:4-8, 21-24; 19:1-4, 6-8, 17-18). In addition to telling John what to do (10:8-11; 11:1-2; 17:1-2; 19:9-10; 21:9), angels also announce judgment (9:13-14; 10:5-7; 14:6-11, 15, 17-18; 16:5-6; 18:2-3) and interpret John's vision (17:1-2, 7-18). Finally, a voice from the heavenly temple, presumably God's,[6] endorses the carnage (16:1, 17) and announces the new age (21:5-8). When John's vision enters its most objectionable stages, heavenly voices endorse it and silence dissent.

The martyrs represent a final category of the heavenly voices John uses. They first appear asking God how long they must wait until God avenges their blood against the earth's inhabitants (6:9-10).

Commentators debate whether the voices in 7:9-10 and 19:1-3 are also those of martyrs. According to G. R. Beasley-Murray, the

---

[5]According to Charles, the eagle is flying in the sun's zenith, a place between earth and heaven (agreeing with Wilhelm Bousset, *Die Offenbarung Johannis* [Göttingen: Vandenhoeck & Ruprecht, 1906] 297). An eagle also serves as a revelatory messenger in *2 Baruch* 77:19-26 (Charles, *A Critical and Exegetical Commentary on the Revelation of St. John*, 2 vols., ICC [Edinburgh: T.&T. Clark; New York: Scribners, 1920] 1:237). While Roloff speculates about the eagle's possible status as an unclean bird and therefore an unclean messenger (Jürgen Roloff, *The Revelation of John*, trans. John E. Alsup, Continental Commentaries [Minneapolis: Fortress, 1993] 111-12), Baruch addresses the eagle as "higher than any other bird." Malina argues that the eagle is Pegasus, one of the four constellations on the celestial equator. The other three are Leo (Lion), Taurus (Bull), and Scorpio (human-faced), each resembling one of the four living creatures in Rev 4:7 (Bruce J. Malina, *On the Genre and Message of Revelation: Star Visions and Sky Journeys* [Peabody MA: Hendrickson, 1995] 100).

[6]Henry Barclay Swete, *The Apocalypse of St. John: The Greek Text with Introduction, Notes, and Indices*, 3rd ed. (London: Macmillan and Co., 1911) 200. But Rev 21:3-5 distinguishes between a voice from the throne and the one seated on the throne.

majority of modern commentators, though lacking textual warrant, read them as martyrs.[7] And Collins notes that the robes of the crowd in 7:9-10 are white because they have been washed in the Lamb's blood, not necessarily through their own martyrdom.[8] Schüssler Fiorenza adopts a middle position, suggesting that the crowd has survived eschatological suffering and somehow speculating that the crowd might not consist exclusively of Christians.[9] Richard provides good reasons for associating them with the martyrs in 6:9-10, pointing to their white robes and conquest imagery.[10] Because the martyrs' white robes in 6:11 are echoed in 7:9, and the song of triumph in 19:1-3 strongly resembles the one in 7:10,[11] I suggest that the same crowd appears in all three passages.

So what do the martyrs do? They endorse God's judgment against John's enemies and God's protection of the elect. In 6:9-10 they cry out for vengeance against humanity (the "inhabitants of the earth"), whom they hold accountable for their blood. In 7:9-10 they praise God and the Lamb, presumably for sparing the saints from some of the eschatological plagues, and in 19:1-3 they praise God's righteous judgments, especially the destruction of Babylon. Because the martyrs have crossed the boundaries between earthly and heavenly existence, their songs carry special pathos for John's audience. As those who have lost their lives for their testimony, the martyrs are especially persuasive when they cry for vengeance against humanity. Since John's audience would likely be reluctant to desire indiscriminate judgment upon all human beings, the martyrs give them reasons to do so. Read rhetorically, the heavenly martyrs are more persuasive on debatable issues than would be John's own voice.

The Apocalypse closes with a cacophony of heavenly voices and John's, all endorsing the book's significance in some form or another. Those who would do evil, whether old-fashioned evil like

---

[7]G. R. Beasley-Murray, *Revelation*, rev. ed., NCB (Grand Rapids MI, Eerdmans, 1981) 145.

[8]Adela Yarbro Collins, *The Apocalypse*, New Testament Message 22 (Collegeville MN: Michael Glazier, 1979) 53.

[9]*Revelation*, 68.

[10]*Apocalypse*, 74.

[11]Caird, *Revelation*, 100, 232.

sorcery or *porneia* (22:15) or less traditional offenses like altering John's message (22:18-19), are excluded from the city.

All early Jewish and Christian apocalypticists used heavenly voices to authorize their visions, so much so that their role figures in John J. Collins's influential definition of an apocalypse ("in which a revelation is mediated by an otherworldly being to a human recipient . . . ").[12] In many cases, the heavenly voices authorize the apocalypses' functions, sometimes justifying difficult positions, purposes similar to those we find in Revelation. A striking example of this pattern occurs in *4 Ezra*. Ezra challenges the angel Uriel to explain why Israel, the only nation to know God and believe the covenants, suffers while the "inhabitants of the earth" prosper. The answer is difficult to hear, so it comes from Uriel's mouth. Uriel defies Ezra to explain fire's weight, to measure the wind, and to bring back the past, demonstrating that mortals cannot understand God's mysteries (3:28-4:11). John pushes this device even farther, consistently using heavenly voices—Christ, the angels, the voice from the throne, the martyrs, and unspecified voices—to attack his various enemies.

(Dis)Identification, Remythologization

Kenneth Burke's concept of identification helped us grasp John's attempts to win his audience's credibility. But the other side of John's task is to promote hostility toward his opponents by identifying them with persons, places, or values his audience is likely to hate. John accomplishes this goal by drawing upon Israel's stories and contemporary mythology.

One of John's techniques is to assign allusive names to his enemies. This technique applies to two of his opponents in the letters to the churches, and possibly to a third. John names one Christian prophet Balaam and another Jezebel; he also refers to the Nicolaitans, a Christian movement, but we do not know the origin of that name.[13] For "Balaam" and "Jezebel," however, we can see

---

[12]"Towards the Morphology of a Genre," 9.

[13]While Balaam is a non-Israelite prophet in Numbers, the name Balaam and the term Nicolaitan mean roughly the same thing in Hebrew and Greek, respectively: "lord/conqueror of the people" (Charles, *Revelation*, 1:52-53). For Hemer,

how John's characterization works. As we saw in chapter 1, these two probably advised Christians to participate in the broader cultural life by eating food that had been sacrificed to idols. Doing so would allow Christians to attend civic and social functions, but John objected that it would also imply apostasy. So John assigns the names of two Hebrew Bible villains to these opponents.

Balaam and Jezebel have a lot in common. John distinguishes them by applying gender-specific charges and punishments to Jezebel, but otherwise both names hearken back to non-Israelite HB figures who "suggest an association of royal authority and disloyalty to God,"[14] particularly through assimilation with other peoples. Balaam's story is somewhat elusive. In Num 22–24 Balaam accepts money to curse Israel on its path into Canaan, but YHWH prevents him. The next chapter of Numbers explains that the Israelites began worshiping the Baal of Peor and other deities because the Israelite men were having relations with Moabite women (25:1-3). Through a slip in the literary sources, the Moabite controversy becomes one involving Midianites, and YHWH tells Moses to defeat the Midianites (25:6-17). Balaam is slaughtered along with the Midianites (31:8), and he is blamed—as are the Midianite women—for the earlier incident of apostasy (31:16).

Jezebel likewise serves as a hindrance to biblical Israel. As soon as Ahab begins to rule the Northern Kingdom, he marries Jezebel the Sidonian. Immediately, he begins to serve Baal (1 Kgs 16:31-32). Jezebel herself becomes an active promoter of Baal, persecuting YHWH's prophets (18:4) and threatening to kill Elijah (19:2). She later conspires to steal a vineyard from a landowner by arranging his sham trial and execution (21:1-17). For that offense, Elijah

---

"Balaam and the Nicolaitans are alike in the name and alike in nature" (Colin J. Hemer, *The Letters to the Seven Churches of Asia in Their Social Setting*, JSNTSup [Sheffield UK: JSOT, 1986] 89). But it is doubtful that John simply draws the name Nicolaitan from a play on the Hebrew Balaam, since several early Christian writers mention the Nicolaitans or the teaching of Nicolaus the Antiochene (cf. Acts 6:5; and Irenaeus, *Haer.* 1.26.3; cf. 3.11.1; Hippolytus, *Refutat.* 7.36; Clement of Alexandria, *Strom.* 3.4.25; and Eusebius, *H.E.*, 3.29.1, all cited in Caird, *Revelation*, 31).

[14]Laws, *In the Light of the Lamb*, 44.

predicts that dogs will eat Jezebel's corpse in Jezreel (21:24), a prophecy that is fulfilled in 2 Kgs 9:30-37.

By identifying his Christian opponents with Balaam and Jezebel, John creates a host of negative associations. Both figures connote sexual relations outside the sacred community. In both instances exogamy leads to idolatry, and to such a degree that the one implies the other. And in both cases the results for the sacred community are disastrous: a breakdown of group distinctiveness combined with divine judgment. Balaam's offense leads to a plague upon Israel (Num 31:16), while Jezebel may be the most compelling figure in the Deuteronomistic History's depiction of the Northern Kingdom's apostasy and ultimate destruction. The results of Jezebel's activity are somewhat ambiguous, but they include drought (1 Kgs 17–18), defeat (1 Kgs 22), and internal chaos (2 Kgs 9), not to mention her own grisly death.

John uses identification against cities as well as persons. He twice alludes to city names with resonances in the Hebrew Bible: "the great city, which is spiritually called Sodom and Egypt, where [the] Lord was crucified" (11:8) and "Babylon the great" (14:8; 16:19–19:3). While commentators stumble over how to decode the great city in 11:8,[15] John's use of identification is evident. Just as his charges against Balaam and Jezebel are implied in the names he assigns to them, these city names carry specific implications.

---

[15]Scholars rarely dissent from the view that Babylon points to Rome. With respect to 11:8, critics generally choose among three primary options. Among those who read 11:8 as referring to Jerusalem is Bousset, *Offenbarung*, 321. Those who associate 11:8 with Rome include: Caird, *Revelation*, 137-38; John M. Court, *Myth and History in the Book of Revelation* (Atlanta: John Knox, 1979) 101-102; Richard, *Apocalypse*, 92; and Schüssler Fiorenza, *Revelation*, 78 (tentatively). A middle route is to blend Jerusalem into Rome and the larger resistant world. Critics who find such a broader spiritual or world-historical significance for the city are: Beasley-Murray, *Revelation*, 185-86; Charles, *Revelation*, 1:287-88 (claiming that the author has modified a source that originally referred to Jerusalem); Austin Farrer, *The Revelation of St. John the Divine* (Oxford: Clarendon, 1964) 135; Harrington, *Revelation*, 122; Krodel, *Revelation*, 225-26; Pierre Prigent, *L'Apocalypse de Saint Jean*, CNT 14 (Lausanne: Delachaux & Niestl, 1981) 168; Roloff, *Revelation*, 133; Swete, *Apocalypse*, 138; and Wall, *Revelation*, 146-47. Adela Yarbro Collins, for whom 11:8 points to Jerusalem ("Oppression from Without: The Symbolization of Rome as Evil in Early Christianity," *Concilium* 200 [1988]: 68), also links the city to non-Christian Jews (*Apocalypse*, 73).

Sodom is traditionally associated with arrogance and injustice (Ezek 16:48-50; Wis 19:14-15) and later comes to stand for sexual immorality (Jude 7). Egypt and Babylon are the models for the Israel's oppression. Babylon is also distinguished as the city that destroyed Jerusalem and the Temple, an association with echoes in Daniel and later apocalyptic literature. It is likely that here John is stacking up identifications against Rome. Rome is the "great city"—Sodom, plus Egypt, plus Babylon, all the great bad cities rolled up into one. In addition, Rome has become Jerusalem, "the city where [the] Lord was crucified"; when Christ's witnesses are executed and raised after three days, they fulfill the pattern set by Jesus.[16] In Rev 11 John accuses Rome, the great city, of Jesus' death and the deaths of his followers.

Besides biblical allusions, John also draws upon Near Eastern mythological types that have resonances in the Hebrew Bible and in early Jewish apocalyptic literature.[17] Struggles between chaos monsters and the divine forces of order pervade Near Eastern mythology, and they sometimes appear in the Hebrew Bible in more or less sublimated forms (Ps 74:13-14; 89:9-10; Job 9:13; 26:12-13; Isa 27:1; and perhaps Gen 3). The myth almost always links chaos monsters with the sea. Several times international powers

---

[16]Why not read 11:8 as a direct reference to Jerusalem? Several factors argue against that choice. (1) The combination of terms, "Sodom and Egypt, where their Lord was crucified," is to be understood πνευματικῶς, a designation that does not apply to "the great city" and invites allegorical interpretation. (2) Outside the letters in Rev 2–3, every other city name in the apocalypse is metaphorical. (3) Jerusalem plays no other role in the Apocalypse, except as a model for the eschatological New Jerusalem. (4) John calls Rome the "great city" in Rev 16–18, the only other occurrences of the phrase. (5) Rev 11:4 stands the two witnesses "before the Lord of the earth," implying their presence in Rome (and possibly indicating an association with Peter and Paul). (6) Given other evidence that Revelation was written *after* Jerusalem's fall, when there would have been no Temple, and the considerations above, it seems reasonable to read Rev 11:8 "spiritually," identifying Sodom, Egypt, and Jerusalem with the other "great city," Babylon/Rome. I do not regard this reading as certain; however, our interest lies more with *how* John attacks his opponents than with *who* they are. In this case we can observe John's use of identification without claiming certainty for identifying the great city of 11:8 with Rome.

[17]More detailed discussions include: Cohn, *Cosmos, Chaos*; Court, *Myth and History*; Adela Yarbro Collins, *The Combat Myth in the Book of Revelation*, HDR 9 (Missoula MT: Scholars Press, 1976); *Crisis and Catharsis*, 147-49.

are identified with figures of chaos (Isa 30:7; Ezek 32:2-8), and Isa 51:9-11 combines a purely mythological reference to the sea monster Rahab with an overt reference to the Exodus account of YHWH drying up the sea.[18]

Particularly well woven is John's tapestry of identifications among the Dragon, the Beast, and the Other Beast. By identifying emperor, Empire, and populace as beastly, and by linking the two Beasts to the Dragon, John uses the chaos monster myth against them. The Dragon is Satan (12:9), who opposes God's people (the Woman Clothed with the Sun) throughout time. A heavenly figure, the Dragon is cast down to the earth and the sea, and uses floods to persecute the Woman, her child, and her other offspring (12:3-17). As I argued in Chapter 1, the Beast is John's cipher for emperor and Empire. Its functions are to oppress people, support the imperial city (Babylon; 17:3), draw worship to itself, and persecute believers. Like the Dragon, from whom it receives its power (13:2), the Beast has seven heads and ten horns (12:3; 13:1). The Other Beast is Dragon-like in its speech (13:11), and its purpose is to promote worship of the Beast. It seems to represent popular or official pressure to participate in the imperial cult. So the Beast and the Other Beast are empowered by and derive from the Dragon, the ultimate force of evil and chaos.

While the two beasts are identified with the Dragon, they are also set against God and the Lamb. Both the Lamb and the Beast have received new life after mortal wounds (5:6; 13:3; 17:9-11). The risen Christ is "the first and the last, yes, the living One" (1:17-18), and God is "the Alpha and the Omega . . . who is and who was and who is coming" (1:8), but the Beast "was and is not, but is about to ascend" (17:8). Riding on the white horse, Christ has a secret name, which is the Word of God (19:12-13); the Beast, upon whom the Whore rides, also has a secret name, which is blasphemous (13:1; 17:3). The Other Beast has "two horns like a lamb" (13:11) and marks the Beast's followers on the right hand or forehead (13:16), just as the Lamb's are marked on the forehead (7:3; 14:1). Most important, just as the Lamb is worshiped with

---

[18]Laws, *In the Light of the Lamb*, 39.

God (5:13; 7:10; 11:15; 12:10), so is the Beast worshiped along with the Dragon (13:4).[19]

Biblical allusion meets cosmic beast in John's depiction of Babylon the Whore and her relationship with the Beast (Rev 16:19–19:3). John first hears of "the great city" Babylon through announcements of its destruction (14:8; 16:19), but he fully characterizes Babylon in a flashback (17–18). Babylon comes with triple identifications: (a) to Rome; (b) to biblical condemnations of πορνεία; and (c) to the Babylon that destroyed Jerusalem and conducted the Exile. After an angel announces her arrival, John sees her riding on the Beast. The Beast's seven heads, ten horns, and mortal wound indicate its identity with the Beast of Rev 13 (17:3, 8). Further linking the Beast to Rome is one half of the interpretation of its seven heads: they are seven mountains where the woman dwells (17:9), a pointed allusion to Rome's seven hills.[20] Rome alone possessed the characteristics John might associate with the Whore: allegiance from people and rulers around the world (17:2), authority over international trade, and the will and ability to kill Christians (17:6).[21]

In addition to using the mythological Beast to characterize Babylon, John draws upon biblical resources. The LXX labels Gomer's activity πορνεία as a means of depicting Israel's infidelity to God (e.g., Hosea 1:2; cf. Lev 20:5; Jer 3:1-9; Ezek 23); John accuses his Christian opponents, Balaam and Jezebel, of πορνεία as well. But the Whore is not linked to John's Christian enemies as are Balaam and Jezebel. Here John is using πόρνη in a different sense: to indicate Rome's international involvement. In the Bible Israel is not alone in being vilified as a whore; the title also applies to cities like Nineveh (Nah 3:4) and Tyre (Isa 23:1-18), both of which are condemned for their international politics. Like Nineveh, Rome dominates by international coalitions and by violence; like Tyre, Rome is a commercial network known for generating wealth.

---

[19]Laws, *In the Light of the Lamb*, 41-42.

[20]See Charles (*Revelation*, 2:69) for references to Rome as "the city on seven hills" in Latin literature.

[21]John did not invent the designation of Rome as Babylon. Cf. *Sib. Or.* 5.143, 159; *2 Baruch* 67:7 (Roloff, *Revelation*, 175).

Only those who benefit from its political and commercial power weep over Babylon's destruction.[22] Rome, in Asia Minor often imaged through the mother goddess Roma,[23] is not to be regarded as a divine life-giver but as a murdering whore.

In biblical tradition, Babylon is the city responsible for the destruction of Jerusalem and the first Temple just as Rome had ruined the city and the Temple in 70 C.E. Jeremiah 50:21–51:64 complains of the Judeans' oppression in Babylon (50:33) and imagines the city's destruction as God's vengeance for Israel and Judah, and for the Temple in particular (50:28). And Isaiah 13–14, which most scholars date to the Exile,[24] depicts Babylon as a wicked oppressor soon to be destroyed like Sodom and Gomorrah. For the prophets, Babylon's defeat by the Persians represented God's judgment. By associating Rome with Babylon, John characterizes a conquering and oppressive power soon to face its own destruction.

John also manages to provide a counteridentification for Babylon/Rome. While Babylon is the Whore, the New Jerusalem is Christ's Bride. Each woman is introduced by one of the bowl-bearing angels who says, "Come and I will show you . . . " (17:1; 21:9). Babylon is "the great city"; the New Jerusalem is "the holy city" (21:2). The Bride wears bright linen (19:8) and is adorned with jewels (21:19-21); the Whore is "decked out in purple and scarlet" (17:4).[25] The Bride descends from heaven (21:2); the Whore is seated upon many waters (17:1). Most important, the Bride marries the Lamb, while the Whore rides upon the Beast.[26] By identifying the Whore with the Beast, πορνεία, and images of Babylon in the Hebrew Bible, and by counteridentifying her with the New Jerusalem, John effectively characterizes Rome as a center

---

[22]Míguez, "Apocalyptic and the Economy."

[23]Adela Yarbro Collins, "Feminine Symbolism in the Book of Revelation," *Biblical Interpretation* 1 (1993): 27; Boring, *Revelation*, 179.

[24]John F. A. Sawyer, "Isaiah, the Book of," in *The Oxford Companion to the Bible*, ed. Bruce M. Metzger and Michael D. Coogan (New York: Oxford University Press, 1993) 326.

[25]Yarbro Collins, "Feminine Symbolism," 25-26.

[26]For John's gender-specific degradation of Babylon, see the section on "Debasing" below.

of corruption and oppression, and as the antithesis of what is good.

Through identification John also manages to connect Jews and humanity in general with the demonic. By referring to Jews as the "synagogue of Satan" (2:9; 3:9),[27] John chooses to dismiss their perspective by attacking their collective ethos. Essentially the same function is performed by describing "the inhabitants of the earth" as worshiping the Beast (13:8-14; cf. 17:8) and being intoxicated by the Whore (17:2). Since the Whore rides the Beast, and the Beast is empowered by the Dragon, it is no wonder the "inhabitants" are so evil: They kill Christians (6:10; 11:10), they are incapable of repentance (9:20-21), and they curse God for their punishments (16:9).

Today's Bible prophecy readers bear witness to John's effectiveness. His rhetoric enables Hal Lindsey to characterize entire population groups by labels one can only call prejudicial. "Russia Is a Gog," "Sheik to Sheik," and "The Yellow Peril" serve as chapter titles in *The Late Great Planet Earth*.[28] His identifications of characters within the Apocalypse (and other biblical literature) may stun critical readers, but one must admit that John's rhetoric empowers such pungent characterizations.

Edward Said names this process: textual characters become "real" by simple reinscription.

> Such "images" of the Orient as [Mohammed the imposter] are images in that they represent or stand for a very large entity, otherwise impossibly diffuse, which they enable one to grasp or see.[29]

In the case of Revelation it is not only the corporate characters who become reified. John's Christian opponents in the seven letters actually become who John says they are. These persons, code-named the Nicolaitans, Balaam, and Jezebel, whose actual names

---

[27]Whether the allusions in 2:9 and 3:9 are in fact to Jews remains a matter of debate. See the discussion in chap. 1.

[28]Also notable is Lindsey's identification of the 144,000 sealed persons from Israel's twelve tribes as "144,000 Jewish Billy Grahams turned loose on this earth" (*Late Great Planet Earth*, 99). How does he identify 12,000 Zebulunites as Jewish?

[29]*Orientalism*, 66.

and characters are lost to us, now function as paradigms for various sorts of evil. In fact, it becomes necessary for some commentators to identify them authoritatively. Prophecy teacher Grant R. Jeffrey, for example, traces the etymology of "Nicolaitan" (people-conqueror?) to a particularly dangerous heresy: Some Christians must be claiming spiritual authority over others. Not surprisingly, Jeffrey locates this heresy as the root of the later Christian priesthood and "the spiritual 'Dark Ages' of the medieval period."[30]

Critical biblical scholars no less than popular commentators follow John's characterization. How can a commentator claim to be doing a good job if she does not wrestle with such details as identifying John's opponents? It is the nature of commentary as a genre to follow John's characterization wherever it may lead. Though more resistant voices are being heard (mostly from outside the commentary traditions), the vast majority of commentators vary little from Jeffrey's strategy of accepting John's representation as reflective of some "reality."[31]

Identification provides John with an exquisitely flexible tool. Just as he builds his own ethos by linking himself with the martyrs, apostles, prophets, Christ, and other heavenly beings, he can also use identification against his opponents. They are all the same. Ultimately, other-minded Christians, Jews, and Gentile neighbors are all tied to the Dragon through their associations with the Beast and the Whore. According to John, his Christian opponents accommodate themselves to the Beast, while his Jewish neighbors use the Beast's resources to harm Christians. Other people, mesmerized by the Beast and intoxicated by the Whore, participate in oppressive, finally blasphemous, systems and present a danger to John and his audience. Through identification, John levels all differences among these diverse antagonists.

---

[30]*Apocalypse*, 73.

[31]Prime examples of scholarly efforts to pin the name on the heretic occur in Hemer, *Letters*.

Parody and Satire

Though parody is a primary resource of resistance authors today, it has long served political ends. Parody, which takes available modes of discourse and makes them the objects of representation and criticism,[32] and satire, which does the same with persons and institutions, were staples of the Greco-Roman literary scene. According to Richard Terdiman, such texts work

> by exaggerating traits of an individual argument or style in such a way that we experience the deformation, but as one consistent with characteristics recognizable in the original.[33]

Parody and satire could range from Aristophanes' gentle needling of Socrates in *Clouds* ("I tread on air and contemplate the sun.") to Seneca's gleeful shaming of Claudius in the *Apocolocyntosis* ("Let him die; allow a better man to reign in his empty court.").[34]

When they served political ends, parody and satire could be particularly sharp—and dangerous. Ramsey Macmullen offers a litany of Roman poets who suffered exile or execution for their witty critique.[35] Persius's fifth satire celebrates Stoic freedom and advances that assassin of emperors, Brutus, as an example of the free person (lines 83-87). Somewhat safer were Seneca and Juvenal, who only poked fun at emperors who were already dead.

How did classical parody and satire work? They were a mixture of the serious and the fantastic, the comic and the fabulous.[36] According to Mikhail Bakhtin, the inappropriate is a leading topos among Latin satires. One finds:

---

[32]Bakhtin, *Dialogic Imagination*, 51.

[33]*Discourse/Counter-Discourse*, 202.

[34]*Clouds*, in *The Complete Plays of Aristophanes*, trans. Moses Hadas, Bantam Classics (New York: Bantam Books, 1962) 108; *Apocolocyntosis Divi Claudii*, ed. and trans. Apostolos Athanassakis (Lawrence KS: Coronado Press, 1973) 63.

[35]*Enemies of the Roman Order: Treason, Unrest, and Alienation in the Empire* (New York: Routledge, 1992; [1]1966) 36-45.

[36]Bakhtin, *Dialogical Imagination*, 26-27; H. K. Riikonen, *Menippean Satire as a Literary Genre with Special Reference to Seneca's Apocolocyntosis*, Commentationes Humanarum Litterarum 83 (Helsinki: Finnish Society of Sciences and Letters, 1987) 31.

> scandal scenes, eccentric behavior, . . . violations of the generally accepted and customary course of events and the established norms of behavior and etiquette.[37]

While comic, these transgressions are deadly serious at the same time. They serve to unsettle norms and disturb monologic discourses. Bakhtin again: They provide

> the creation of *extraordinary situations* for the provoking and testing of a philosophical idea, a discourse, a *truth*, embodied in the image of a wise man, the seeker of this truth.[38]

Perhaps the most frequent topos of Greek and Latin parody was *hybris*, or presumptuous behavior. In a society in which the economy of honor was paramount, what could be more offensive than an overly presumptuous person or institution? And what better form for characterizing *hybris* than parody or satire? An example: Domitian was noted for reinstating strict moral laws. But he had hidden his incestuous relationship with his niece by ordering an abortion procedure in which she died. Juvenal brings Domitian's *hybris* "before the eyes": Domitian awakens the old laws even as Julia's abortuses—which look very much like their uncle—are being delivered (*Satire* 2.29-33).

So ancient Greek and Roman parody and satire had a biting edge; they could be serious, sometimes dangerous, business. And their primary political use was to criticize those who were, as we Southerners say, "getting too big for their britches." The best way to point out human follies and frailties in those persons or institutions which seemed untouchable or self-evident was to identify them with thc ridiculous.

Contemporary resistance literatures employ parody to subvert colonial discourses. Unable to avoid the language of the empire, they twist it for their own purposes, a tactic Ashcroft, Griffiths, and Tiffin call "abrogation and appropriation."[39] Whether or not

---

[37]*Problems of Dostoevsky's Poetics*, ed. and trans. Caryl Emerson, Theory and History of Literature 8 (Minneapolis: University of Minnesota Press, 1984) 117.

[38]Ibid., 114.

[39]Bill Ashcroft, Gareth Griffiths, and Helen Tiffin, *The Empire Writes Back:*

John realizes that "cultural practices [cannot] return to some 'pure' and unsullied cultural condition,"[40] he turns imperial discourse against itself by appropriating its language, imagery, and mythology.

John especially digs at claims to imperial supremacy. He describes God as the *Pantocrator* (παντοκράτωρ), the term that translates *YHWH Ṣĕbāôt* (יהוה צבאות) in the LXX, and a term unique in the NT (with the exception of 2 Cor 6:18, which follows a pastiche of LXX quotations).[41] Reflecting "Revelation's deep theological concern about power,"[42] the term reaches beyond allusion to the LXX. Instead, the term is revolutionary. Some of Domitian's coins, for example, represented the emperor's deceased son sitting on a globe, a symbol of dominion over the entire world, and others depict the emperor holding Jupiter's thunderbolt.[43] But for John, God, not the Emperor, rules the world, and God's realm is radically democratic. God's people are a priestly dominion (1:6; 5:10): they will wear crowns (2:10; 3:11; 4:4, 10), and those who resist the Beast will rule with Christ in the millennium (20:4).[44] John flatly rejects imperial authority by substituting a radically democratic vision.

We have seen that John identifies the Empire with mythological chaos monsters. But these mythological motifs also parody imperial uses of mythology. The common myth of a woman (Leto or Isis) pursued by a dragon (Python or Seth-Typhon) and delivered by Apollo (cf. Rev 12) served to convey the message that the emperor is the divine restorer of order, as emperors identified

---

Theory and Practice in Post-Colonial Literatures, New Accents (New York: Routledge, 1989) 38-39.

[40]Ibid., 41-42.

[41]Rev 1:8; 4:8; 11:17; 15:3; 16:7, 14; 19:6, 15; 21:22.

[42]Schüssler Fiorenza, *Revelation*, 45. Schüssler Fiorenza goes on to note that it is God's identity as παντοκράτωρ that guarantees John's ethos.

[43]Ernest P. Janzen, "The Jesus of the Apocalypse Wears the Emperor's Clothes," *SBLSP* 33 (1994): 644-48.

[44]Is the identity of those who rule with Christ restricted to martyrs? The καί that joins the martyrs with "those who had neither worshiped the Beast nor its image and had not accepted its mark upon their foreheads or hands" may well be paratactic (BDF §444).

themselves with Apollo and Zeus.[45] Revelation's combat myth reverses these imperial identifications by making a Beast out of the Emperor, even painting the Beast red like Seth-Typhon (12:3).[46] Rome's emperors create not order but chaos in John's mythological twist.

Revelation features several examples of internal parody, in which one aspect of the Apocalypse plays against others. One example is the marks on the right hand and forehead given to the Beast's followers (13:16). R. H. Charles, who posits a Hebrew original beneath Rev 13,[47] maintains that the marks are "full of significance." Some Jews wore phylacteries on the left hand and on the head, but the Beast's followers are marked on the right hand and the forehead.[48] Because Charles's suggestion depends upon his source-critical conclusions, it overlooks the other ancient practices that may have served as a background for John's image. Among these are the imperial stamp on documents and coins, the branding of slaves and captives, and perhaps priestly ornaments in the imperial cult.[49] It may be that the most significant thing about the marks is that they are a poor imitation of those borne by God's servants, who have God's seal upon their foreheads (7:3; cf. Ezek 9:4, 6).

As we have seen, John plays the Beast against the Lamb at several other points. According to Sophie Laws, both figures are characterized by: life after a mortal wound; past, present, and future significance; physical resemblances; secret names; and receiving worship.[50] The Beast rises out of the sea, and the Dragon stands on the shore (12:18–13:1), but the Lamb opposes them from Mount Zion (14:1). The parallels do not end yet. Beast and Lamb oppose each other in terms of speech and presence. Both figures speak through prophets, but the Beast is known through an image. Though the Lamb is the true Lion (5:5), the beast utters blasphemy

---

[45]Jan Willem van Henten, "Dragon Myth and Imperial Ideology in Revelation 12-13," *SBLSP* 33 (1994): 496-515.

[46]Ibid., 504.

[47]*Revelation*, 1:lxiv.

[48]Ibid., 1:362.

[49]Caird, *Revelation*, 172-73.

[50]*Light of the Lamb*, 41-42.

toward God (13:5-6) with a mouth like a lion's (13:2). Humans can only hear the Beast speak through the Other Beast's magic (13:14-15). By contrast, the Lamb's speech is "real" and terrible: the Lamb's mouth is a weapon (1:16; 2:16; 19:15, 21). And the Lamb's presence is overwhelming, always provoking worship (1:17; 5:8-14; 14:1-3), while the Other Beast must compel people to worship the first Beast (13:12). Finally, the Beast carries the Whore on his back, but the Lamb awaits a heavenly bride, the New Jerusalem.

John uses parody to unmask imperial *hybris*. The Empire and its rulers represent not order but chaos; God, and not the emperor, rules the world. Neither Empire nor emperor is eternal, but God is. John does not employ parody so much against Jews, other Christians, and "the inhabitants of the earth" as he does against the Empire. References to the "synagogue of Satan" (2:9; 3:9) and "the so-called deep things of Satan" (2:24) represent not so much parody as invective. It is likely that John's decision to apply parody against the Empire reveals the seriousness with which he regards it. Parody is especially appropriate when appearances are deceptive; it is the perfect tool for revealing imperial pretensions.

Taunting and Debasing

Many readers have noticed that the Apocalypse expresses a certain glee over the suffering it imagines for others. Arthur P. Mendel writes, "Virtually the whole of [Revelation] is an account of the violence, devastation, suffering, and death necessary to purge the world and clear the way for the pure and perfect Kingdom."[51] And because "Revelation works against the values of humanization and love" by "[involving] the degradation of others," Adela Yarbro Collins suggests that it represents "a partial and imperfect vision."[52] But aside from theological and ethical evaluation, what rhetorical purposes are served when John and his characters praise God over the harm others suffer? And what purpose is served by the way John mocks his opponents?

---

[51]*Vision and Violence* (Ann Arbor: University of Michigan Press, 1992) 39.
[52]*Crisis and Catharsis*, 172.

David Spurr's study of colonial rhetoric may help us understand why John taunts and debases his opponents. Spurr argues that debasement, characterizing people in terms of filth or defilement, has more to do with writers or speakers than with their subjects. In colonial discourse, debasement typically involves abjection, the claim that the colonized need the intervention of civilized nations. It offers a negative pole against which colonizers can affirm their own values and social codes as civilized. In other words, debasement enables colonizers to cope with self-doubt in the face of sociocultural stress.[53]

While they promise a kind of certainty over John's opponents, debasement and taunting may actually betray his uncertainty. Those boundaries that John would maintain, which would separate Christians from the rest of humanity and would define Christian superiority, are crumbling. Even some Christian voices have been suggesting accommodation to the larger society. Rather than *argue* why complete withdrawal is the appropriate Christian response to the rest of society, John applies debasement and taunting to undermine his opponents' legitimacy.

Unlike the writers Spurr surveys, John writes from the underside of the colonial equation. Revelation is resistance literature. He does not argue that his audience should lift the Empire or his neighbors out of their depravity; instead, he totally belittles them. Christ's return is not good news for the rest of society—"on his account all the tribes of the earth will wail" (1:7).

In the previous chapter I argued that John spends tremendous energy justifying his vision, especially when it is likely to estrange his audience. In the Apocalypse the underside of justification is taunting. By imagining his opponents' humiliation, John suggests that they are unworthy of sympathy. One day Jews will bow before his audience's feet, forced to acknowledge the divine favor Christians enjoy (3:9). The general population will suffer ugly and evil sores, and their sources of water will become blood—after all, "they deserve it" (16:5-6). It is true that John enjoys fantasizing about suffering for his opponents, as taunting them offers one means of dismissing their claims for legitimacy or sympathy.

---

[53]*Rhetoric of Empire*, 76-78.

John's disposition toward the world is evident in his critique of Babylon/Rome.[54] In predicting Babylon's fall John both debases and taunts the city and those who associate with it. Forced to acknowledge Rome's grand reputation among his neighbors, John first perceives the city as a regal woman. "Decked out in purple and scarlet . . . [and] adorned with gold and precious stones and pearls" (17:4), she rides the scarlet Beast. John then works against Rome by debasing it. As John has been told (17:1), the regal woman is in fact a drunken, cannibalistic Whore. Intoxicated by human blood, she rides the hideous Beast. Upon her destruction, the heavenly multitude rejoices: "Allelujah! Her smoke rises for ever and ever" (19:3).

The Whore is grotesque in the fullest possible sense, at once both repulsive and attractive. The modern reader might recall Kurtz's African lover in Conrad's *Heart of Darkness*, the "wild and gorgeous apparition of a woman":

> She walked with measured steps, draped in striped and fringed cloths, treading the earth proudly, with a slight jingle and flash of barbarous ornaments. . . . She must have had the value of several elephant tusks upon her. She was savage and superb, wild-eyed and magnificent; there was something ominous and stately in her deliberate progress.[55]

Even though John depicts Babylon/Rome as an oppressor, many people mourn its destruction (18:9-19). Does John's representation of their distress express a sympathy for Rome in its impending suffering?[56] According to G. B. Caird, John depicts Babylon's fall "with exemplary restraint"; "with infinite pathos" he observes her destruction.[57] But there is nothing in Rev 18 to conceal

---

[54]Significantly, Spurr notes affinities to Rev 17–18 in particular examples of colonial discourse (*Rhetoric of Empire*, 90).

[55]Joseph Conrad, *Heart of Darkness* (New York: Dover, 1990; [1]1902) 55-56.

[56]On primarily structural and form-critical grounds, Adela Yarbro Collins argues that the dirges in Rev 18 "express no sympathy or regret on the part of the author" ("Revelation 18: Taunt-Song or Dirge?" in *L'Apocalypse johannique et l'Apocalyptique dans le Nouveaux Testament*, ed. J. Lambrecht, BETL 53 [Gembloux: J. Duculot, 1980] 203).

[57]*Revelation*, 227.

John's glee over the catastrophe. From a literary perspective, Babylon's fall is John's creation. Four times the event is heralded by heavenly voices (14:8; 17:1; 18:2, 4), and the mourners are silenced by the pronouncements that frame their appearances. In 18:4-8, a heavenly voice calls God's people to withdraw from the sinful and arrogant city, and 18:20 invites the audience to *rejoice* over its destruction. John taunts Babylon's mourners along with the city. Even as they put dust on their heads and cry out for her, a voice (probably John's) calls the audience to rejoice (18:19-20).[58]

Something at once violent and erotic is at work in John's image of the Whore. Tina Pippin has argued that this familiar combination participates in Revelation's larger fascination with death, especially the high value placed upon martyrdom. Pippin, who acknowledges that the Whore's death has everything to do with resistance against "the dominant ideology of power and oppression,"[59] opts to emphasize the misogynist over the liberative potential of this scene. Her choice spotlights John's partial submission to the Whore's attractiveness.[60] The Whore's destruction affixes violence to the erotic, but it is also subversive—subversive of Rome and subversive of John's vision itself. According to Spurr, debasement is an attempt to repel the longing to "go native"; it is the ultimate recognition of something desirable in the other.[61] As we have seen, that itch is the one John scratches; he is concerned that his audience will accommodate themselves to the larger culture. Though John writes from the underside of the colonial relation, his fear is that Rome's desirability will seduce his audience. To a degree, it seduces John himself as he fixes his gaze on the Whore.

In the same ways John's characterization of Jezebel (2:20-24) combines fascination with erotic debasement. With a wave of the hand John dismisses Balaam and the Nicolaitans, but he cannot look away from Jezebel, whose teaching is apparently identical to the others'. John belittles her teaching as "the so-called deep things of Satan" (2:24), but he cannot stop there. John's Christ has given

---

[58]Inexplicably, the RSV, NRSV, NIV, NAB, and NASB all assign 18:20 to the mourners!

[59]*Death and Desire*, esp. 57-68.

[60]Ibid., 73.

[61]*Rhetoric of Empire*, 82-87.

her an opportunity to repent, but she remains obstinate. Her gender determines her punishment: her partner/followers will face great distress (θλῖψιν μεγάλην),[62] while Christ will cast her onto a bed (κλίνη) and kill her children. Jezebel's bed offers several interpretive options, with even more connotations than attend the word "bed" today. In various contexts, a bed was a place where people slept, ate (in the sense of a dining couch),[63] had sex, recovered from illness, and died. Bed is an ideal place for John to put Jezebel, whose offenses he associates with diet and sexual immorality.[64] As Babylon must be made desolate and exposed (17:16), so Jezebel faces her own humiliation.

Like Cicero, John taunts and debases his opponents in moments of crisis. Even when Cicero appeared to have suppressed Catalina's rebellion, his own position was tenuous. Only a few of the conspirators had been caught, while others remained in the Senate house and the city. It is when pressing a fragile advantage that Cicero taunts Catalina, saying that, "No single thing you do, nothing you attempt or even contemplate, escapes my notice."[65] And the situation had improved little when Cicero accused his enemy of being behind "every type of criminality and wickedness that you can think of."[66]

John shares Cicero's intensity. Indeed, his use of vivid description (ἐναργεία) to taunt and debase his opponents follows the advice of Cicero and other ancient theorists, who sought character-

---

[62]Though Revelation is filled with allusions to θλίψσις, only Jezebel's partners undergo "great distress."

[63]Following Adolf Deissmann, Hemer notes that κλίνη sometimes referred to dining couches at guild feasts (*Letters*, 252n.62).

[64]Charles argues forcefully that Jezebel's is a sickbed, and that her punishment combines with that of her partners as "a clear instance of Hebrew parallelism" (*Revelation*, 1.71). Reading with Charles are Beasley-Murray (who offers the same argument; *Revelation*, 91), Collins (*Apocalypse*, 22), Pippin (*Death and Desire*, 72), Pierre Prigent (also citing parallelism; *L'Apocalypse de Saint Jean*, CNT 14 [Lausanne: Delachaux & Niestl, 1981] 58), and Wall, (*Revelation*, 78). Though they overlook its possible allusion to meals, Swete (*Apocalypse*, 44), Harrington (*Revelation*, 64), Krodel (*Revelation*, 125), and Roloff (*Revelation*, 55) all note the double entendre built into Rev 2:22.

[65]*Political Speeches*, 79.

[66]Ibid., 97.

ization so graphic that it came "before the eyes."[67] But the techniques denote more than just good strategy. Taunting and debasing also reveal an ambivalence toward John's opponents. John recognizes that other prophets, the synagogue, and the larger culture might attract his audience or draw their sympathy, and his intense rhetoric—especially in its erotic dimensions—suggests his own fascination with his opponents.

Dehumanizing and Negating

Taunting and debasing increase the distance between John and his opponents. Two other techniques that serve a similar function are duhumanizing and negating. John removes from his opponents those signs and behaviors that would give away their humanity.[68] By dehumanizing and negating his opponents, John alienates them from his audience. As Wayne C. Booth claims:

> Every literary work of any power—whether or not its author composed it with his audience in mind—is in fact an elaborate system of controls over the reader's involvement and detachment among *various* lines of interest.[69]

Spurr's study of colonial discourse again provides an avenue for understanding what John is about. Colonial discourse strips the colonized society's history and culture, thus denying its identity. This process gives colonizers a blank slate, making it possible for them to construct their others however they would like.

> A people without history is one which exists only in a negative sense; like the bare earth, they can be transformed by history, but they cannot make history their own.[70]

Having stripped his opponents of their own stories and internal perspectives, John can do with them whatever he likes.

---

[67]Cicero, *De Or.* 2.184; *Style* 208-22; Aristotle, *Poet.* 17.1; Aristotle, *Rhet.* 1.9-10; 3.16.10; Longinus, *Sublime* 15.1; *ad Her.* 4.63-66; Quintilian, *Inst. Or.* 4.1.15.

[68]Booth, *Rhetoric of Fiction*, 155-59; Lanser, *Narrative Act*, 201-22.

[69]*Rhetoric of Fiction*, 123.

[70]*Rhetoric of Empire*, 98.

From a theological perspective, one of the defining marks of human being is the ability to repent. Repentance is a major theme in the seven letters, which include repeated invitations to repent (2:5, 16; 3:3, 19). Jezebel, however, has lost her opportunity (2:21), though John even gives her followers time to repent (2:22). Even more telling is the state of the "inhabitants of the earth." When the general population faces the eschatological plagues, they continue in their ways. They continue to worship idols and pursue crimes (9:20-21); eventually they become so bitter that they curse God (16:9, 11). But never do they repent. Heavenly voices proclaim God's glory and warn that following the Beast leads to destruction, (14:6-11)—but this is hardly a chance to repent. After a brief pause, judgment continues with the reaping of the earth (14:14-16).

William Klassen has written that in Revelation "the purpose is always to bring men to repentance through the tragedies of history."[71] I find this assessment stunning. Revelation's catastrophes have nothing to do with history; they are the direct judgments of God.[72] Nowhere does Revelation indicate that anyone outside the churches will repent; even his audience's hope is in doubt. Instead, an angel tells us, "Let the unjust still do injustice, and let the filthy still be filthy, but let the righteous still do righteousness and let the holy be holy" (22:11). Even when John subordinates other people to his perspective, as when Jews bow before the Christians' feet (3:9) and when every living creature gives glory to the Lamb (5:13; cf. 15:3-4), the purpose seems not so much to hope for their salvation as to erase their perspectives in the service of his own.

Negation can have a leveling effect. Just as Paul's erasure of distinctions between Jew and Greek, slave and free, and male and female promises liberating potential, John does away with status barriers. "Kings, magnates, generals, rich and powerful people—all people, slave and free" undergo God's judgment (6:15-17), whether great or small (20:12-15). But does leveling always lead to liberation? In my opinion, it is too easy to say with Richard that the persons of high status who undergo these upheavals "all . . . are

---

[71]"Vengeance in the Apocalypse of John," *CBQ* 28 (1966): 304.
[72]Caird would disagree (*Revelation*, 90-91).

wicked, since by their power or wealth they are structurally integrated into the Roman Empire."[73] As Schüssler Fiorenza observes, the disasters of Revelation 6 would "devastate especially the poor."[74] Indeed, the powerful suffer, but so do the weak. Revelation simply erases the distinction, offering equal judgment—but not opportunity—to all.

Richard Bauckham would disagree. Bauckham argues that Rev 15:3-4 employs Moses' song in Exodus 15 to express hope for the conversion of the nations.

> And they sing the song of Moses, God's slave,
> and the song of the Lamb:
> "Great and marvellous are your works,
> O Lord God Ruler-of-All;
> Righteous and true are your ways,
> O Ruler of the nations;
> Who would not fear you, O Lord;
> and glorify your name?
> For you alone are holy,
> since all the nations will come
> and bow down before you,
> because your judgments have been revealed."

Bauckham acknowledges that this song is followed by global pictures of judgment for the inhabitants. He accounts for this "tension" by arguing that while Revelation *hopes* for "the faithful witness of the church leading to the repentance and faith of all the nations," it also regards the inhabitants who resist this testimony as "necessarily subject to final judgment."[75]

Bauckham's reading, while attractive, itself falls into the tensions that plague John's vision. John's ethos repeatedly promises more hope than it delivers, but in this case Bauckham has found mercy when there is none. The visions of judgment that follow make perfect sense of the song itself. Nothing about coming and worshiping implies conversion or redemption. Instead, these acts

---

[73]*Apocalypse*, 72.
[74]*Revelation*, 62.
[75]*The Theology of the Book of Revelation*, New Testament Theology (New York: Cambridge University Press, 1993) 103.

are simply the acknowledgment of God's greatness, given the fact of God's judgment. That the inhabitants' worship is motivated primarily by fear simply confirms Revelation's morbid fascination with vengeance. It is the worship of an imperial conquerer by a vanquished people.

Moreover, Bauckham's reading underscores the tensions within John's ethos. His case is strengthened by his reading of Rev 21:3 as an echo of both Ezek 37:27-28 and Zech 2:10-11.[76] While the hope for acceptance of Gentiles is weak at best in Ezekiel, the evidence is stronger for Zechariah. Nevertheless, Zechariah envisions the nations recognizing YHWH as God through Israel's mediation, with God continuing to dwell in the midst of Israel. One might even argue that the issue is Israel's vindication, not the Gentiles' inclusion (cf. Zech 2:12). And since John's churches almost certainly consist of a sampling from the nations, Rev 21:3 amounts to a recentering of John's perspective, along with those who submit to it, over against all competing options.

When push comes to eschatological shove, "the inhabitants" are less than human. John shows less regard for them than he does for plants and animals. It is not surprising that Christians escape, but heavenly orders tell the locusts to spare even the *plants* and afflict only *humans* (9:4). Here John indulges in a little pathos for his opponents: So painful is this ordeal that "the inhabitants" want to die, but they cannot (9:6). Another context in which John erases the boundaries that define the human is Rev 19:17-21, "God's great supper." Here people become food, as the Beast's army literally is offered to the birds. This is the ultimate in unclean dining, as human corpses are devoured by unclean birds.[77]

The prevalence of allusive names in Revelation is consistent with this pattern. What do we really know about the false apostles, Nicolaitans, Balaam, or Jezebel? Does Jezebel really have children (2:23)? John uses these nicknames to mask their true identities. By identifying the emperor with the Beast and Rome with the Whore,

---

[76]Ibid., 103-104.

[77]Lev 11:13-19, 24-28, 39-40; Deut 14:11-21; cf. Jerome H. Neyrey, "The Symbolic Universe of Luke-Acts: 'They Turn the World Upside Down,' " in *The Social World of Luke-Acts: Models for Interpretation*, ed. Jerome H. Neyrey (Peabody MA: Hendrickson, 1991) 286-87.

John has silenced Rome's claims to splendor or beauty. Why should we object when John's enemies are exposed, tortured, and destroyed? Without face or history, John's opponents have nothing to recommend them.

John paints the earth's inhabitants with blank faces. By erasing their humanness, he renders them malleable and frees himself to do whatever he wants with them. They are lower than plants and animals, with no distinctions among them. They lack religious potential since they cannot or will not repent.

Conclusion

There is a tension in ancient rhetorical theory between ethical modesty and the desire for vivid characterization of oneself and one's opponents. John reflects that tension by constructing his ethos as brother, fellow slave, and coparticipant, then abandoning caution in attacking his opponents. Here he sounds more like the Cicero who is menacing Catalina than Cicero the rhetorical theorist.

John's own ethos demands that he tear down opposing claims to authority, particularly those aligned with Rome. Because Revelation is resistance literature, calling out against the Empire from its underside, John adopts a monologic mode of discourse. Given the Empire's vitality, even popularity, and the radical nature of his opposition to it, John cannot afford to acknowledge its voice. Nor can he represent the speech of those who cooperate with the Empire—other Christian preachers, some Jews, and the general population.

Like any good orator in a difficult situation, John takes an indirect approach. His program depends not so much on his arguments against his opponents as upon his own ability to represent them effectively. Rather than prove his case against them, he appeals to his audience's sensibilities by constructing stories and images that align his audience against the Empire and those who support it.[78] Apocalyptic discourse provides just the means for this sort of attack. It offers especially powerful resources for representa-

[78]Cf. *De Part. Or.* 71.

tion and the control of multiple voices. In apocalyptic John finds vivid myths and images with which to characterize his visionary world: composite humans and animals, dragons, visions of heaven and the abyss, and so forth. But perhaps more important, apocalyptic discourse enables John to characterize his opponents without giving voice to their perspectives. Without his vision, John could not claim to see into the future, to learn about the Whore and witness destruction. Apocalyptic also enables John to learn about the Whore from an angel and to hear human mourners from around the world.

Though it is indirect, John's vision is also bold. Rarely does he blink in condemning his enemies. The sole exception may be the pathos when people beg the rocks to fall on them and hide them from God and the Lamb (6:15-17). While it is common to hear that the Apocalypse's intense symbolism is a means of hiding John's program from hostile readers, his condemnation of Rome could scarcely be more obvious. Indeed, John applies the same techniques to his Jewish and Christian enemies. Rather than protect him from official persecution, John's indirect approach shields him from his audience's potential disfavor. It enhances his ethos by allowing him to disparage his opponents even as it distances him from the polemic aspects of his vision.

Chapter 6
Negotiating Ethos?

In its own day the Book of Revelation was a public document. Addressed to Christian communities in Asia Minor, it advocated a particular community practice that at once engaged and resisted the realities of life in the imperium. Almost certainly the Apocalypse met a mixed reception. John's Christian opponents would have understood his message as a direct challenge to their own praxis; others in the audience would also have grasped its implications. While Revelation's first readers and hearers may have differed in their responses, John's subversive characterization of the Empire and his polemic against his Jewish and Christian opponents would have been clear to them all.

Today, however, Revelation is an elusive apocalypse. Despite the near-consensus among scholars as to its basic context and message, in public discourse Revelation's meanings and audiences are fragmented. For example, millenarian readers have effectively constructed a discursive world of their own. Their Apocalypse paints a detailed landscape of earth's last days, and this generation is in the picture. Despite Hal Lindsey's astonishing initial popularity, most outsiders regard the prophecy teachers as curious at best, dangerous at worst, and bizarre all around. The prophecy teachers have a ready response: those who dismiss them are either enemies of the faith or victims of secular indifference.

Likewise, liberationist readers have created their own reading community, with its distinctive interpretation. As John resisted the idolatrous imperial systems of his day, Revelation inspires an alternative praxis for the present. Contemporary imperialism, militarism, and commercialism all resound in John's same Beast. The faithful refuse to participate, testifying to the Beast's true identity. If most readers do not respond to the Apocalypse with such urgent resistance, it is because they are too entangled with the idolatrous Beast to see or act upon the truth.

Ironically, both interpretive communities bear the traces of John's ethos. For one thing, each reflects a sense of alienation from the broader current of society, and each offers an alternative vision to alleviate the tension. But it is the common ethos that configures these that has attracted my interest. Millenarians and liberationists alike reveal a tension between the authoritarian and the egalitarian. Millenarians claim that their literal interpretive strategy is accessible to anyone, but one must submit to it to understand the truth. Their liberationist counterparts insist that domination runs counter to John's prophetic vision, while they also denounce the millenarians. After all, "false prophets in the churches echo those in the wider society."[1] In either case one's response to the prophecy determines whether one stands inside or outside the truth.

Biblical scholars have generated their own insider discourse with respect to the Apocalypse. Their interpretations often resemble those of the liberationists, while they attack millenarian readers as obscurantist, dangerous, or misguided. Nevertheless, the ethos of biblical critics bears its own internal friction. Biblical scholars may insist that their expertise is accessible to anyone willing to learn the discipline, and they may share their insights through teaching and writing. But at the end of the day they remain the arbiters of exegetical and, presumably, theological truth.

Just as the Apocalypse was and is a public document, I want to submit my reading of it to public conversation. I believe that Revelation is so elusive largely because John's ethos is at once divided and divisive. Just as John's ethos participates in the larger flow of early Christian discourse, so has it contributed to the distinctive blend of egalitarianism and authoritarianism that we find in its modern appropriations. Milleniarians, liberationists, and biblical scholars alike have a stake in John's construction of authority. By taking each of their readings seriously, and by foregrounding my own involvement as a critical biblical scholar, I am

---

[1]Dale Aukerman, *Reckoning with Apocalypse: Terminal Politics and Christian Hope* (New York: Crossroad, 1993) 62.

developing an interpretive practice that seeks public and ethical accountability.

I have modeled my own interpretive practice after that of Elisabeth Schüssler Fiorenza, who insists that readers should foreground their own engagement with the text.[2] I have sketched why I am interested in the Apocalypse and what I believe is at stake in its interpretation. Public reflection about the Apocalypse calls for more than honesty from isolated readers, however, and for a model of such public negotiation I have turned to the work of Jürgen Habermas.

Revelation and Discourse Ethics

The traditional method of New Testament scholarship has been for a scholar to judge (be a *critic* of) the text, exegetically and often morally.[3] This paradigm results from a Kantian notion of a universal subject, someone who is able to project *him*self into global judgments through a process of abstract reasoning.[4] The critic assumes that reason enables him or her to apply textual and practical (i.e. moral) judgments with validity to every conceivable situation.

While objections to this universalist model are now a commonplace in biblical studies,[5] I am interested in applying Jürgen

---

[2]See especially her "The Ethics of Biblical Interpretation: Decentering Biblical Scholarship," *JBL* 107 (1988): 3-17.

[3]Robert M. Fowler, "Who Is 'the Reader' in Reader-Response Criticism?" *Semeia* 31 (1985): 9-10.

[4]Cf. Jürgen Habermas, *Justification and Application: Remarks on Discourse Ethics*, Studies in Contemporary German Social Thought (Cambridge MA: MIT, 1993) 13.

[5]One cannot provide an adequate bibliography for these objections. Especially important for my own reflections have been Schüssler Fiorenza, "Ethics of Biblical Interpretation"; Fernando F. Segovia, "'And They Began to Speak with Other Tongues': Competing Modes of Discourse in Contemporary Biblical Criticism," in *Reading from This Place*, vol. 1, *Social Location and Biblical Interpretation in the United States*, ed. Fernando F. Segovia and Mary Ann Tolbert (Minneapolis: Fortress, 1995) 1-32; Mary Ann Tolbert, "When Resistance Becomes Repression: Mark 13:9-27 and the Poetics of Location," in *Reading from This Place*, vol. 2, *Social Location and Biblical Interpretation in Global Perspective*, ed. Fernando F. Segovia and Mary Ann Tolbert (Minneapolis: Fortress, 1995) 331-46; Tolbert, "Feminists and the Bible: On the Horns of a Dilemma" *USQR* 43 (1989): 1-17; Renita J. Weems, "Reading *Her Way* through the Struggle: African American Women and the Bible," in *Stony the Road We Trod: African American Biblical Interpretation*, ed. Cain

Habermas's work on communicative action and discourse ethics for an interpretive strategy.[6] Dealing with the question of authority in Revelation requires both exegetical and moral or ethical discernment, a process that *ought* to take place in public. According to Habermas, moral discourse[7] assumes (a) that normative claims are meaningful and subject to critical examination and assent and (b) that justifying normative claims requires an authentic dialogue.[8] Ideally, the conversation would include participants from "all those possibly affected" by how Revelation is interpreted, representing a variety of specific contexts.[9] Habermas proposes a universal standard for identifying a valid norm in moral discourse:

> *All* affected can accept the consequences and the side effects its *general* observance can be anticipated to have for the satisfaction of *everyone's* interests (and these consequences are preferred to those of known alternative possibilities for regulation).[10]

Hope Felder (Minneapolis: Fortress, 1991) 57-77; Vincent Wimbush, "Reading Texts through Worlds, Worlds through Texts," *Semeia* 62 (1993): 129-40; A. K. M. Adam, *What Is Postmodern Biblical Criticism?*, Guides to Biblical Scholarship (Minneapolis: Fortress, 1995); Daniel Patte, *Ethics of Biblical Interpretation: A Reevaluation* (Louisville: Westminster/John Knox, 1995); and Brian K. Blount, *Cultural Interpretation: Reorienting New Testament Criticism* (Minneapolis: Fortress, 1995).

[6]Among Habermas's works that have been helpful to this project are: *Knowledge and Human Interests* (Boston: Beacon, 1971); *Legitimation Crisis* (Boston: Beacon, 1973); *Theory and Practice* (Boston: Beacon, 1973); *The Theory of Communicative Action*, vol. 1, *Reason and the Rationalization of Society* (Boston: Beacon, 1984); *The Theory of Communicative Action*, vol. 2, *Lifeworld and System: A Critique of Functionalist Reason* (Boston: Beacon, 1987); *The Philosophical Discourse of Modernity: Twelve Lectures*, Studies in Contemporary German Social Thought (Cambridge MA: MIT, 1987); *Moral Consciousness and Communicative Action*, Studies in Contemporary German Social Thought (Cambridge MA: MIT, 1990); and *Justification and Application*. The critical literature on Habermas is immense. Especially useful to me have been Paul Lakeland, *Theology and Critical Theory: The Discourse of the Church* (Nashville: Abingdon, 1991); McCumber, *Poetic Interaction*; and Steven Seidman, *Contested Knowledge: Social Theory in the Postmodern Era* (Oxford: Blackwell, 1994) 159-93.

[7]Habermas uses "moral" to refer to what most North Americans would call "ethics," that field of action that affects others. By "ethical" Habermas means human action that defines the sort of life an individual would lead (*Justification and Application*, 4-8).

[8]*Moral Consciousness*, 68.

[9]*Justification and Application*, 12-13.

[10]*Moral Consciousness*, 65 (Habermas's emphasis). While Habermas draws upon

Might it be possible to adapt this standard toward a public reading of the Apocalypse? Can one imagine the process by which professional biblical scholars might submit their readings to evaluation by millenarians and liberationists, along with the many communities who have been victimized by modern Christian authoritarianism?

Admittedly, Habermas's program is idealistic. Perhaps Steven Seidman exaggerates when he says, "Habermas aimed to recover the modern utopian faith in the beneficent power of reason."[11] But Seidman correctly wonders whether Habermas's "ideal speech situation" is even possible in postindustrial societies.[12]

Habermas is aware of these challenges. It does not seem to be the case that participants in moral discourse often submit their own interests to general criticism. Indeed, Habermas argues that the reality we encounter is constituted only within the realm of our interests. And our interests are themselves contextual; we live in a world that includes relations of production, symbolic interaction, and cultural tradition.[13] Viewed this way, our world is thoroughly political and absolutely interested. None of our knowledge-generating activity is conceivable without this self-interest. Even the desire to spend a lifetime in disinterested inquiry requires a cultural and financial superstructure designed to make such leisure possible.[14] That the ideal speech situation may never actually be realized does not eliminate the utility of Habermas's project, however. We may approximate his ideal, since fully participatory discourse appears to be our most viable opportunity to resolve differences fairly.[15]

At first glance, Habermas's work holds little promise for interpreting Revelation. As John McCumber indicates, "Habermas's

---

Kantian moral theory, he is careful to distinguish this principle of universalization from the categorical imperative (63).

[11]*Contested Knowledge*, 174.

[12]Ibid., 190-91.

[13]*Knowledge and Human Interests*, 130-39, 194-99.

[14]Even positivism bears its own ideological freight. For positivism, a disposition toward knowledge with technical application determines the forms of legitimate knowledge. See Habermas, *Theory and Practice*, 268-69.

[15]Lakeland, *Theology and Critical Theory*, 48-49.

discussion of works of art is admittedly incomplete and peripheral to his main concerns."[16] And Habermas rarely discusses religion. But there are solid reasons for applying discourse ethics to biblical interpretation. First, Habermas proposes a rationality for aesthetic and interpretive judgment. To the degree that one can bring others to see particular value or authenticity in a work, one uses discourse to interpret cultural products.[17] Unfortunately, Habermas shows a stunted awareness that works of art, such as literary texts, can present validity claims beyond the expressive realm.[18]

A second justification for employing discourse ethics in biblical interpretation may be more persuasive. If public argumentation is appropriate for interpreting difficult moral problems, why not use it in interpreting texts? Not only do we judge interpretations aesthetically, as Habermas proposes, we also evaluate them according to their ethical and theological effects. As the conflicts between millenarian and liberationist readings show, interpretations often legitimate practice. By bringing readings of the Bible into free and inclusive discourse, we may increase hermeneutical, theological, and political accountability.[19]

From the perspective of discourse ethics Revelation would become subject to rational public discourse; the conversation would extend beyond any particular reading community, whether the biblical studies guild, liberationist readers, or prophecy students. This debate is not likely to result in some grand meta-understanding of the Apocalypse or of discursive authority; however, it would (ideally) promote a public theological sensitivity to authority as it functions in Revelation and in Christian discourse in general.

Few of Revelation's readers would agree to enter free and participatory discourse about Revelation. Biblical studies people often prefer to limit their discourse to trained insiders, those who have

---

[16]*Poetic Interaction*, 366.

[17]*Theory of Communicative Action*, 1:20.

[18]McCumber, *Poetic Interaction*, 366-67.

[19]In seeking a clearer Roman Catholic voice on political theology, Lakeland proposes that discourse ethics can lead to a clearer, more authoritative, articulation of justice (*Theology and Critical Theory*, 90-93).

"[learned] certain things that one may not say."[20] Prophecy students, who draw upon fundamentalist absolutism, are likely to label those who disagree as persons of bad (or no) faith. And liberationists, engaged in acute struggles for justice, tend to identify millenarian readers with their political enemies, an association often grounded in hard reality.

In any case, biblical scholars typically resent the infringement of popular readers on their expertise. At one level, these three ways of reading the Apocalypse cannot be reconciled. Nevertheless, by taking them seriously and in the context of my own interests and identity, I have shaped my own appraisal of Revelation's discourse of authority.

Negotiating John's Ethos

How does John get his authority? Speakers who resist those powers that are self-evident, or who call for radical resistance to the larger society, face tremendous rhetorical obstacles. In particular, their extreme claims demand that they win credibility. I have adopted a rhetorical approach to this problem, one which assumes that John must contend for his audience's trust, shouting for attention by representing himself and his opponents in certain ways.

John's first task is to construct his own ethos. By associating himself with the generic conventions of prophets, apostles, and visionaries, John enhances his own status. He then uses apocalyptic conventions to make direct claims for his own narrative and religious authority. Harmonizing the levels of discourse within his own narrative, John "speaks with the tongues of mortals and angels"—not to mention of Christ—subordinating divine and heavenly voices to his own program. To prevent his elevated claims from alienating his audience, John seeks to identify with them. He shares their values, struggles, and experiences; he and they aspire to be faithful witnesses like Christ. Finally, John employs saints and other heavenly voices to justify more objectionable aspects of his vision such as the devastation of the earth and its inhabitants.

---

[20]Adam, *What Is Postmodern Biblical Criticism?* 22.

Simply establishing his own ethos is not sufficient. Demanding absolute rejection of the Empire and the larger culture of Asia Minor, John must decenter other authoritative voices within and without the Asian churches. Because Rome is so compelling in its power, productivity, and stature, and because most people want to participate in the larger society, many in John's audience are likely to wonder why he cannot compromise. John's task is to overturn the Empire, his Gentile and Jewish neighbors, and those Christians who would accommodate themselves to the imperial culture. His only resources are rhetorical. Perhaps unable to take them on himself, John employs other authoritative voices to condemn his enemies. He promotes hostility toward them by linking them to contemptible persons, places, and concepts from the Bible and popular mythology. He uses parody and satire to ridicule the ambitious claims of the Empire and its rulers. Further, John pushes his opponents as far down as possible by taunting and debasing them, especially in terms of sexual immorality. In order to further distance his audience from his enemies, John erases their humanity through dehumanization and negation.

John's apocalyptic ethos creates an internal conflict: John is building and tearing down at the same time. This internal tension is more profound than a simple reversal of imperial discourse. Revelation certainly contends with Rome, but it also orders relationships between John and his audience. Revelation's promise of a "priestly dominion for God" (1:6) turns against itself: John's ethos cannot sustain both resistance and mutuality. John subordinates every other voice to his own. He demands absolute obedience from his audience, and anyone—Christian or otherwise—who would diverge from John's vision stands under his curse. The Apocalypse reduces even heavenly figures—Christ, the angels, and the martyrs—to the status of witnesses for John's authority.

Readers of the Apocalypse have long noticed an internal tension, but they have not identified its rhetorical motivation. A prominent critical reader such as W. D. Davies could cite its "abortive hatred that can only lead, not to [the Roman authorities'] redemption, but to their destruction."[21] And a nonprofessional reader like C. G. Jung specifically argued that Revelation suffers from an internal struggle, John's inability to keep his conscious and unconscious apart. Jung attributes its violence to "less a metaphysical mystery than the outburst of long pent-up feelings such as can frequently be observed in people who strive for perfection."[22]

Biblical scholars tend to speak more of Revelation's limitations than of its internal tensions. Adela Yarbro Collins calls Revelation "a partial and imperfect vision" because its "imagery does not suggest a new order in which all people will achieve personal dignity and autonomy."[23] Her assessment comes near the mark, but it fails to engage Revelation on its own terms: The Apocalypse never promises inclusion for *all* people. Revelation is no post-Enlightenment utopia. As Elisabeth Schüssler Fiorenza suggests, it is doubtful that John conceives of modes of power other than "power over."[24] The problem *within Revelation's rhetoric* is that it cannot sustain its own vision—that of a priestly dominion in which John is a partner under God's rule (1:9).

A recent study by Robert M. Royalty, Jr., comes closer to the point. Focusing upon the imagery of wealth in the Apocalypse, Royalty argues that Revelation simply mimics dominant perceptions of wealth and status by reversing the tables, replacing the dominant culture with a Christianized version. Babylon, which once wore jewels and fine clothing, is replaced by the New Jerusalem, the Bride who wears white linen (19:8), whose streets are pure gold, and whose walls are "decorated with every precious stone" (21:19).[25] Royalty has identified the irony inherent in Revelation's appropriation of imperial discourse; like Collins, however, he does not investigate its internal instability.

---

[21]Cited in Klassen, "Vengeance," 301, from "Ethics in the New Testament," *IDB* E–J:176.

[22]Cited in Klassen, "Vengeance," 301, from *Answer to Job*, trans. R. F. C. Hull (London: Routledge & Keegan Paul, 1954) 125.

[23]*Crisis and Catharsis*, 172.

[24]*Revelation*, 123.

[25]*The Streets of Heaven: The Ideology of Wealth in the Apocalypse of John* (Macon GA: Mercer University Press, 1998).

Neither Collins nor Royalty is at fault for passing by John's ethos problem. Both authors fairly assess the dimensions of Revelation with which they are concerned. Schüssler Fiorenza, however, comes closest to identifying the tensions within John's ethos. Noting that John cloaks his voice with divine authority, even going so far as to curse those who resist it, she discerns that John falls short of his own vision. The curses negate John's invitations for his audience to participate in his vision. This self-consciousness betrays John's "great anxiety" about his authority. Citing its popular reception, Schüssler Fiorenza also points out that this dimension of the Apocalypse has contributed to authoritarian thought and practice.[26]

Schüssler Fiorenza's analysis indicates that we may trace Revelation's instability to a fundamental rhetorical problem: John's ethos. She also suggests that John's ethos motivates conflicting theological and ethical practices. But with respect to two issues Schüssler Fiorenza's assessment invites us to pay even closer attention to this problem. First, she works so hard to resist authoritarian appropriations of Revelation that she pays little attention to the potential problems of liberationist readings. Might their practice include traces of domination and exclusion? More importantly, while she recognizes that John's authority would have suffered stresses even in its own context, she suggests that only some contemporary readers—those who are excluded from power—can produce "fitting" readings of Revelation. She refuses to acknowledge that John's ethos sustains authoritarian readings as well.[27] If Schüssler Fiorenza would submit popular liberationist readings (that so strongly resemble her own) to critical scrutiny, and if she would take authoritarian interpretations more seriously, she might be able to assess the *causes* of John's authority problem more precisely. The promise of her insights has encouraged this more detailed examination of John's ethos.

A turn to theories of resistance literature may sharpen our understanding of John's predicament. Richard Terdiman argues that, "Counterdiscourses are always interlocked with the domi-

---

[26]*Revelation*, 137-38.
[27]Ibid., 138-39.

nation they contest."[28] Does he overstate the case by insisting that it is impossible for resistance literatures to escape oppressive discourses? When John seeks to assert his own ethos in contrast to the prevailing sources of authority, Terdiman would regard his frustration as inevitable:

> The paradox of any social distinction is that the heterogeneity sought is determined by what it excludes: situated thus, one never gets outside.[29]

John, at least, does not escape the exclusions and hierarchies he is resisting. No less totalitarian than imperial discourses, his argument demands that he silence every competing voice. Revelation is one early example of the process described by Averil Cameron: "Christians . . . talked and wrote themselves into a position where they spoke and wrote the rhetoric of empire."[30] Revelation subverts imperial authority even as it contributes to the foundations of a new discourse of domination.

Revelation's contemporary readers reflect John's authority conflict. Most scholars are sympathetic to liberationist readers who emphasize Revelation's passion for justice and its criticism of imperial domination and wealth. On the other side are the contemporary prophecy students who connect right-wing politics with chiliastic readings of Revelation. For them, Revelation is a key for discerning righteous from evil persons in the last days and for assigning favor and condemnation to nations and continents. The intense register of Revelation's claims demands eschatological action: absolute support for Israel, distrust toward Russia and the Arab nations. In my opinion, this interpretive clash is rooted in Revelation's own rhetorical ethos: a struggle between resistance and repression.

---

[28]*Discourse/Counter-Discourse*, 16.
[29]Ibid., 278.
[30]*Christianity and the Rhetoric of Empire*, 14.

Appropriating John's Ethos: Possible Mitigating Factors

Why would John go so far? Why does his ethos require that he silence other voices? And how should contemporary readers respond to the dualistic dimension of John's ethos? These questions, perhaps less pressing for Revelation's secular critics than for more theologically inclined readers, disclose that John's ethos problem is symptomatic of Christian discourse in general. Once sectarian, Christian discourse has become the language of church and empire. That it makes claims to truth about ultimate matters—however confessional those claims may be—poses a fundamental problem for contemporary reflection.

According to theologian David Tracy, the appeal or authority of the religious classic—and Tracy would include Revelation—is nonviolent. By empowering rather than demanding obedience from the religious self, the classic conveys an appeal of its own.[31] Yet Revelation *demands* that its readers acknowledge its own authority. John's ethos dominates the book. Expressing Tracy's sensibilities about what a religious classic *ought* to be, many readers have advanced possible mitigating factors or excuses for John's coercive claims to authority.

1. In its own historical context, John's rhetoric would have sounded less offensive than it appears to many of today's readers. Vilification and other aggressive language were common features of ancient polemic, used both to define communities over against their opponents and to incriminate enemies.[32] We have observed Cicero in action, accusing Catalina of responsibility for every immoral act committed in Rome. And we have noted that classical rhetorical theorists advised vivid description of opponents' flaws.

At the same time, we should also keep in mind why ancient speakers often used such highly charged language: they were in danger. Real threats often accompanied ancient polemic; violent language emanated from violent situations. Cicero's speeches

---

[31]*The Analogical Imagination: Christian Theology and the Culture of Pluralism* (New York: Crossroad, 1981) 177.

[32]Borgen, "Polemic," 204. Cf. Johnson, "New Testament's Anti-Jewish Slander"; and Freyne, "Vilifying the Other and Defining the Self."

against Catalina were intended to drive the rebel out of the city and to expose his conspirators, leading to their deaths or imprisonment. Failure could cost Cicero his life.

But ancient polemics could also take the more sinister turn of exposing one's opponents to danger in order to further one's own interests. For example, a common means of injuring one's enemies was to bring extremely serious charges against them in court. The excuses that John's coercive language was "normal" in its context, or that one can sift out the cultural baggage of how he represents his opponents from his true liberating message, overlook the Apocalypse's rhetorical nature.[33] As the resistance theorists insist, one never encounters "mere rhetoric." The boundaries between characterization and the "real world" are quite fluid, as we observe when critical commentators collaborate in John's disapproval of Jezebel and her colleagues. Revelation may reflect a perceived crisis, but John's attacks against his opponents do nothing to enhance his security. Rather, they are a carefully woven fabric of characterizations designed to advance John's message at the expense of other perspectives.

2. Others might suggest that John's use of apocalyptic rhetoric results from his own powerlessness.[34] Unlike Cicero, John could not imagine turning the forces of the Empire to his own advantage. But one cannot maintain a direct link between apocalyptic language and the oppressed. For one thing, apocalyptic discourses serve multiple functions. It is likely that some early Jews used apocalyptic to deal with imperial oppression, as we see in Daniel, *2* and *3 Baruch, 4 Ezra,* and some of the *Sibylline Oracles*. But oppression, like beauty, is in the eye of the viewer. The apocalyptic perspective we find at Qumran appears to express an opposition to Jerusalem that results from disillusionment and alienation rather than oppression. Even persons of relative comfort may experience intense dissatisfaction with the present order. As we have seen, Paul used apocalyptic to maintain his authority in Corinth and

---

[33]Cf. Schüssler Fiorenza, *Revelation*, 123-24, 131-32.

[34]E.g., Efird, *Revelation for Today*, 129-30. This argument is especially prominent among liberationist readers. See Boesak, *Comfort and Protest*, 29-34; Richard, *Apocalypse*, 4.

Galatia, yet he was a person with significant human and material resources at his disposal. Sometimes an apocalyptic perspective expresses radical dissatisfaction with the present order with no grounding in concrete experiences of oppression, as we may observe among many of Revelation's contemporary readers.[35]

The supposed connection between oppression and apocalypticism does not excuse John's violent rhetoric for a second reason. People respond to perceived oppression in various ways. They turn to revolution, healing, or even to attempts to convert or reform the present order. An apocalyptic turn is not inevitable.[36]

But there is an even more basic reason not to use John's powerlessness to excuse his coercive ethos. Many visionaries use apocalyptic to address perceived crises without resorting to such aggressive rhetoric. One prominent example is *4 Ezra*, which responds to the destruction of Jerusalem in 70 CE. As Philip F. Esler argues, its first three visions express concern for all of humanity.[37] Ezra protests:

> It would have been better if the earth had not produced Adam, or else, when it had produced him, had restrained him from sinning. For what good is it to all that they live in sorrow now and expect punishment after death? (7:116-17)

Though its emphasis narrows from the world to Israel,[38] *4 Ezra* offers a simple solution for humanity: obedience to Torah. *4 Ezra* appeals to the Law to distinguish between the saved and the damned. In contrast, Revelation is the first apocalypse to claim that salvation depends upon response to its own message.

3. A third means of mitigating the offense of John's vision has been offered by Richard Bauckham, who argues that Revelation

---

[35]We might ask whether the traditional association of apocalyptic discourse with contexts of oppression reflects the degree to which scholars' romantic attachment to apocalyptic influences their historical reconstructions.

[36]Bryan R. Wilson, *Magic and the Millennium: A Sociological Study of Religious Movements of Protest Among Tribal and Third-World Peoples* (New York: Harper & Row, 1973) 19-28.

[37]"The Social Function of 4 Ezra," in *The First Christians in Their Social World*, 129.

[38]Ibid.

balances its emphasis on judgment with hope for conversion of the nations.[39] Bauckham further argues that Revelation sides with history's victims. It offers them a vision of a transcendent God and an alternative future. It even provides a strategy of engagement with the world through witness, including hope for the nations' conversion.[40]

Attractive as Bauckham's proposal is, it is grounded in the conviction that "Revelation is overwhelmingly concerned with the *truth* of God."[41] Indeed, insistent witness to the truth is among the most effective tools available to those in solidarity with history's victims. And such insistence differs greatly from the abuse of power to enforce conformity. It is too simple to dismiss John as an authoritarian megalomaniac who will not tolerate dissent. Nevertheless, Bauckham is apparently unaware of the implications of John's ethos, especially for modern readers. Bauckham writes, "The church's witness will be of value only if it knows truth worth dying for,"[42] but he never questions the nature, authority, or detail of that truth in the way that John does. Compliant readers must identify the "truth of God" with the truth of John.

4. Elisabeth Schüssler Fiorenza appeals to another strategy for minimizing John's polemic: He didn't really mean it. When the Apocalypse predicts disaster for human beings, Schüssler Fiorenza repeatedly appeals to their rhetorical function, warning Christians away from certain behaviors.

> One may not, however, construe the punishment of the beast's worshipers [Rev 13:9-11] as an accurate description or a literal prediction of their fate. Rather, it functions as a prophetic threat and rhetorical exhortation which is expressed in symbolic language.[43]

---

[39]*Theology of Revelation*, 98-104.

[40]Ibid., 160-61.

[41]Ibid., 160; emphasis his.

[42]Ibid.

[43]*Revelation*, 89-90. Schüssler Fiorenza also calls the bird's supper at the last battle (Rev 19:17-18) "an urgent warning," not a "concrete depiction of cruel judgment" (106).

Schüssler Fiorenza reduces rhetoric to stylistics and fails to appreciate its seriousness. When John resorts to threats and proclaims doom for his enemies, he invites his audience to side against them, even to desire their suffering. Even if John is not conjuring literal punishments, his characterization of his opponents is still violent. By paying attention to the ways popular readers like Hal Lindsey and John Walwoord adapt these attacks against their enemies, we may discern how Schüssler Fiorenza's appeal to rhetoric actually muffles rhetorical sensitivity. Rhetoric involves more than stylistics; it lures audiences toward particular dispositions and behaviors.

5. Perhaps the most intriguing attempt to mitigate the offense of the Apocalypse has been offered by David L. Barr.[44] Barr notes two reasons that traditional readings of Revelation are morally objectionable. Such interpretations suggest that God triumphs over evil simply because God is supremely powerful, rendering power the ultimate value in the universe. And one must ask why God allows innocent suffering to continue in the present if God can put a stop to it in the future.[45] Barr's response to both questions is to read the Apocalypse as a story—the story of Jesus as experienced by John and his community.[46] In the story of Jesus, God triumphs through the Lamb's death; in the experience of the early Christians, God triumphs through the martyrs.[47] According to Barr, God does not rely on might but instead works through the suffering of the Lamb and of the holy ones to restore the world. Rather than being charged to God, the violence and suffering depicted in Revelation are the natural consequences of human brutality.[48]

Unfortunately, Barr leaves out a great deal. Indeed, John does envision a redemptive role for faithful endurance. And, as Barr notes, John offers his audience an egalitarian handshake. He would be their brother and partner. As Barr puts it, "by telling the story

---

[44]*Tales of the End;* "Towards an Ethical Reading of the Apocalypse: Reflections on John's Use of Power, Violence, and Misogyny," *SBLSP* 36 (1997): 358-74.

[45]"Towards an Ethical Reading," 359.

[46]*Tales of the End*, 3; "Towards an Ethical Reading," 367.

[47]"Towards an Ethical Reading," 360-63.

[48]Ibid., 362.

through the point of view of those abused by Roman power, the discourse persuades the audience to resist such power."[49] But we have seen that John's ethos is much more complicated than that. John at once offers solidarity with his audience while he demands their submission. And if the Apocalypse does envision a suffering that conquers evil, it also glories in the suffering of John's opponents, from Balaam, the Nicolaitans, and Jezebel, to the "synagogue of Satan," to Babylon/Rome, and even to the "inhabitants of the earth." "They deserve it," announces the voice from the altar (16:6). Barr's optimistic (one-dimensional?) reading of the Apocalypse simply will not withstand John's ethos.

The problem persists. In its historical context, Revelation's claims to authority are extremely high and its use of apocalyptic discourse to silence opposition almost as extreme. Adela Yarbro Collins notes an intereting phenomenon: While some fundamentalists appropriate its extreme vilification against China and the former Soviet Union, some liberation theologians find such rhetoric useful in criticizing oppressive structures.[50] Collins's observation parallels the tension I have been suggesting: both prophecy students and liberationists are appropriating Revelation's ethos, despite their conflicting purposes. One wonders whether Collins's reading minimizes Revelation's potential destructiveness, however. By arguing that it has a social function—to define monotheistic Christianity against other options—she implies a constructive purpose. Might John have had other, less ambivalent, alternatives?

Negotiating Alternatives

As I argued in Chapter 2, Chinua Achebe's novels present one case in which subversion avoids the sort of dualism we find in Revelation. Being resistance literature, Revelation leans toward what Ashcroft, Griffiths, and Tiffin call "counterdetermination"—the tendency to reinscribe what one opposes.[51] Indeed, resistance literatures often wrestle with a dualism of their own, vilifying the

---

[49] Ibid., 373.
[50] "Vilification," 318-19.
[51] *Empire Writes Back*, 170.

oppressor and idealizing those who work for resistance.[52] One misreading of Achebe demonstrates how easy it is to move from criticizing the colonizer to reinscribing colonial oppositions. Reflecting on Achebe's characterization of colonial administrators in *Things Fall Apart,* Ernest N. Emenyonu says:

> The actual truth is that those who suffered blindness and folly were not the dwellers of the "Dark Continent," but those who came with "light" on a civilizing mission.[53]

Emenyonu can point to ample evidence for his reading. Achebe's colonial administrators usually combine arrogance and ignorance to an amazing degree. Yet Achebe avoids the sort of dualism Emenyonu's reading suggests. The tragedy of *Things Fall Apart* demands contributions from both colonizer and colonized. Mr. Brown, the missionary who seeks some degree of dialogue with the Ibo and shows appreciation for their culture, exemplifies the complexity of the colonial situation. His mission is to destroy the Ibo culture's foundations, but he is not an evil person and he does not intend harm for the Ibo. On the Ibo side, the conflict between Okonkwo and his son Nwoye reveals how multifaceted is the situation of the colonized. Okonkwo hears the missionaries' message as foolishness; for Nwoye, it offers a resolution for his own questions about Ibo life.[54] Achebe demonstrates that one may criticize the imperial power without resorting to demonization.

Surely there are other ways of dealing with John's ethos. One avenue would be to participate in it from the start. Jürgen Roloff, for example, argues that, "What gives [John's] message full authority is the word of the exalted Christ itself which is issued through it."[55] By yielding to John's authority, one avoids his judgment and conforms to Revelation's divine perspective. But is

---

[52]Harlow, *Resistance Literature*, 29.

[53]"Chinua Achebe's *Things Fall Apart*: A Classic Study in Colonial Diplomatic Tactlessness," in *Chinua Achebe: A Celebration*, ed. Kirsten Holst Peterson and Anna Rutherford (Oxford: Heinemann, 1990) 84.

[54]My own hunch is that Achebe would avoid the sort of moralizing in which I am indulging here. But the contrast between Revelation and *Things Fall Apart* bears the weight I am putting upon it.

[55]*Revelation*, 8; cf. 20, 32.

such monologic complicity appropriate or helpful for contemporary Christian discourse?

Concerned that unitary discourse leans toward conservatism and centralization,[56] Mikhail Bakhtin defined the ideal novel in terms of heteroglossia. The true novel gives full expression to the diverse, even conflicting discourses we encounter in daily life. Authoritarian discourse cannot dominate the true novel because the novel is inherently dialogic.[57] "Authoritative discourse cannot be represented—it is only transmitted."[58] In the novel, even those authors who speak in their own voices betray an awareness that their perspectives are neither self-evident nor incontestable. Their apologetic or polemic language cannot escape the multiplicity of voices (heteroglossia) that define the novel.[59]

Revelation is no novel, but John's rhetoric embodies a striking confirmation of Bakhtin's hypothesis. The Apocalypse is a model case of an attempt to elevate one voice above the clamor its audience would have confronted daily. Using them and then destroying them, John would assimilate all other voices to his own vision. Ironically, the only traces that remain of John's Jewish and Christian opponents are those he himself inscribes. Certainly we did not need the Apocalypse to learn about the Empire's influence. But John's extreme polemic gives itself away: Without John, we would never have known that positions like those of the Nicolaitans, Balaam, and Jezebel ever existed. By going so far to nullify other points of view, the Apocalypse reveals how insecure John's authority is. John's tenuous ethos neither justifies nor mitigates his rhetorical attacks, but it promises insights into the Apocalypse and Christian discourse in general.

Conclusion

Despite the obstacles posed by Revelation and its readers, this project has sought to contribute a public interpretation of the Apocalypse. The unique contributions of this study are its

---

[56]*Dialogic Imagination*, 271.
[57]Ibid., 342-44.
[58]Ibid., 344.
[59]Ibid., 332.

thoroughly rhetorical approach to Revelation's ethos and its refusal to exclude popular readings—including my own experience—from the conversation. I began with discord among real readers, asking why different readers—particularly prophecy students and liberationists—use the Apocalypse for opposing ends. My conclusion is that conflicting understandings of authority lie beneath these interpretive struggles.[60] Then I have applied my own reading conventions, those of a biblical scholar trained in rhetorical criticism, to wrestle with authority in Revelation as a rhetorical problem. In an important sense, my study of John's ethos has confirmed liberationist as well as millenarian readings. John does envision a priestly dominion that resists imperialistic claims to authority; in doing so, however, he reinscribes his own authoritarian ethos. John's ethos inspires both egalitarian and dualistic interpretations.

I find myself in the precarious situation of a postmodern critic, what Linda Hutcheon characterizes as "complicity and critique."[61] Hutcheon suggests that postmodern discourse "takes the form of self-conscious, self-contradictory, self-undermining statement."[62] Her proposal rests upon the insight that our resources for resistance—thought, language, symbol, culture—are grounded in the very systems we would undermine. Hutcheon's words apply to my reading of Revelation as well:

> this is a strange kind of critique, one bound up, too, with its own *complicity* with power and domination, one that acknowledges that it cannot escape implication in that which it nevertheless still wants to analyze and maybe even undermine.[63]

---

[60]Gerald West adopts a similarly pragmatic approach to the Cain and Abel story. West uses conflicting interpretations (by Allen Boesak and Itumeleng J. Mosala) to provoke his own suggestions about the most useful way to read the story (*Biblical Hermeneutics of Liberation: Modes of Reading the Bible in the South African Context*, rev. ed., Bible and Liberation Series [Maryknoll NY: Orbis, 1995] 60-82).

[61]*The Politics of Postmodernism*, New Accents (London and New York: Routledge, 1989) 11.

[62]Ibid., 1.

[63]Ibid., 4; Hutcheon's emphasis.

Despite my dissatisfaction with Revelation, it articulates a fundamental liberating vision that has motivated my own practice and inspired countless others. If I can criticize the Apocalypse, I must begin from within, appropriating its own subversive resources. The result is profoundly ironic. Like so many others, I am following John's example.

Bibliography

Modern Translations of Ancient Sources

Aristophanes. "Clouds." In *The Complete Plays of Aristophanes*. Translated by Moses Hadas. Bantam Classics. New York: Bantam, 1962. 101-41.

Aristotle. *The Art of Rhetoric*. Translated by J. H. Freese. Loeb Classical Library. Cambridge MA: Harvard University Press, 1926.

________. *The Poetics*. Translated by W. Hamilton Fyfe and W. Rhys Roberts. Loeb Classical Library. Cambridge MA: Harvard University Press, 1927.

Charlesworth, James H., editor. *The Old Testament Pseudepigrapha*. Volume 1. *Apocalyptic Literature and Testaments*. New York: Doubleday, 1983.

Cicero. *De Oratore*. Translated by H. Rackham. Loeb Classical Library. Cambridge MA: Harvard University Press, 1942.

________. *De Partitione Oratoria*. Translated by H. Rackham. Loeb Classical Library. Cambridge MA: Harvard University Press, 1942.

________. *Selected Political Speeches of Cicero*. Revised edition. Edited and translated by Michael Grant. New York: Penguin, 1973.

Pseudo-Cicero. *Rhetorica ad Herennium*. Translated by Harry Caplan. Loeb Classical Library. Cambridge MA: Harvard University Press, 1954.

Pseudo-Demetrius. *On Style*. Translated by W. Hamilton Fyfe and W. Rhys Roberts. Loeb Classical Library. Cambridge MA: Harvard University Press, 1927.

Gaylord, H. E., Jr. *3 (Greek Apocalypse of) Baruch*. In *The Old Testament Pseudepigrapha*. Volume 1. *Apocalyptic Literature and Testaments*. Edited by James H. Charlesworth, 653-79. New York: Doubleday, 1983.

Isaac, E., translator. *1 (Ethiopic Apocalypse of) Enoch*. In *The Old Testament Pseudepigrapha*. Volume 1. *Apocalyptic Literature and Testaments*. Edited by James H. Charlesworth, 5-89. New York: Doubleday, 1983.

Juvenal. *Satires, with the Satires of Persius*. Translated by William Gifford. Everyman's Library. Rutland VT: Charles E. Tuttle, 1992.

Klijn, A. F. J., translator. *2 (Syriac Apocalypse of) Baruch*. In *The Old Testament Pseudepigrapha*. Volume 1. *Apocalyptic Literature and Testaments*.

Edited by James H. Charlesworth, 617-52. New York: Doubleday, 1983.

ten Kortenaar, Neil. *Beyond Authenticity and Creolization: Reading Achebe Writing Culture,* 30-42. PMLA 110 (1995).

Longinus. *On the Sublime*. Translated by W. Hamilton Fyfe and W. Rhys Roberts. Loeb Classical Library. Cambridge MA: Harvard University Press, 1927.

Metzger, Bruce M., translator. *The Fourth Book of Ezra*. In *The Old Testament Pseudepigrapha*. Volume 1. *Apocalyptic Literature and Testaments.* Edited by James H. Charlesworth, 517-59. New York: Doubleday, 1983.

Seneca. *Apocolocyntosis Divi Claudii*. Edited and translated by Apostolos Athanassakis. Lawrence KS: Coronado Press, 1973.

Secondary Sources

Aberle, David F. "A Note on Relative Deprivation Theory as Applied to Millenarian and Other Cult Movements." In *Millennial Dreams in Action: Studies in Revolutionary Religious Movements*. Edited by Sylvia L. Thrupp, 209-14. New York: Shocken, 1970.

Achebe, Chinua. "An Image of Africa." *Massachusetts Review* 18 (1977): 782-94.

________. *Things Fall Apart*. African Writers Series 1. Portsmouth NH: Heinemann, 1962; [1]1958.

Adam, A. K. M. *What Is Postmodern Biblical Criticism?* Guides to Biblical Scholarship. Minneapolis: Fortress Press, 1995.

Alexander, Loveday, editor. *Images of Empire*. Journal for the Study of the Old Testament Supplement Series 122. Sheffield UK: Sheffield Academic Press, 1991.

Anderson, Janice Capel, and Jeffrey L. Staley. "Taking It Personally: Autobiographical Biblical Criticism." *Semeia* 72 (1995).

Appelbaum, S. "The Legal Status of the Jewish Communities in the Diaspora." In *The Jewish People in the First Century: Historical Geography, Political History, Social, Cultural, and Religious Life and Institutions.* Edited by S. Safrai and M. Stern. Compendia Rerum Iudaicarum ad Novum Testamentum. Assen: Van Gorcum & Comp. B.V., 1974. 1:420-63.

Ashcroft, Bill, Gareth Griffiths, and Helen Tiffin. *The Empire Writes Back: Theory and Practice in Post-Colonial Literatures*. New Accents. New York: Routledge, 1989.

Aukerman, Dale. *Reckoning with Apocalypse: Terminal Politics and Christian Hope*. New York: Crossroad, 1993.

Aune, David E. "The Apocalypse of John and the Problem of Genre." *Semeia* 36 (1986): 65-96.

________. "Intertextuality and the Genre of the Apocalypse." *Society of Biblical Literature Seminar Papers* 30 (1991): 142-60.

________. *Prophecy in Early Christianity and the Ancient Mediterranean World*. Grand Rapids MI: Eerdmans, 1983.

______. *Revelation 1–5*. Word Biblical Commentary 52A. Dallas: Word Books, 1997.

______. "The Social Matrix of the Apocalypse of John." *Biblical Research* 26 (1981): 16-33.

Bakhtin, Mikhail M. *The Dialogic Imagination: Four Essays*. Edited and translated by Michael Holquist and Caryl Emerson. University of Texas Press Slavic Series 1. Austin: University of Texas Press, 1981.

______. *Problems of Dostoevsky's Poetics*. Edited and translated by Caryl Emerson. Theory and History of Literature 8. Minneapolis: University of Minnesota Press, 1984.

Barr, David L. *Tales of the End: A Narrative Commentary on the Book of Revelation*. The Storytellers Bible 1. Santa Rosa CA: Polebridge, 1998.

______. "Towards an Ethical Reading of the Apocalypse: Reflections on John's Use of Power, Violence, and Misogyny." *Society of Biblical Literature Seminar Papers* 36 (1997): 358-74.

Bauckham, Richard J. "The Economic Critique of Rome in Revelation 18 (with Note on Sibylline Oracles)." In *Images of Empire*. Edited by Loveday Alexander, 47-90. Journal for the Study of the Old Testament Supplement Series. Sheffield UK: Sheffield Academic Press, 1991.

______. *The Theology of the Book of Revelation*. New Testament Theology. New York: Cambridge University Press, 1993.

Baumlin, James S. "Introduction: Positioning *Ethos* in Historical and Contemporary Theory." In *Ethos: New Essays in Rhetorical and Critical Theory*. Edited by James S. Baumlin and Tita French Baumlin, xi-xxvii. SMU Studies in Composition and Rhetoric. Dallas: Southern Methodist University Press, 1994.

Baumlin, James S., and Tita French Baumlin, editors. *Ethos: New Essays in Rhetorical and Critical Theory*. SMU Studies in Composition and Rhetoric. Dallas: Southern Methodist University Press, 1994.

Beasley-Murray, G. R. *Revelation*. Revised edition. New Century Bible. Grand Rapids: Eerdmans, 1981.

Beker, J. Christiaan. *Paul the Apostle: The Triumph of God in Life and Thought*. Philadelphia: Fortress Press, 1980.

Berrigan, Daniel. *Beside the Sea of Glass: The Song of the Lamb*. New York: Seabury, 1978.

Bhabha, Homi K. "Postcolonial Criticism." In *Redrawing the Boundaries: The Transformation of English and American Literary Studies*. Edited by Stephen Greenblatt and Giles Gunn, 437-65. New York: Modern Language Assocation of America, 1992.

Bible and Culture Collective, The (George Aichele et al.). *The Postmodern Bible*. New Haven CT: Yale University Press, 1995.

Blass, F., A. Debrunner, and R. W. Funk. *A Greek Grammar of the New Testament and Other Early Christian Literature*. Chicago: University of Chicago Press, 1961.

Blount, Brian K. *Cultural Interpretation: Reorienting New Testament Criticism*. Minneapolis: Fortress Press, 1995.

Blue, J. Ronald. "Major Flaws in Liberation Theology." *Bibliotheca Sacra* 147 (1990): 89-103.

Böcher, Otto. "Die Johannes-Apokalypse in der Neueren Forschung." *Aufstieg und Niedergang der Römishen Welt*. Berlin and New York: Walter de Gruyter, 1988. 2.25.3850-93.

Bockmuehl, Markus. *Revelation and Mystery in Ancient Judaism and Pauline Christianity*. Grand Rapids MI: Eerdmans, 1997.

Boesak, Allan A. *Comfort and Protest: Reflections on the Apocalypse of John of Patmos*. Philadelphia: Westminster, 1987.

Booth, Wayne C. "Are Narrative Choices Subject to Ethical Criticism?" In *Reading Narrative: Form, Ethics, Ideology*. Edited by James Phelan, 57-78. Columbus: Ohio State University Press, 1989.

________. *The Company We Keep: An Ethics of Fiction*. Berkeley: University of California Press, 1988.

________. *The Rhetoric of Fiction*. Second edition. Chicago: University of Chicago Press, 1983; [1]1961.

________. "Distance and Point of View: An Essay in Classification." *Essays in Criticism* 11 (1961): 60-79.

Borgen, Peder. "Polemic in the Book of Revelation." In *Anti-Semitism and Early Christianity*. Edited by Craig A. Evans and Donald A. Hagner, 199-211. Minneapolis: Fortress Press, 1993.

Boring, M. Eugene. *Revelation*. Interpretation. Louisville: John Knox, 1989.

Bousset, Wilhelm. *Die Offenbarung Johannis*. Göttingen: Vandenhoeck & Ruprecht, 1906.

Boyer, Paul. *When Time Shall Be No More: Prophecy Belief in Modern American Culture*. Cambridge MA: Harvard University Press, 1992.

Briggs, John. "Reflectaphors: The (Implicate) Universe as a Work of Art." In *Quantum Implications: Essays in Honour of David Bohm*. Edited by B. J. Hiley and F. David Peat 414-35. London and New York: Routledge & Keegan Paul, 1987.

Burke, Kenneth. *A Rhetoric of Motives* (repr.: Berkeley: University of California Press, 1969; [1]1950).

Caird, G. B. *The Revelation of Saint John*. Black's New Testament Commentary. Peabody MA: Hendrickson, 1966.

Cameron, Averil. *Christianity and the Rhetoric of Empire: The Development of Christian Discourse*. Sather Classical Lectures 55. Berkeley, Los Angeles, and Oxford: University of California Press, 1991.

Charles, R. H. *A Critical and Exegetical Commentary on the Revelation of St. John*. International Critical Commentary. Two volumes. Edinburgh: T.&T. Clark; New York: Charles Scribner's Sons, 1920.

Cohn, Norman. *Cosmos, Chaos and the World to Come: The Ancient Roots of Apocalyptic Faith*. New Haven: Yale University Press, 1993.

Collins, Adela Yarbro, editor. "Early Christian Apocalypticism: Genre and Social Setting." *Semeia* 36 (1986).

________. *The Apocalypse*. New Testament Message. Collegeville MN: Michael Glazier, 1979.

______. *The Combat Myth in the Book of Revelation*. Harvard Dissertations in Religion 9. Missoula MT: Scholars Press, 1976.

________. *Crisis and Catharsis: The Power of the Apocalypse*. Philadelphia: Westminster, 1984.

________. "Feminine Symbolism in the Book of Revelation." *Biblical Interpretation* 1 (1993): 20-33.

________. "Insiders and Outsiders in the Book of Revelation and Its Social Context." In *"To See Ourselves as Others See Us": Christians, Jews, "Others" in Late Antiquity*. Edited by Jacob Neusner and Ernest S. Frerichs, 187-218. Scholars Press Studies in the Humanities. Chico CA: Scholars Press, 1985.

______. "Oppression from Without: The Symbolization of Rome as Evil in Early Christianity," *Concilium* 200 (1988): 66-74.

______. "The Political Perspective of the Revelation to John." *Journal of Biblical Literature* 96 (1977): 241-56.

________. "Revelation 18: Taunt-Song or Dirge?" In *L'Apocalypse Johannique et L'apocalyptique dans le Nouveaux Testament*. Edited by J. Lambrecht, 185-204. Bibliotheca Ephemeridum Theologicarum Lovaniensium 53. Gembloux: J. Duculot, 1980.

________. "Vilification and Self-Definition in the Book of Revelation." *Harvard Theological Review* 79 (1986): 308-20.

Collins, John J. *The Apocalyptic Imagination: An Introduction to the Jewish Matrix of Christianity*. New York: Crossroad, 1984.

_______. "Introduction: Towards the Morphology of a Genre." *Semeia* 14 (1979): 1-20.

Conrad, Joseph. *Heart of Darkness*. New York: Dover, 1990; [1]1902.

Conzelmann, Hans. *The Theology of St. Luke*. Translated by Geoffrey Buswell. Philadelphia: Fortress Press, 1961.

Cook, Stephen L. *Prophecy and Apocalypticism: The Postexilic Social Setting*. Minneapolis: Fortress Press, 1995.

Corbett, Edward P. J. *Classical Rhetoric for the Modern Student*. Second edition. New York: Oxford University Press, 1971.

Court, John M. *Myth and History in the Book of Revelation*. Atlanta: John Knox, 1979.

Cox, Harvey G. *Religion in the Secular City: Towards a Postmodern Theology*. New York: Simon & Schuster, 1984.

Culler, Jonathan. *On Deconstruction: Theory and Criticism After Structuralism*. Ithaca: Cornell University Press, 1982.

de Andrade, Paulo Fernando Carniero. "Reading the Bible in the Ecclesial Base Communities of Latin America: The Meaning of Social Context." In *Reading from This Place*. Volume 2. *Social Location and Biblical Interpretation in Global Perspective*. Edited by Fernando F. Segovia and Mary Ann Tolbert, 237-49. Minneapolis: Fortress Press, 1995.

Dehandschutter, B. "The Meaning of Witness in the Apocalypse." In *L'Apocalypse Johannique et L'Apocalyptique dans le Nouveau Testament*. Edited by J. Lambrecht, 283-88. Bibliotheca Ephemeridum Theologicarum Lovaniensium 53. Leuven: Leuven University Press, 1980.

deSilva, David A. "The Revelation to John: A Case Study in Apocalyptic Propaganda and the Maintenance of Sectarian Identity." *Sociological Analysis* 53 (1992): 375-95.

Eagleton, Terry. *Literary Theory: An Introduction*. Minneapolis: University of Minnesota Press, 1983.

Eco, Umberto. "The Poetics of the Open Work." In *The Role of the Reader: Explorations in the Semiotics of Texts*, 47-66. Bloomington: Indiana University Press, 1984.

Eddy, Samuel K. *The King is Dead: Studies in Near Eastern Resistance to Hellenism 334–31 B.C.* Lincoln: University of Nebraska Press, 1961.

Efird, James M. *Revelation for Today*. Nashville: Abingdon Press, 1989.

Ehrman, Bart D. *The New Testament: A Historical Introduction to the Early Christian Writings*. New York: Oxford University Press, 1997.

Emenyonu, Ernest N. "Chinua Achebe's *Things Fall Apart*: A Classic Study in Colonial Diplomatic Tactlessness." In *Chinua Achebe: A Cele-*

bration. Edited by Kirsten Holst Peterson and Anna Rutherford, 83-88. Oxford: Heinemann, 1990.

Enos, Richard Leo, and Karen Rossi Schnakenberg. "Cicero Latinizes Hellenic *Ethos*." In *Ethos: New Essays in Rhetorical and Critical Theory*. Edited by James S. Baumlin and Tita French Baumlin, 191-209. SMU Studies in Composition and Rhetoric. Dallas: Southern Methodist University Press, 1994.

Esler, Philip F. "The Social Function of 4 Ezra." In *The First Christians in Their Social Worlds: Social-Scientific Approaches to New Testament Interpretation*, 110-30. New York: Routledge, 1994.

________. "Sorcery Accusations and the Apocalypse." In *The First Christians in Their Social Worlds: Social-Scientific Approaches to New Testament Interpretation*, 131-46. New York: Routledge, 1994.

Evans, Craig A., and Donald A. Hagner, eds. *Anti-Semitism and Early Christianity*. Minneapolis: Fortress Press, 1993.

Farrer, Austin. *The Revelation of St. John the Divine*. Oxford: Clarendon, 1964.

Felder, Cain Hope, editor. *Stony the Road We Trod: African American Biblical Interpretation*. Minneapolis: Fortress Press, 1991.

Fish, Stanley. "Literature in the Reader: Affective Stylistics." In *Reader-Response Criticism: From Formalism to Post-Structuralism*. Edited by Jane P. Tomkins, 70-100. Baltimore: Johns Hopkins University Press, 1980.

Floyd, John. "The Relevance of Inerrancy for Missions." *Mid-America Theological Journal* 6 (1982): 59-85.

Fowler, Robert M. "Who Is 'the Reader' in Reader Response Criticism?" *Semeia* 31 (1985): 5-23.

Franke, William. *Dante's Interpretive Journey*. Religion and Postmodernism. Chicago: University of Chicago Press, 1996.

Freyne, Sean. "Vilifying the Other and Defining the Self: Matthew's and John's Anti-Jewish Polemic in Focus." In *"To See Ourselves as Others See Us": Christians, Jews, "Others" in Late Antiquity*. Edited by Jacob Neusner and Ernest S. Frerichs, 117-43. Scholars Press Studies in the Humanities. Chico, CA: Scholars Press, 1985.

Gager, John G. "Judaism as Seen by Outsiders." In *Early Judaism and Its Modern Interpreters*. Edited by Robert A. Kraft and George W. E. Nickelsburg, 99-116. Atlanta: Scholars Press, 1986.

Garrett, Susan R. "Revelation." In *The Women's Bible Commentary*. Edited by Carol A. Newsom and Sharon H. Ringe, 377-82. Louisville: Westminster John Knox, 1992.

Graham, Billy. *Approaching Hoofbeats*. Dallas: Word Books, 1983.

Habermas, Jürgen. *Justification and Application: Remarks on Discourse Ethics*. Translated by Ciaran P. Cronin. Studies in Contemporary German Social Thought. Cambridge MA: MIT Press, 1993.

________. *Knowledge and Human Interests*. Translated by Jeremy J. Shapiro. Boston: Beacon, 1971.

________. *Legitimation Crisis*. Translated by Thomas McCarthy. Boston: Beacon, 1975.

________. *Moral Consciousness and Communicative Action*. Translated by Christian Lenhardt and Shierry Weber Nicholsen. Studies in Contemporary German Social Thought. Cambridge MA: MIT Press, 1990.

________. *The Philosophical Discourse of Modernity: Twelve Lectures*. Translated by Frederick G. Lawrence. Studies in Contemporary German Social Thought. Cambridge MA: MIT Press, 1987.

________. *Theory and Practice*. Translated by John Viertel. Boston: Beacon, 1973.

________. *The Theory of Communicative Action. Volume One. Reason and the Rationalization of Society*. Translated by Thomas McCarthy. Boston: Beacon, 1984.

________. *The Theory of Communicative Action. Volume Two. Lifeworld and System: A Critique of Functionalist Reason*. Translated by Thomas McCarthy. Boston: Beacon, 1987.

Halsell, Grace. *Prophecy and Politics*. Chicago: Lawrence Hill, 1986.

Hanson, Paul D., editor. *Visionaries and Their Apocalypses*. Issues in Religion and Theology. Philadelphia: Fortress Press, 1983.

________. *The Dawn of Apocalyptic: The Historical and Sociological Roots of Jewish Apocalyptic Eschatology*. Revised Edition. Philadelphia: Fortress Press, 1979.

Harlow, Barbara. *Resistance Literature*. New York: Methuen, 1987.

Harrington, Wilfrid J., O.P. *Revelation*. Sacra Pagina. Collegeville MN: Michael Glazier, 1993.

Harris, Stephen L. *The New Testament: A Student's Introduction*. Mountain View CA: Mayfield Publishing Company, 1988.

Haynes, Stephen R. *Reluctant Witnesses: Jews and the Christian Imagination*. Louisville: Westminster John Knox, 1995.

Hellholm, David, editor. *Apocalypticism in the Mediterranean World and the Near East: Proceedings of the International Colloquium on Apocalypticism, Uppsala, August 12-17, 1979*. Tübingen: Mohr, 1983.

Hellholm, David. "The Problem of Apocalyptic Genre and the Apocalypse of John." *Semeia* 36 (1986): 13-64.

Hemer, Colin J. *The Letters to the Seven Churches of Asia in Their Social Setting*. Journal for the Study of the New Testament Supplement Series 11. Sheffield: JSOT, 1986.

Holquist, Michael. *Dialogism: Bakhtin and His World*. New Accents. London and New York: Routledge, 1990.

Hutcheon, Linda. *The Politics of Postmodernism*. New Accents. London and New York: Routledge, 1989.

Innocenti, Beth. "Towards a Theory of Vivid Description as Practiced in Cicero's Verrine Orations." *Rhetorica* 12 (1994): 355-81.

Iser, Wolfgang. *The Act of Reading: A Theory of Aesthetic Response*. Baltimore: Johns Hopkins University Press, 1978.

Isichei, Elizabeth. *A History of Christianity in Africa*. Grand Rapids MI: Eerdmans, 1995.

Janzen, Ernest P. "The Jesus of the Apocalypse Wears the Emperor's Clothes." *Society of Biblical Literature Seminar Papers* 33 (1994): 637-51.

Jasper, David. *Rhetoric, Power and Community: An Exercise in Reserve*. Louisville: Westminster/John Knox, 1993.

Jeffrey, Grant R. *Apocalypse: The Coming Judgment of the Nations*. New York: Bantam, 1992.

Johnson, Luke T. "The New Testament's Anti-Jewish Slander and the Conventions of Ancient Polemic." *Journal of Biblical Literature* 108 (1989): 419-41.

______. *The Writings of the New Testament: An Interpretation*. Philadelphia: Fortress Press, 1986.

Jones, Donald L. "Christianity and the Roman Imperial Cult." *Aufstieg und Niedergang der Römischen Welt*. New York: Walter de Gruyter, 1980. 2.23.2.1023-54.

Joüon, Paul. *A Grammar of Biblical Hebrew*. Two volumes. Translated and revised by T. Muraoka. Subsidia Biblica 14. Rome: Editrice Pontificio Instituto Biblico, 1991.

Kee, Howard Clark. *Understanding the New Testament*. Fourth edition. Englewood Cliffs NJ: Prentice-Hall, 1983.

Kennedy, George A. *Classical Rhetoric and Its Christian and Secular Tradition from Ancient to Modern Times*. Chapel Hill: University of North Carolina Press, 1980.

______. *Comparative Rhetoric: A Historical and Cross-Cultural Introduction*. New York: Oxford University Press, 1998.

Klassen, William. "Vengeance in the Apocalypse of John." *Catholic Biblical Quarterly* 28 (1966): 300-11.

Koch, Klaus. "What Is Apocalyptic? An Attempt at a Preliminary Definition." In *Visionaries and Their Apocalypses*. Edited by Paul D.

Hanson, 16-36. Issues in Religion and Theology. Philadelphia: Fortress Press, 1983.

Kraybill, J. Nelson. *Imperial Cult and Commerce in John's Apocalypse*. Journal for the Study of the New Testament Supplement Series 132. Sheffield: Sheffield Academic Press, 1996.

Krodel, Gerhard A. *Revelation*. Augsburg Commentary on the New Testament. Minneapolis: Augsburg, 1989.

Kwok Pui Lan. "Discovering the Bible in the Nonbiblical World." *Semeia* 47 (1989): 25-42.

LaHaye, Tim. *No Fear of the Storm: Why Christians Will Escape All the Tribulation*. Sisters OR: Multnomah, 1992.

Lakeland, Paul. *Theology and Critical Theory: The Discourse of the Church*. Nashville: Abingdon Press, 1990.

Lambrecht, J., editor. *L'Apocalypse Johannique et L'Apocalyptique dans le Nouveau Testament*. Bibliotheca Ephemeridum Theologicarum Lovaniensium 53. Leuven: Leuven University Press, 1980.

Lanser, Susan Snaider. *Fictions of Authority: Women Writers and Narrative Voice*. Ithaca: Cornell University Press, 1992.

________. *The Narrative Act: Point of View in Prose Fiction*. Princeton: Princeton University Press, 1981.

Laws, Sophie. *In the Light of the Lamb: Imagery, Parody, and Theology in the Apocalypse of John*. Good News Studies 31. Wilmington DE: Michael Glazier, 1988.

Leitch, Vincent B. *Cultural Criticism, Literary Theory, Poststructuralism*. New York: Columbia University Press, 1992.

Lindsey, Hal. *The Final Battle*. Palos Verdes CA: Western Front, 1995.

________, with Carole C. Carlson. *The Late Great Planet Earth*. Grand Rapids MI: Zondervan, 1970.

Linton, Gregory. "Reading the Apocalypse as an Apocalypse." *Society of Biblical Literature Seminar Papers* 30 (1991): 161-86.

McCumber, John. *Poetic Interaction: Language, Freedom, Reason*. Chicago: University of Chicago Press, 1989.

Mack, Burton L. *The Lost Gospel: The Book of Q and Christian Origins*. San Francisco: HarperSanFrancisco, 1993.

________. *A Myth of Innocence: Mark and Christian Origins*. Philadelphia: Fortress Press, 1988.

________. *Who Wrote the New Testament? The Making of the Christian Myth*. San Francisco: HarperSanFrancisco, 1995.

MacMullen, Ramsay. *Enemies of the Roman Order: Treason, Unrest, and Alienation in the Empire*. London and New York: Routledge, 1992; [1]1966.

Mailloux, Steven. *Rhetorical Power*. Ithaca: Cornell University Press, 1989.
Malina, Bruce J. *On the Genre and Message of Revelation: Star Visions and Sky Journeys*. Peabody MA: Hendrickson, 1995.
Mann, Michael. *The Sources of Social Power. Volume 1: A History of Power from the Beginning to A.D. 1760*. New York: Cambridge University Press, 1986.
Marshall, John W. "Parables of the War: Reading the Apocalypse within Judaism and during the Judean War." Ph.D. dissertation, Princeton University Press, 1997.
Martin, Dale B. "Heterosexism and the Interpretation of Romans 1:18-32." *Biblical Interpretation* 3 (1995): 332-55.
________. *Slavery as Salvation: The Metaphor of Slavery in Pauline Christianity*. New Haven: Yale University Press, 1990.
Meeks, Wayne A. "Social Functions of Apocalyptic Language in Pauline Christianity." In *Apocalypticism in the Mediterranean World And the Near East: Proceedings of the International Colloqium on Apocalypticism, Uppsala, August 12-17, 1979*. Edited by David Hellholm, 687-705. Tübingen: Mohr, 1983.
Mendel, Arthur P. *Vision and Violence*. Ann Arbor: University of Michigan Press, 1992.
Metzger, Bruce M. *A Textual Commentary on the Greek New Testament*. Corrected edition. Stuttgart: United Bible Societies, 1975; [1]1971.
______. *Breaking the Code: Understanding the Book of Revelation*. Nashville: Abingdon Press, 1993.
Míguez, Néstor. "Apocalyptic and the Economy: A Reading of Revelation 18 from the Experience of Economic Exclusion." In *Reading from This Place*. Volume 2. *Social Location and Biblical Interpretation in Global Perspective*. Edited by Fernando F. Segovia and Mary Ann Tolbert, 250-62. Minneapolis: Fortress Press, 1995.
Morson, Gary Saul. *The Boundaries of Genre*. Austin: University of Texas Press, 1981.
Neusner, Jacob, and Ernest S. Frerichs, eds. *"To See Ourselves as Others See Us": Christians, Jews, "Others" in Late Antiquity*. Scholars Press Studies in the Humanities. Chico CA: Scholars Press, 1985.
Neyrey, Jerome H., editor. *The Social World of Luke-Acts: Models for Interpretation*. Peabody MA: Hendrickson, 1991.
________. "The Symbolic Universe of Luke-Acts: 'They Turn the World Upside Down'" In *The Social World of Luke-Acts: Models for Interpretation*. Edited by Jerome H. Neyrey, 271-304. Peabody MA: Hendrickson, 1991.

O'Leary, Stephen D. *Arguing the Apocalypse: A Theory of Millennial Rhetoric*. New York and Oxford: Oxford University Press, 1994.

Packer, J. I. "Implications of Biblical Inerrancy for the Christian Mission." In *The Proceedings of the Conference on Biblical Inerrancy, 1987*, 245-50. Nashville: Broadman, 1987.

Patte, Daniel. *Ethics of Biblical Interpretation: A Reevaluation*. Louisville: Westminster John Knox, 1995.

________. "Textual Constraints, Ordinary Readings, and Critical Exegesis: An Androcritical Perspective." *Semeia* 62 (1993): 59-79.

Perkins, Pheme. *Reading the New Testament*. Revised edition. New York: Paulist, 1988.

Perrin, Norman, and Dennis C. Duling. *The New Testament: An Introduction*. Second edition. San Diego: Harcourt Brace Jovanovich, 1982.

Pettegrew, Larry D. "Liberation Theology and Hermeneutical Preunderstandings." *Bibliotheca Sacra* 148 (1991): 274-87.

Pilch, John J. "Lying and Deceit in the Letters to the Seven Churches." *Biblical Theology Bulletin* 22 (1992): 126-34.

Pippin, Tina. *Death and Desire: The Rhetoric of Gender in the Apocalypse of John*. Literary Currents in Biblical Interpretation. Louisville: Westminster/John Knox, 1992.

Pregeant, Russell. *Engaging the New Testament: An Interdisciplinary Introduction*. Minneapolis: Fortress Press, 1995.

Prigent, Pierre. *L'Apocalypse de Saint Jean*. Commentaire du Nouveau Testament 14. Lausanne: Delachaux & Niestlé, 1981.

Richard, Pablo. *Apocalypse: A People's Commentary on the Book of Revelation*. Maryknoll NY: Orbis, 1995.

________. "The Hermeneutics of Liberation: A Hermeneutics of the Spirit." In *Reading from This Place*. Volume 2. *Social Location and Biblical Interpretation in Global Perspective*. Edited by Fernando F. Segovia and Mary Ann Tolbert, 263-80. Minneapolis: Fortress Press, 1995.

Riikonen, H. K. *Menippean Satire as a Literary Genre with Special Reference to Seneca's Apocolocyntosis*. Commentationes Humanarum Litterarum 83. Helsinki: Finnish Society of Sciences and Letters, 1987.

Roloff, Jürgen. *The Revelation of John*. Translated by John E. Alsup. Continental Commentaries. Minneapolis: Fortress Press, 1993.

Rosen, Moishe. Assisted by Bob Massie. *Overture to Armageddon? Beyond the Gulf War*. San Bernardino CA: Here's Life, 1991.

Rowland, Christopher. *The Open Heaven: A Study of Apocalyptic in Judaism and Early Christianity*. New York: Crossroad, 1982.

Royalty, Robert M., Jr. *The Streets of Heaven: The Ideology of Wealth in the Apocalypse of John*. Macon GA: Mercer University Press, 1998.

Ruiz, Jean Pierre. "Hearing and Seeing but not Saying: A Look at Revelation 10:4 and 2 Corinthians 12:4." *Society of Biblical Literature Seminar Papers* 33 (1994): 182-202.
Ryrie, Charles C. *The Final Countdown*. Wheaton IL: Victor, 1982.
Saffrey, H. D. "Relire L'Apocalypse à Patmos." *Revue Biblique* 82 (1975): 385-417.
Said, Edward W. *Orientalism*. New York: Random House, 1978.
______. "Orientalism Reconsidered." *Cultural Critique* 1 (1985): 89-107.
______. "Representing the Colonized: Anthropology's Interlocutors." *Critical Inquiry* 15 (1989): 205-25.
______. "The World, the Text, and the Critic." In *Critical Theory Since Plato*. Revised edition. Edited by Hazard Adams, 1211-22. Fort Worth: Harcourt Brace Jovanovich, 1992.
Sallis, John. *Spacings—of Reason and Imagination in Texts of Kant, Fichte, Hegel*. Chicago: University of Chicago Press, 1987.
Sanders, J. N. "John on Patmos." *New Testament Studies* 9 (1963): 75-85.
Sanders, Jack T. *Schismatics, Sectarians, Dissidents, Deviants: The First One Hundred Years of Jewish-Christian Relations*. Valley Forge PA: Trinity Press International, 1993.
Sawyer, John F. A. "Isaiah, the Book Of." In *The Oxford Companion to the Bible*. Edited by Bruce M. Metzger and Michael D. Coogan, 325-29. New York and Oxford: Oxford University Press, 1993.
Scholes, Robert, and Robert Kellogg. *The Nature of Narrative*. Oxford: Oxford University Press, 1966.
Schüssler Fiorenza, Elisabeth. "The Ethics of Biblical Interpretation: Decentering Biblical Scholarship." *Journal of Biblical Literature* 107 (1988): 3-17.
______. *Revelation: Vision of a Just World*. Proclamation Commentaries. Minneapolis: Fortress Press, 1991.
Scott, James C. "Revolution in the Revolution: Peasants and Commissars." *Theory and Society* 7 (1979): 97-134.
Segovia, Fernando F. "'And They Began to Speak with Other Tongues': Competing Modes of Discourse in Contemporary Biblical Criticism." In *Reading from This Place*. Volume 1. *Social Location and Biblical Interpretation in the United States*. Edited by Fernando F. Segovia and Mary Ann Tolbert, 1-32. Minneapolis: Fortress Press, 1995.
Segovia, Fernando F., and Mary Ann Tolbert, eds. *Reading from This Place*. Volume 1. *Social Location and Biblical Interpretation in the United States*. Volume 2. *Social Location and Biblical Interpretation in Global Perspective*. Minneapolis: Fortress Press, 1995.

Seidman, Steven. *Contested Knowledge: Social Theory in the Postmodern Era*. Oxford: Blackwell, 1994.

Short, Bryan C. "Literary Ethos: Dispersion, Resistance, Mystification." In *Ethos: New Essays in Rhetorical and Critical Theory*. Edited by James S. Baumlin and Tita French Baumlin, 367-87. SMU Studies in Composition and Rhetoric. Dallas: Southern Methodist University Press, 1994.

Sine, Tom, "Suspicions of Conspiracy: How a Spirit of Fear Can Distort Scripture and History." *Sojourners* 24 (July-August 1995): 26-30.

Sleeper, C. Freeman. *The Victorious Christ: A Study of the Book of Revelation*. Louisville: Westminster John Knox, 1996.

Smith, Jonathan Z. "Wisdom and Apocalyptic." In *Map is not Territory: Studies in the History of Religions*, 67-87. Studies in Judaism in Late Antiquity. Leiden: Brill, 1978.

Smith, Morton. "On the History of ΑΠΟΚΑΛΥΠΤΩ and ΑΠΟΚΑΛΥΨΙΣ." In *Apocalypticism in the Mediterranean World and the Near East: Proceedings of the International Colloquium on Apocalypticism, Uppsala, August 12-17, 1979*. Edited by David Hellholm, 9-20. Tübingen: Mohr, 1983.

Snyder, Barbara Wooten. "Triple-Form and Space/Time Transitions: Literary Structuring Devices in the Apocalypse." *Society of Biblical Literature Seminar Papers* 30 (1991): 440-50.

Spivey, Robert A., and D. Moody Smith. *Anatomy of the New Testament*. Second edition. New York: Macmillan, 1974.

Staley, Jeffrey L. *Reading with a Passion: Rhetoric, Autobiography, and the American West in the Gospel of John*. New York: Continuum, 1995.

Strozier, Charles B. *Apocalypse: On the Psychology of Fundamentalism in America*. Boston: Beacon, 1994.

Suleiman, Susan R. "Introduction: Varieties of Audience-Oriented Criticism." In *The Reader in the Text: Essays on Audience and Interpretation*. Edited by Susan R. Suleiman and Inge Crosman, 3-45. Princeton: Princeton University Press, 1980.

Suleiman, Susan R., and Inge Crosman, editors. *The Reader in the Text: Essays on Audience and Interpretation*. Princeton: Princeton University Press, 1980.

Swete, Henry Barclay. *The Apocalypse of St. John: The Greek Text with Introduction, Notes, and Indices*. Third edition. London: Macmillan and Co., 1911; ^{2}1907; ^{1}1906.

Talbert, Charles H. *The Apocalypse: A Reading of the Revelation of John*. Louisville: Westminster John Knox, 1994.

Terdiman, Richard. *Discourse/Counter-Discourse: The Theory and Practice of Symbolic Resistance in Nineteenth-Century France*. Ithaca: Cornell University Press, 1985.

Theissen, Gerd. *The Social Setting of Pauline Christianity*. Philadelphia: Fortress Press, 1982.

Thompson, Leonard L. *The Book of Revelation: Apocalypse and Empire*. New York: Oxford University Press, 1990.

Thrupp, Sylvia L., editor. *Millennial Dreams in Action: Studies in Revolutionary Religious Movements*. New York: Shocken, 1970.

________. "Millennial Dreams in Action: A Report on the Conference Discussion." In *Millennial Dreams in Action: Studies in Revolutionary Religious Movements*. Edited by Sylvia L. Thrupp, 11-27. New York: Shocken, 1970.

Tolbert, Mary Ann. "Feminists and the Bible: On the Horns of a Dilemma." *Union Seminary Quarterly Review* 43 (1989): 1-17.

Tolbert, Mary Ann. "When Resistance Becomes Repression: Mark 13:9-27 and the Poetics of Location." In *Reading from This Place*. Volume 2. *Social Location and Biblical Interpretation in Global Perspective*. Edited by Fernando F. Segovia and Mary Ann Tolbert, 331-46. Minneapolis: Fortress Press, 1995.

Tompkins, Jane P., editor. *Reader-Response Criticism: From Formalism to Post-Structuralism*. Baltimore: Johns Hopkins University Press, 1980.

________. "The Reader in History: The Changing Shape of Literary Response." In *Reader-Response Criticism: From Formalism to Post-Structuralism*. Edited by Jane P. Tompkins, 201-32. Baltimore: Johns Hopkins University Press, 1980.

Tracy, David. *The Analogical Imagination: Christian Theology and the Culture of Pluralism*. New York: Crossroad, 1981.

Trites, Allison A. "Μάρτυς and Martyrdom in the Apocalypse: A Semantic Study." *Novum Testamentum* 15 (1973): 72-80.

van Henten, Jan Willem. "Dragon Myth and Imperial Ideology in Revelation 12-13." *Society of Biblical Literature Seminar Papers* 33 (1994): 496-515.

Vielhauer, Philipp, and Georg Strecker. "Apocalypses and Related Subjects: Introduction." In *New Testament Apocrypha*. Two volumes. Revised edition. Edited by Wilhelm Schneemelcher; translated by R. McL. Wilson, 2:542-68. Louisville: Westminster/John Knox, 1994.

Vorster, W. S. " 'Genre' and the Revelation of John: A Study in Text, Context and Intertext." *Neotestamentica* 22 (1988): 103-23.

Wainwright, Arthur W. *Mysterious Apocalypse: Interpreting the Book of Revelation*. Nashville: Abingdon Press, 1993.

Wall, Robert W. *Revelation*. New International Biblical Commentary. Peabody MA: Hendrickson, 1991.

Walvoord, John F, and John E. Walvoord. *Armageddon, Oil, and the Middle East Crisis: What the Bible Says about the Future of the Middle East and the End of Western Civilization*. Revised edition. Grand Rapids: Zondervan, 1990; [1]1974.

Webber, Randall C. "The Apocalypse as Utopia: Ancient and Modern Subjectivity." *Society of Biblical Literature Seminar Papers* 32 (1993): 104-18.

Weems, Renita J. "Reading Her Way through the Struggle: African American Women and the Bible." In *Stony the Road We Trod: African American Biblical Interpretation*. Edited by Cain Hope Felder, 57-77. Minneapolis: Fortress Press, 1991.

West, Gerald. *Biblical Hermeneutics of Liberation: Modes of Reading the Bible in the South African Context*. Second edition. The Bible and Liberation Series. Maryknoll NY: Orbis, 1995.

West, Gerald, and Musa W. Dube, eds. " 'Reading with' African Overtures." *Semeia* 73 (1996).

Wilson, Bryan R. *Magic and the Millennium: A Sociological Study of Religious Movements of Protest Among Tribal and Third-world Peoples*. New York: Harper & Row, 1973.

Wilson, J. Christian. "The Problem of the Domitianic Date of Revelation." *New Testament Studies* 39 (1993): 587-605.

Wilson, Stephen G. *Related Strangers: Jews and Christians, 70-170 C.E.* Minneapolis: Fortress Press, 1995.

Wimbush, Vincent. "Reading Texts through Worlds, Worlds through Texts." *Semeia* 62 (1993): 129-40.

Wisse, Jakob. *Ethos and Pathos from Aristotle to Cicero*. Amsterdam: Adolf M. Hakkert, 1989.

Index of Ancient Texts

Hellenistic and Ancient Near Eastern Literature

Jewish Scriptures

Apocrypha

Noncanonical Jewish Sources

New Testament

Noncanonical Christian Sources

Elusive Apocalypse.
Reading Authority in the Revelation to John.
by Greg Carey.
Studies in American Biblical Hermeneutics 15 (StABH 15)

Mercer University Press, Macon, Georgia 31210-3960 USA.
Isbn 0-86554-632-0. Catalog and warehouse pick number: MUP/P186.
Text and interior designs, cover design, composition, and layout
by Edmon L. Rowell, Jr.
Cover illustration: Cover. *St. John on the Island of Patmos,* from a 19th-century, illuminated-Bible woodcut by H. M. Snyder.
Camera-ready pages composed on a Gateway 2000
via WordPerfect 5.1/5.2 (with WpWin 6.1 and Corel WP 7)
and printed on a LaserMaster 1000.
Text fonts: (Adobe) Palatino 11/13, 10/12; ATECH Hebrew and Greek.
Display font: (Adobe) Palatino 24-, 12-, and 11-point bf.
Printed and bound by BookCrafters, Chelsea, Michigan 48118-0370.
Printed (offset lithography) on 55# Booktext Natural Hi Bulk (360ppi).
Perfectbound in 10-pt. c1s stock, printed one PMS color,
and lay-flat laminated (matte film).

[June 1999]

050799elr